MW00812376

THE BEST OF LOWELL L. BENNION

SELECTED WRITINGS 1928-1988

Introduction - True religion is based in social morality -

Three types of love - unconditional or Christ-like
- Friendship
- Romantic

XVIII

XXI

"He's a combination of Old Testament prophet, who wants to give you his vision of what should be, and a New Testament Good Samaritan who doesn't stand back and talk, but steps in to do the good work himself."

Goethe - "Life, divided by reason, leaves a remainder."

William P. Montague, "Religion is the faith that the things that matter most are not ultimately at the mercy of the things that matter least." XXI

"The truly religious person learns to thrill in the satisfaction that comes from freely living in harmony with God's laws."
XXII

"To action alone thou hast a right, not to its fruits" - Hindu Scripture XXII

"Do not marry anyone with whom you have not worked on a committee."
XXII

"Learn to like people, even though some of them may be different ... different from you."
XXIII

"Learn to keep your <u>wants</u> simple and refuse to be controlled by the <u>likes & dislikes of others</u>."

Key - Alma 34 - "Christ's suffering & death can save us, not by paying for our sins after we have repented, but by providing us power to repent while we are still sinners
XXIV

As Amulek says - "The Atonement bringeth about means unto men that they may have faith unto repentance" Alma 34:15

"Religion, like music, philosophy, or science, has no meaning to a person until it becomes his own." - Pg. 21

Memorize Scripture - Pg 23

"Plato "The free individual is one who can direct his energies and labor to purposes of his own choosing." pg 30

THE BEST OF LOWELL L. BENNION

SELECTED WRITINGS 1928-1988

EDITED BY EUGENE ENGLAND

Deseret Book Company
Salt Lake City, Utah

Printed in the United States of America

ISBN 0-87579-186-7

First printing November 1988

Dedicated to Lowell Bennion's students—
past, present, and future.

"One sees what one carries in ones heart." — Goethe   P. 137

A great man made peace with the tragedy of life by his love Pg. 136
for humanity. Albert Schweitzer - French musician, thinker & medical missionary

To the widow who lost her only two sons in the war - "Why don't you
forget yourself by helping folks in this town who need you?" Pg. 137
She became Granny to all in her community

"Things of the Spirit" - truth, beauty, love, integrity & friendship. Pg. 139

If there were no God, our goals would be human goals and would be
destroyed, should man's life end. Pg. 139

"That's the way to do. No boy ever becomes a man until he learns
to love to work!" Bryant S. Hinckley - 82 yr. old grand neighbor - Pg. 141

"I have been a widow for eight years. I live alone. This is the
first time anyone has ever offered to help me in a physical, tangible
way!" THINK OF IT! No neighbor, no Boy Scout troop, no Aaronic or
Melchizedek Priesthood quorum, no MIA group of girls - had ever
"Whatsoever thy hand findeth to do, do with with thy might." Pg. 143
Ecclesiastes 9:10

For give - "If forgiveness must be earned or doubly earned,
the word "give" should be removed from the center of it."
Pg. 226

Contents

SECTION IV: PRACTICAL RELIGION

SECTION V: TEACHING AND LEADING

SECTION VI: LEARNING HOW TO KNOW

SECTION VII: LEARNING HOW TO LOVE

Introduction

The Achievement of Lowell Bennion

What does the Lord require of thee, but to do justly, and to love mercy, and to walk humbly with thy God? (Micah 6:8.)

A unique figure and voice enlivens—and haunts—late twentieth-century Mormonism. The figure is stooped slightly forward, dressed in work clothes or inexpensive, sometimes mismatched, pants and jacket, with blunt farmer's hands protruding, a browned face and pate, and only a fringe of sandy, graying hair. That figure has been seen driving to teach religion at the Salt Lake Institute of Religion or sociology at the University of Utah, or delivering donated food to a Salt Lake widow, all in a battered and ancient Ford truck. He has been seen, looking a bit awkward in academic robes, delivering the baccalaureate address at the university and, more comfortable in grubby Levis, boots, and straw hat, teaching city boys how to ride a horse and to build a pole barn in the Teton Valley in eastern Idaho. He has been seen giving a Brigham Young University devotional address, instructing a conference of Sunday School teachers, conducting sacrament service as bishop of a Salt Lake City ward, and, now with the hint of a shuffle added to his unhurried, bent-forward gait, moving from session to session at the Sunstone Theological Symposium.

Lowell Bennion's voice has not been elegant, but rather rough and homey, quite informal and unself-conscious, even when delivering an eloquent talk to an LDS general conference on preparing for a happy marriage. He is completely fearless, almost old-fashioned, outspoken against unchastity, drugs, intellectual pride, materialism, and prejudice—and willing to be heard and published anywhere. Until authors were no longer identified in the 1970s, his name appeared more often than any other in LDS Church lesson manuals, which he wrote for all the auxiliaries. He has spoken in more essays and books, over a greater variety of subjects, than perhaps any other contemporary Mormon. He is the only one to have written for nearly every independent and official Mormon periodical of the twentieth century.

Why do that voice and figure haunt, as well as enliven, us? Brother Bennion is among the gentlest and meekest of men, constantly conciliatory and nonconfrontive. However, in a time when our quick growth in numbers and material blessings tempts us Mormons to forget some important things, his teaching and writing—and especially his life—provide us with clear, challenging reminders of the central message of the Hebrew prophets and of Christ, reaffirmed by the prophets of the Restoration: that true religion is based in social morality. His voice has spoken, for some sixty years, with a simplicity and clarity like water in a dry land, in favor of positive, integrated religion, in support of a unified philosophy of life, grounded in affirmative and universal principles. His faith is based in Joseph Smith's revelation of the truth that all humans are co-eternal with God—the same kind of beings and thus co-creators with him. Their basic natures are fulfilled and moved to progression through receiving unconditional love and being given opportunities to love and to serve creatively the needs of all such God-like beings, including God, their neighbors, and themselves.

We are haunted by this unique voice because we know that at times we have discriminated against others because of race or sex. We know that sometimes we value programs over people and sometimes break hearts rather than break rules—or sometimes prefer "right doctrine" to simple justice and mercy. We know that with all our growth and great buildings and high activity, we sometimes forget the fatherless and widows, the naked and those in prison, even the ones right among us, as well as strangers and foreigners. We know how hard it is, with busy schedules and a favorable image to preserve and the cumbering responsibilities of a worldwide church, to remember "the least of these."

Brother Bennion is one who has not forgotten. Without patronizing or condemning, he has taught and written to remind us. And he has set a constant, humble example for us. At the same time (and this, I believe, is the reason his ideas and example will continue to haunt us, the reason he will long be a gentle but piercing reminder) he has provided one of the most unified pictures we have of our theology, including a clear explication of its central and most challenging doctrines concerning Christ's atonement and the way of salvation.

One of Lowell Bennion's students, who entered the University of Utah in 1950, remembers attending his small LDS institute classes, where there was no indoctrination but members were led to express their developing thoughts and feelings. "That thrilled me," the former student says. "It confirmed my soul. For the first time in my religious learning I felt the teacher was genuinely interested in the questions he was asking, not simply looking for a set answer, and that he was interested in me and my response. We were soon sitting on the edge of our seats trying to help him—and that was the best help for us!"

I went to the U. from 1951 to 1958, interrupted by a mission to Samoa. I took classes from Brother B., as we called him, and his colleagues. I participated in the LDS fraternity/sorority, Lambda Delta Sigma, which they had created to provide social, service, and spiritual experiences to balance their students' intellectual studies. And I attended the Friday noon devotionals at the institute, where faith and reason were joined in sermons that were both intellectually stimulating and spiritually and emotionally moving—sermons often given by the faculty itself. The faculty during that time—Brother Bennion, T. Edgar Lyon, George Boyd, and Elder Marion D. Hanks (who continued teaching there after being called as a General Authority in 1952)—were all brilliant thinkers and teachers and also devoted Latter-day Saints. And because they were deeply involved, and were known by their students and others to be deeply involved, in serving the poor and deprived throughout the Salt Lake Valley, they spoke with the unique authority of practicing Christians.

Almost every Saturday Brother B. would accompany a Lambda Delta Sigma chapter or two as they cleaned the yard and painted the house of a widow or elderly couple in the valley. We students saw him delivering food in his truck. We knew from personal experience that Elder Hanks often spent a stormy winter evening driving around helping people stalled in the snow, and we had heard that when all the hotels refused rooms to black athletes participating in the NCAA track tournament in Salt Lake City, his family took them in. When that faculty told us the gospel was true and that it called us to a life of selfless service, we believed them. When they told us the Church was true, despite our human failings, we trusted them.

Dr. Bennion's approach to teaching, which greatly influenced the rest of his faculty and gradually his many students, was based partly on the example of his father, who was known as one of the finest Socratic teachers in the Church. But Brother B. added a unique perspective of his own, which he articulated early in his missionary journal and has preached consistently as well as demonstrated for sixty years: that any religious principle must be consistent within its whole context, particularly the great and repeated fundamentals (chief of which are Christ's teachings), and that its reliability is greatly strengthened by verification through a variety of ways of knowing: reason and experience as well as authority and the witness of the Spirit. He has demonstrated that the form of teaching used by Christ, whom he calls "the Master Teacher," and by the great teacher-prophets of the scriptures insists on consistency, openly invites skepticism of itself, and offers a variety of proofs, even asking us to conduct "an experiment" upon his words. (Alma 32:27.) It is aimed at providing foundation principles for dynamic development and a variety of insights with which to respond to life's dynamic variety, not static "answers."

I remember a class at the institute in about 1953 on the nature of God. A student asked why, if God is no respecter of persons, as the scriptures and common sense clearly indicate, a difference existed in God's church between blacks and all others. I immediately answered, as I had been taught all my life, "Well, God is also a God of justice, and since blacks were not valiant in the preexistence, they are cursed with the just consequences." In the discussion following my remark, Brother Bennion—who in my experience never mentioned this issue except when directly questioned—pronounced no answers, quoted no dogma. He simply asked me how I knew blacks had not been valiant. When I had no answer but tradition, he gently suggested that the God revealed in Christ would surely let blacks know what they had done wrong and how they could repent, rather than merely punishing them—and since God had done no such thing, it seemed better to believe that blacks had been, and were, no different spiritually from the rest of us. As I thought about this, my way of thinking about the gospel was changed, and not merely concerning this issue. I came to realize with stunning clarity that many of my beliefs, ones that profoundly affected my relationships to others, were based on flimsy and unexamined evidence and were directly contradictory to great gospel principles like the impartial Fatherhood of God, the universal brotherhood of humankind, and the unconditional atonement, which offered sufficient power to all to repent and be both saved and exalted.

That crucial change in me was not imposed from outside by authority. It was educated, educed, led out of me by Brother B. I was able to watch how he did it not long after I left the U. I was sent by the Air Force to study to be a weather officer at Massachusetts Institute of Technology in Boston, and the Bennions visited our Cambridge Branch on their way to New York to meet their son returning from a mission in West Germany. The Sunday School lesson, on ward teaching, was being taught in the usual manner (the teacher simply asking "What word am I thinking of?" questions about the purpose and structure of ward teaching); and the class, as usual, was giving the correct answers but was bored. Knowing how much this pained him, I waited for Brother B. to rise in prophetic fury and denounce the teacher, the lesson manual, or the class. After a while (he was waiting, I realized later, for me or someone else to take the lead), he did raise his hand. But then he simply asked, with what we all recognized as genuine, uncondemning interest, why, since ward teaching was obviously such a wonderful program, true to fundamental gospel principles and human needs, we had such a hard time doing it. He didn't say another word, but we had the best, most honest, helpful, and mutually supportive discussion I remember in that branch. I learned what I should have had sense to see he was teaching us earlier at the U.—that any member of a class or group, even of a large audience, can make the learning situation more successful by asking (either aloud or silently) genuine questions that lovingly and sincerely point toward integrated basics: fundamentals rooted in the eternal, universal human needs as revealed by Christ.

Lowell Bennion is the best teacher I have known. I believe he is also one of the finest practical philosophers The Church of Jesus Christ of Latter-day Saints has produced in the twentieth century. He is both a fine thinker about the great theoretical principles on which our practical, living religion is based and a fine practitioner of those principles. He is good evidence for his own favorite scripture, quoted at the beginning of this introduction, in which the Hebrew prophet Micah tells us that, instead of programs and performance, even instead of sacrifice, what the Lord wants of us is justice and mercy and humble love of him and what he stands for—what Christ called "the weightier matters." All over the world there are former students and colleagues, in business offices and classrooms and kitchens and slums, who go about doing good to "the least of these," Christ's brothers and sisters, because of the teaching and example of Lowell Bennion. This book is intended to help that tribe increase, by extending Brother B. to new minds and hearts.

There are now two Bennion memorials at the University of Utah, the new Lowell L. Bennion Center for Community Service and the education building, named after Lowell's father, Milton Bennion. He was Dean of the College of Education and Professor of Philosophy at the U. and later head of the LDS Sunday Schools, and his *Moral Teachings of the New Testament* and many essays and reviews in Church and professional journals remain a significant contribution to religious education. He was, of course, a major influence on Lowell. Others of great influence were Arthur Beeley, who taught him sociology and involved him in a study of the social habits of young men in Salt Lake Valley before his mission, and Elder John A. Widtsoe, LDS apostle and head of Church Education, who was so impressed when he met Lowell while Lowell was studying in Vienna in 1932 that he hired him two years later, as a mere twenty-six-year-old, to head the new Salt Lake Institute of Religion.

These men influenced Brother Bennion strongly toward rational religion and toward an attempt to integrate all human scholarship and experience with the gospel. Both of these emphases fit naturally with his interest in the great German philosopher and developer of the sociology of religion, Max Weber, who had died in 1922. But before he did his dissertation on Weber, Lowell got married and then served a mission in Germany and Switzerland, and his wife, Merle, joined him in Europe for his graduate work. His diary effectively reveals his intense interest in individuals and relationships. His published writings are all modest, even shy, using personal experiences as Christ used parables, only to teach or illustrate principles, not to reveal or examine himself. Therefore, the diary, from which I have quoted excerpts, is unique in exposing the range and depth of his personality and in detailing his spiritual experiences and humble service. Those certainly helped produce the ethical idealism and personal piety that have characterized his work as much as its rational brilliance and coherence.

Lowell had graduated from the U. in 1928 at age nineteen, because he had skipped two grades. He was married on September 18 and left for his mission one month later. He was extremely lonely without Merle and wrote his diary, full of longings and passionate endearments, essentially as letters to her. He yearned for the time when he could share his experiences and spiritual growth and the culture of Europe with her directly, and a plan to make that possible slowly formed and was realized when his father, who must have sensed his potential, offered to pay his way while he stayed on to do a doctorate at a European university. He studied at Erlangen in Germany and the University of Vienna, but when Hitler came to power, he went to Strasbourg, France, where he wrote *Max Weber's Methodology,* the first full-length study of Weber in English, publishing it in Paris in 1933.

Lowell compares Weber to Karl Marx, tracing the similar origins of their work in an effort to understand humans in the context of the modern capitalistic order and analyzing their very different conclusions. He shows how Weber's passion to base his work in objective, "value-free" methodologies keeps him from the propagandistic and dogmatic tendencies of Marxism. To demonstrate the continuing influence of Weber on Lowell, as well as Lowell's insight into Weber's achievement, I have included an informal speech from 1982, in which he reviews his own life as a sociologist and Weber's main ideas.

The Bennions returned to Salt Lake City on New Year's Day, 1934, penniless and jobless at the bottom of the Depression. They were still sorrowing over their first child, Laurel, born in France, who had died of an infection at six months. Lowell got work as an education director for the Civilian Conservation Corps (Federal public works) in Salina and then Soapstone, Utah, where he and Merle lived in an abandoned sheep camp. In the fall he was asked to head the new Salt Lake Institute of Religion, where he remained until 1962, interrupted only by a two-year term as the first director of the Tucson (Arizona) Institute. He managed to find time in the early part of 1934 to write his first Church manual, *What About Religion?,* a practical study of how religious feelings develop and affect our everyday lives, very much influenced by his knowledge of Weber's studies of world religions and religious forces. By 1937 his reputation had grown to the point he was invited by President Hugh B. Brown of the British Mission to write five articles for the *Millennial Star.* They show his growing confidence, first expressed in his mission diary when he was studying a variety of great religious and philosophical texts, that a life lived accepting the possibility of God's existence is not only intellectually defensible but also exciting, challenging, and much less wasteful than the alternative. He was increasingly convinced—and able to convincingly express—that life is purposeful insofar as it is meaningful, that is, as it is based on clearly conceived principles related to universal human needs. By 1939 his experience in developing a curriculum and in teaching and counseling college students provided the basis for a book review and a long essay on teaching for the new periodical of the Church Education System, *Week-day Religious Education;* for another MIA manual, *Youth and Its Religion;* and for the first version of probably his most important book: *The Religion of the Latter-day Saints.* That book became the standard theology text for the LDS institutes for many years and in 1955 was revised into *An Introduction to the Gospel,* which became a standard Sunday School manual for fifteen years and is still one of the best systematic versions of Mormon theology. It reflects Brother Bennion's characteristic struggle against the tendency to "pulverize" the gospel, to analyze and defend and explain it in small chunks that may have no logical connection and may, in fact, contradict each other. It powerfully demonstrates the coherent moral and spiritual force available in Mormon thought.

During the 1940s Lowell studied the intellectual contributions of Joseph Smith in restoring the gospel and gave radio talks in Salt Lake and the annual Joseph Smith Memorial Lecture at the Logan (Utah) Institute of Religion on the creative mind and generous spirit of the founder of Mormonism. He developed his orthodox, commonsense views of courtship and marriage, based on an analysis of three kinds of love—unconditional or Christ-like, friendship, and romance. He taught the need to build a relationship firmly on the first and second before the third can play its powerful, important role. And he continued to express his ideas in a variety of forums: Primary, Sunday School, and MIA manuals, Relief Society lessons, institute curriculum materials, and his first essay for the Church's official magazine, the *Improvement Era,* "The Fruits of Religious Living in This Life."

In the 1950s and '60s Brother Bennion developed into an amazingly prolific as well as effective writer, producing many excellent lesson manuals, three major books, and scores of fine articles for the *Improvement Era* and the *Instructor.* There were periods in the early '60s when he had an article in every issue of both periodicals and his manuals were being used by two or three different classes in both the Sunday School and the MIA, in English and also in a number of foreign languages. During the '50s he was invited by BYU President Ernest Wilkinson to give devotionals at various times and by University of Utah President Ray Olpin to give the baccalaureate address at the 1956 commencement. President David O. McKay asked him to speak at general conference in 1958 (and again in 1968, one of the few lay Church members so honored). He was asked to keynote a "Religion in Life Week" at the University of Colorado and to speak at the Deseret Sunday School Union Conference in 1962, and he addressed an "Inter-faith Dialogue" of Salt Lake religious leaders on aspects of Mormonism in 1963 and 1964.

During this time of intense intellectual effort, Brother Bennion was continuing his commitment to practical religion, not only through

Lambda Delta Sigma but also by developing a boys' ranch in Teton Valley, near Driggs, Idaho. Since his sociological study of Salt Lake boys in 1927, he had felt the need to provide urban youth with the opportunities for outdoor work and recreation that had blessed him as a boy. A former student offered financing, and Brother Bennion searched all over Mormon country until he found the right ranch. Then, aided by boys themselves (two sessions of forty each summer), he built the dormitories, lodge, and barns. He continued this unique service, at less than cost, helped by young counselors and providing reduced or no fees for the needy, for over twenty years, from 1962 to 1984, when his health would no longer permit. Now former students and counselors are planning to reopen the ranch. I know many—friends, children of friends, and other youths—who remember with enormous pleasure and gratitude the work and responsibility and cooperation, the faith-building discussions and counseling, at the ranch. They were blessed both by a utopian vision and by the ability of Brother B. to make his vision into a reality.

80 kids a summer

In 1962 Lowell Bennion left the Salt Lake Institute to become Assistant (and later Associate) Dean of Students and Professor of Sociology at the University of Utah. He had been courted for a full professorship by various departments of the U. throughout the '50s but had loved what he later called "the most complete relationship I have ever had with students" at the institute of religion too much to leave voluntarily. When he was released by the Church Department of Education from his work as institute director and teacher and invited to write courses of study at BYU, he decided instead to leave the system. He continued his output of manuals and articles for Church magazines for a while and continued to serve on the YMMIA general board and the Church's youth correlation committee (which met weekly to approve and coordinate all Church materials for youth). In 1968 he was asked to speak for the second time in general conference. But his role as a speaker and writer in Church forums was gradually diminished.

In the 1970s and '80s Brother Bennion's voice continued to be heard mainly through a series of short and quite popular books, published by Bookcraft and Deseret Book, and in various independent Mormon journals and forums. The books show his remarkable variety of expertise: a partial listing ranges from *Husband and Wife* and *On Being a College Student* (1972), to *The Things That Matter Most* (1978) and *Jesus the Master Teacher* (1980), to *The Book of Mormon, A Guide to*

Christian Living (1985) and in 1988 *The Unknown Testament,* a book on the Old Testament. His essays and talks have become fewer but more powerful. "By Grace Are Ye Saved," a Christmas sermon published in 1966 in *Dialogue,* a new independent journal of Mormon thought for which he was an advisory editor, is a confession of his own neglect of the central gospel principle of grace and a moving call to all works-oriented Mormons to see and include that central principle of our faith. "The Things That Matter Most," a lecture given at the invitation of leaders of the Boston Massachusetts Stake for their Education Week in 1977, is a beautifully personal testimony of his coherent philosophy of life. And his address to the Washington Sunstone Theological Symposium in June 1987, "What It Means To Be a Christian" (published in the July 1987 issue of *Sunstone),* gives a challenging and mature estimate of the essentials of the Christian life.

Lowell Bennion speaks with the highest authority about the Christian life because of the way he passionately but unostentatiously lives it. In 1972, as he puts it, he "left the halls of ivy for the real world." At age sixty-four, so much valued at the University of Utah that he could have stayed on there after retirement, he was asked to serve on a selection committee for a new executive director of the Community Services Council—and then accepted a draft to take the position himself. This private service agency, funded by United Way, had been mainly engaged in studying service needs and resources in the Salt Lake Valley. Brother Bennion led the council into direct service, which now includes a food bank that collects contributions (often through Brother Bennion himself in his truck) and stocks centers that provide food for thousands of needy households. As director, he also coordinates hundreds of volunteers doing chore services (painting and fixing up houses again as in the institute days, providing mail service and meals, and so forth) for the elderly and handicapped; an independent living center for paraplegics; a program to provide dentures and eyeglasses for indigent senior citizens at greatly reduced cost; and functional fashions to make manageable clothing for the handicapped. As Brother Bennion says, with admitted oversimplification, "I used to teach religion; now I practice it."

During these sixteen years of full-time community service, extending far past normal retirement as he has just passed his eightieth year, Lowell Bennion has also continued to serve his church faithfully and quietly—remaining on the correlation committee until 1972, serving on various high councils, being called as a bishop in 1979, and becoming a gospel doctrine teacher after his term as bishop.

The honors have come mainly from outside the official church and, despite Lowell's obvious embarrassment, have begun to crescendo in the 1980s:

The Phi Kappa Phi Honorary Address at BYU, 1973.

The invited address at the Boston Massachusetts Stake, 1977.

The 1981 Distinguished Service to Humanity Award from the Association of Mormon Counselors and Psychologists.

An honorary degree from the University of Utah, 1982.

Laudatory articles about him in the *Deseret News* (1984), *Sunstone* (1985), and Utah's *Peace News* (1987).

The Good Samaritan Award from Utahns Against Hunger (1985).

An Evening for Lowell Bennion, in October 1986, where he was praised by a poet and student, Emma Lou Thayne; a colleague at Community Services, Elaine Smart; a scholar and friend, Sterling W. McMurrin; and a General Authority and co-teacher, Marion D. Hanks. (He also received a station wagon—more comfortable for aging legs but still useful for delivering groceries—to replace the latest battered truck.)

Election to Utah's honorary society, the Beehive Hall of Fame (1987).

Recipient of the Richard D. Bass award for Distinguished Service by a Utahn in the Humanities (April 1988).

Subject of one of the essays on great LDS teachers in *Teachers Who Touch Lives: Methods of the Masters* (Horizon, 1988) and of an extended review-essay (including a complete, annotated bibliography) in the July 1988 *Sunstone*.

Charles Johnson, executive director of United Way, expressed well what the honors are for: "He's a combination of an Old Testament prophet, who wants to give you his vision of what should be, and a New Testament Good Samaritan, who doesn't stand back and talk, but steps in to do the good work himself."

The vision Lowell Bennion has provided in his teaching and writing is rich in variety and implication but coherent, focused on a few basics: Humans should engage in religious thought and living because otherwise their universal needs for meaning, for creative engagement in causes greater than themselves and extending beyond life, for unconditional love and strength to repent and change their lives, will not be met. He often quotes Goethe, "Life, divided by reason, leaves a remainder," and William P. Montague, "Religion is the faith that the things that matter most are not ultimately at the mercy of the things that matter least." He loves the free, open, creative spirit of the restored gospel, especially Joseph Smith's unique contribution to Christian thought, the idea that all humans have eternal, God-like being in themselves and were not created from nothing and cannot be reduced to nothing, and thus that their very natures require and yearn for expansion, love, meaning beyond the earthly and material, in fact, for eternal progression. He does not see the gospel as prohibition and restriction, not as doggedly earning rewards or being subjected to either irresistible grace or predestined damnation from an inscrutable Deity. For him the gospel is a call to respond freely and rationally to the grace and knowledge given by Divine Beings that enable us to fulfill our own natures as their literal children. "The truly religious person," he writes, "learns to thrill in the satisfaction that comes from freely living in harmony with God's laws." But he is also a stern realist; he knows that faith brings inner and eternal satisfactions but not relief from this world's evil and pain, and that loving service will not solve all problems or inevitably produce individual wealth or social utopias. He quotes the Hindu scripture, "To action alone thou hast a right, not to its fruits."

Brother Bennion has experienced and studied a great range of human life in detail and teaches practical guides: "Do not marry anyone with whom you have not worked on a committee." "A student should not come out of a class in religion with all the prophecies dated, the celestial kingdom landscaped, the past and future of the Creator understood, and himself ready to step into a place in the council of Deity." "Try a 'work party' sometime, where you have [groups of young people] helping the widows of the ward—serving with their hands, then coming together afterward for an old-fashioned supper, for singing, for prayer." "We should never hold a meeting, teach a class, or plan an activity without asking ourselves: How is this going to affect the people who will participate in the realization of their full potential as children of God?" Along with the practical advice, he is capable of creating memorable phrases: "In the realm of knowledge, one conforms to what is; in the realm of faith, one creates life after the image carried in the heart." "Even as I prefer marriage to living alone, so do I prefer to live in a world of both faith and rationality rather than in a world of either alone." "A Christian believes in plain and simple living and high thinking." Brother B. even indulged himself once in a set of poetic lines, which provide a concise version of his philosophy of life:

Learn to like what doesn't cost much.
Learn to like reading, conversation, music.
Learn to like plain food, plain service, plain cooking.
Learn to like fields, trees, brooks, hiking, rowing, climbing hills.
Learn to like people, even though some of them may be different . . . different from you.
Learn to like to work and enjoy the satsifaction of doing your job as well as it can be done.
Learn to like the songs of birds, the companionship of dogs.
Learn to like gardening, puttering around the house, and fixing things.
Learn to like the sunrise and sunset, the beating of rain on the roof and windows, and the gentle fall of snow on a winter day.
Learn to keep your wants simple and refuse to be controlled by the likes and dislikes of others.

Lowell Bennion's greatest and most lasting intellectual contributions, I believe, are his insistence on rational coherence in theology and his use of such a coherent, rational approach to give an understandable and personally moving explanation of the Atonement, the way in which Christ saves us from mortality, ignorance, and sin. Our theology has tended to be developed piecemeal in response to continuous revelation in complex and changing historical conditions. Lowell's writing has been a major factor both in giving it elegant intellectual shape and in revealing its powerful moral implications. He shows that its diverse teachings, which seem heretical to traditional Christian thought and elicit mockery from some non-Mormon thinkers and baldly inconsistent beliefs from some Mormon extremists, nevertheless have great rational consistency. Those diverse ideas, united into a systematic theology, lead directly from a marvelous affirmation of the eternal God-like nature of all humans and culminate in the call to respond to Christ's uniquely saving power and to serve him in the world in ways that fulfill our own and others' needs and nature.

Brother B's teachings are founded in the scriptures. I noticed as a student that his standard works were not marked up like most other teachers' (probably because of his aversion to proof-texting and to analyzing the gospel into disconnected, dogmatic fragments), but they were worn, throughout, to frazzled edges. He knows them well, all of them. It was through a more careful study than most others had made of the Book of Mormon teachings on the Atonement, particularly Alma 34, that he made his key discovery about how Christ's suffering and death can save us, not by paying for our sins after we have repented, but by providing us incentive and power to repent while we are still sinners. As Amulek says, the Atonement "bringeth about means unto men that they may have faith unto repentance." (Alma 34:15.) That simple change in emphasis, first articulated by Brother Bennion in his *Religion of the Latter-day Saints*, has, I know from much personal experience, released many Mormons from the burden of guilt they previously carried because they were focusing on paying and justice rather than on responding to Christ's mercy, his free gift. They have learned to look with assurance to Christ for strength to repent.

Despite his love for the scriptures, Brother B. has taken a helpfully rational approach to them—and to all other authority, again insisting on consistency, especially on harmony with Christ's teachings, and on individual responsibility. "I do not accept any interpretation of scripture that denies the impartiality or love of God or the free agency and brotherhood of man," he has said. His *Religion and the Pursuit of Truth* (1959) and *Understanding the Scriptures* (1981) remain among the very best works on epistemology in Mormon thought; they provide a comprehensive analysis of how we can effectively go about answering the most fundamental and difficult question we face: How do we know something is true, worthy of our commitment?

Finally, of course, Brother Bennion rightly sees his greatest contribution in his trying to live the Mormon religion rather than in his teaching and writing. The "best of Lowell Bennion" is not really in this selection of his writings but in his life. However, the two aspects of theory and practice, of word and action, as he well knows, are inseparable. In one of his first published essays, "Teaching Religion by Word of Mouth," he recognizes the great value of learning religion though experience and example but then explores the enormous value of a third way, through the spoken and written word: "The skillful writer with eyes to see and ears to hear and the talent to express his keener insight and deeper understanding singles out tragedy, builds a plot around it, holds our attention to it until we feel it more intensely than life itself." He recommends Jesus, "the artist in parable," as the great example, an example he explores in detail in *Jesus the Master Teacher* (1980). He himself is such an artist, constructing parables from his own and others' experience and using the scriptures with great power. But the particular power in his writing derives less from its literary beauty than from the moral authority of his life and the felt presence of that life in his teachings.

I offer as a primary example of Lowell Bennion's unique literary and spiritual achievement the short essay, "The Weightier Matters" (1978). It has been placed first in this collection because it is an excellent introduction to the values of his life and writing—and one of the very best essays written by anyone in our time.

These selected writings are arranged under eight subjects, but they have also been chosen so as to give a sense of the range and development of Lowell Bennion's ideas and approaches. They include work that taken together gives a comprehensive survey of his major contributions to Mormon thought, but not at the sacrifice of quality: The best essays, addresses, and chapters from his books are here, including most of those mentioned above. For readers who would like to read the selections in order of their writing or to trace the development of his thought, a chronological listing is provided on pages 285-86, as well as the thematically arranged table of contents. Each chapter has information about the original context and source. I have silently corrected any typographical errors or misquotations in the original printings, occasionally improved punctuation or syntax for clarity, and changed a few outdated spellings and words. Any substantive changes or additions are indicated with brackets; deletions are marked by ellipses.

EUGENE ENGLAND
PROVO, UTAH
JULY 1988

I
PERSONAL WITNESS

FAREWELL TESTIMONIAL
IN HONOR OF
Elder Lowell L. Bennion
PRIOR TO HIS DEPARTURE FOR THE
SWISS-GERMAN MISSION
TO BE GIVEN IN THE
FOREST DALE WARD CHAPEL
ASHTON AVENUE & 7TH EAST
THURSDAY EVE., OCTOBER 11th, 1928
PROGRAM 8:15 O'CLOCK VOLUNTARY CONTRIBUTIONS

Missionary farewell program, 1928

1

The Weightier Matters

Near the center of the Salt Lake Valley at the end of a picturesque lane lives a little lady of seventy-five in a two-room shack. Her house is heated by a coal range, which has a broken grate and a big hole between the firebox and the oven that prevents her from baking. The pipe from the stove to the chimney has a large crack that releases smoke and soot into her kitchen. She heats water for dishes and a sponge bath on top of the stove. Since the drainage system doesn't work, she throws her waste water out the front door. Years ago a leaky roof rotted away the bedroom ceiling and caved it in, so she now sleeps on the living room couch and looks up at another ceiling that is bowed toward her. The kitchen floor is covered with pieces of linoleum to cover up the cracks.

Her Social Security income is about $173 per month, so she can't fix up the house herself. Her husband died nineteen years ago, her only son eight years later. She has two daughters—one divorced with four children, the other chronically ill with six children and a husband of modest means.

Less than a block away stands an LDS chapel where the faithful meet regularly to praise God, to take upon them the name of Jesus Christ, and to discuss the Lord's poor in priesthood quorums. A few miles to the east other Saints live in luxurious homes with many bedrooms and multiple bathrooms.

While this woman's condition is extreme, it is not wholly unique. In the Salt Lake Valley there are 58,000 persons over sixty-five, 22 percent (about 12,000) of whom live below the federal poverty level.

This personal essay, published in the January-February 1978 Sunstone *and reprinted in the February 24, 1988,* BYU Student Review, *was a major influence in helping Brigham Young University students form a Service Association to replace student government. It captures in just a few paragraphs Lowell Bennion's central theme and the spirit of his central contribution to twentieth-century Mormonism.*

They must go without food or heat or medical care to survive. How can these conditions exist in Zion?

Similar conditions were found in ancient Israel in the days of Amos (760 B.C.). Large class distinctions had developed, a few people becoming rich while many suffered in poverty. The wealthy had no regard for the plight of the poor, but denied the poor their legal rights and sold debtors into servitude. Amos, in the fury of the Lord, lashed out against those who lived in luxury, indifferent to the suffering of their fellow Israelites.

"Woe to them that are at ease in Zion, . . . that lie upon beds of ivory, and stretch themselves upon their couches, and eat the lambs of the flock, and the calves out of the midst of the stall; that chant to the sound of the viol, and invent to themselves instruments of musick, like David; that drink wine in bowls, and anoint themselves with the chief ointments: *but they are not grieved for the affliction of Joseph.*" (Amos 6:1, 4-6; emphasis added.)

The scene Amos describes might be compared to a ward dinner or social. The Saints are busy enjoying the food and entertainment, and they do not sorrow for the suffering of their brothers. Somehow these affluent Saints lack any concern for those beyond their eyesight who are in need. Perhaps the greatest modern convenience is the ability to insulate against the poor—to assume either that there are no poor nearby or that some church or government program will take care of them.

There is a couple in their sixties in the south end of the Salt Lake Valley who have had neither teeth nor dentures for four years. They each have a pair of old misfit uppers they put in their mouths to go to funerals. The rest of the time they stay home, social isolates, surviving on soft and liquid foods. One set of dentures costs $350, but the cost is not covered by Medicare. Most of the health needs of the elderly—tooth, eye, and ear care—are not covered by Medicare. Government programs are not the answer. The generosity of some physicians is not enough. Occasional fits of charity are not sufficient.

Another woman, an intelligent, cultured lady of eighty-three, lives alone in her comfortable Salt Lake home. She is not in need financially, but she is nearly blind. Just cooking a meal is difficult, even dangerous for her. After she has eaten, she worries that she has forgotten to turn off the stove. When she answers the door, she wonders if it could be an intruder. Once a voracious reader, now she is unable to read her mail, write a letter, or look up a number in the phone book. She sits alone hour after hour in a dark room reviewing her life again and again, trying to keep her mind from slipping into forgetfulness and aimless wandering. She longs for conversation. She would like to have someone read to her. Friends and neighbors are good to her, but their occasional visits take up only a small fraction of her waking moments.

Yet Latter-day Saint youths in the surrounding area have time for skiing, shows, popular concerts, television, and sports events. In church the list of announcements often includes fathers and sons' outings, Halloween and Christmas parties, even money-raising projects to finance a trip from Salt Lake City to Disneyland. Seldom is a planned service project announced. It seems we are more often motivated by personal excitement and entertainment than by a sense of brotherhood or community.

In a village in Idaho a few years ago, my neighbor's haystack caught fire and burned to the ground. It was his winter's supply of hay to feed ten cows—his whole livelihood. Neighbors rushed to the scene, contained the fire with a bucket brigade, and saved his barn. Then they went home and each returned with a load of hay to rebuild their brother's stack.

Perhaps it is difficult in an urban society to reach out to the stranger, to the nonmember as well as to the co-believer. But we must become personally involved. Our time and means are desperately needed, not only to build human relationships but also to save the health and lives of the poor in our midst. Otherwise how can we escape the wrath of Amos or the condemnation of Jesus, who said in his day:

"Woe unto you, scribes and Pharisees, hypocrites! for ye pay tithe of mint and anise and cummin, and have omitted the weightier matters of the law, judgment, mercy, and faith: these ought ye to have done, and not to leave the other undone." (Matthew 23:23.)

2

Selections from Missionary Diary, 1928-31

T*hurs. Oct. 18th, 1928.* I left Salt Lake Wed. Oct. 17th at 6 P.M. Mother, father, Wayne, Merle, Paul, Eloise, Mr. & Mrs. Spencer & Ione saw me off. It was the hardest break away I have ever made. . . . I spent 2 hours with Bishop Woodruff in Denver. He showed the town and we exchanged friendship. I choked in trying to express my gratitude to him; and I perceived tears in his eyes.

Bonn Jan. 2, 1929. Arrived at 11 A.M. with "Hap" Carlson and Harold Calder. We tramped the streets from then until 9 P.M. Finally coming back to this place. . . .

Thurs. Jan. 3, '29. Spent the day freezing. Met Calder at 1:30 P.M. Looked over the situation here; . . . and wound up by a D. & C. reading for my spiritual pleasure. I thought of many things to write Merle about. . . .

[Undated cover letter, with pages from diary, from about this time.] Merle dear, I love you. My love and appreciation grows daily. I had a fine dinner today and spent the afternoon talking about the Gospel and you and life, my three favorites.

Merle dear I thank you and the Lord with all my heart. God bless that dear heart of yours. Tomorrow I should hear from you. All your Hubby's love and affection and blessings. Lowell.

Wed. Jan. 16th. Had a usual day of tracting. Went to Beule with Bro.

Lowell Bennion's only diary (October 1928 to May 1931) provides unique insight into his private reflections very early in what was to rapidly become a public life as teacher and administrator. It is handwritten, with almost daily entries, from which I have selected some that reveal tender and self-analytical dimensions not as apparent in his other work.

Weseman and "Hap." Bro. Weseman gave a fine talk and Herr Schwann followed with a rebuttal of every point. I realized my promise that I could discern spirits. I left the meeting happy and with increased faith. Wish I could talk and share my experiences with Merle. I saw and heard plenty of grief in married life here.

Sun. Jan. 20, '29. Ran all the way to the depot. Spent a very enjoyable day in Cologne. Heard Bro. Weseman's story of coming into the church and enjoyed his spirit and testimony. On the way home I read Dr. [Max] Haenle's article ["Some Inter-relations Between Religion and Economics"] and others in the Improvement Era [November and December 1929. Haenle, a non-Mormon professor of economics at the University of Erlangen, Bavaria, had been invited to give this address at the University of Utah]. I was greatly encouraged and determined. I arrived home and read two lovely-spirited letters from my dear Merle and one from father. I retired with love and joy in my heart for Merle and the gospel and determined to hit the work harder. . . .

Sun. Jan. 27, '29. . . . I read today a little blue book, The Philosophy of Herbert Spencer by Will Durant. It was very interesting, especially when I compared it with Christ's teachings in Matthew. The first was largely an admission that we didn't know anything fundamental about life, that religion was for primitive man and an outgrowth of myth. It is very faith promoting to me to compare as little (far) as I know the influence of Christ and other men.

True enough our religion is based on faith but the evidences are so great that it would amount to assurance in other fields.

It's a great life, Merle dear. I love your sweet spirit. Believe me the gospel certainly shows in one. You are more distinctive, original and <u>the only one</u> more than ever before. . . .

Tues. 5:30, 5ten Marz. . . . I have quite enjoyed the day. This morning I tracted alone for 3 1/2 hours and enjoyed a half-dozen good conversations and a good spirit. I like to go alone, then I have to talk and I'm a little funny but I like the way I preach the gospel better than my pardner. I try to go from what we agree on to something else instead of hitting up a debate right off. . . .

Sunday. 8 A.M. den 24ten Marz, 29 [1929]. I love you on our day Merle my own dear. Yesterday I visited Bethel but couldn't get inside the buildings without a guide on Sat. afternoon. Bethel is the institution for Epileptics. It is a regular little town—with its own police force, bookstore, factories, graveyards, tombstones for sale, bakeries and all. It is a marvelous Institution and I want to take time to study it.

10 P.M. . . . I'm happy tonight dear, in our love and the blessings of the gospel. Tonight I spoke again. I hadn't had the chance to prepare anything, only a plan in my head, and really Merle dear I enjoyed a fine spirit. I told them with assurance of the days to come. It always strengthens me to bear my testimony and I need all the strength I can get.

We had a very sad case in the branch. A fellow beat up his wife—came home drunk at 3 A.M. The sister has been putting up with it for years but now it looks like divorce and cutting someone off the church. I do my best to cheer the folks up and reassure them. A sister we blessed Montag is again well and gives the Lord the credit for it. Tomorrow night we are going to hear a famous Russian Chorus, one of the best in the world. . . .

[*About one year later*] After writing my diary at times, to my dear Merle, I've decided to keep a daily account. My first winter was spent in Siegen, Bonn and Cologne am/ Rhein. I worked happily with Harold J. Carlson of Ogden. I shall never forget the night Hap and I crossed the bridge between Bonn and Buel, which Bonn built and paid for. We visited the meeting of some apostate adventists in January 1929. The Lord blessed me with the gift of tongues that night. I bore testimony with tears in my eyes. Hap and I couldn't talk afterward for joy. I shouldn't forget the woman I met tracting who sat me on a chair and she took the table and wanted to hear everything from beginning to end. We made several friends in Bonn. The old bearded tailor, the political science writer, the professor, the young teachers. . . . Those days were happy, humble, and sincere. Hap and I have lived happily together and are still the closest of friends. . . . I worked [in Bielefeld] with Hans Beckmann from Feb. 7 to May 13 and with Kenneth Huber until Sept. 23rd, when I was transferred to Minden. That was the hardest separation since I left home. . . . It is too late to make a report of my Bielefeld days, but I'll never forget. . . . I was a sick man [with chronic appendicitis] as I saw the Minden Branch that Monday evening Sept. 24th. Billy Howell and I hit out in the villages to tract and enjoyed a splendid winter. . . . [A] joy has been to visit Mrs. Hofstätter almost weekly. She is beginning to understand our teachings better. Our bi-weekly meetings at Sis. Schödel's in Bückeburg are indeed wonderful. Her art, conversation, and suppers are choice. She needs and appreciates help and company. . . . One evening a workman spoke up in church, the same one who got married to keep out of the insane asylum. . . .

Sat. Mar. 29th [1930]. I read Plato, "Guest Meal," a talk on love by Socrates and friends, also a bit in Infidelity. Towards evening we visited Herr Stein, enjoying his paintings and life's history. He's a bachelor of 62. Lived for two years on two white biscuits a day only. . . . Toward 9 o'clock we heard that Noah's Ark was playing in the New Theatre. Floyd and I went for 15 cents a piece and enjoyed it greatly. . . .

Thurs. April 3. The papers arrived this morning. L.D.S. beat Logan 25-27, Jim starring for L.D.—it surely thrilled me. We tracted this morning, met only one interesting person. . . . Sometimes life seems like a dream. My memories are sweet and are satisfied by my assurance and hope of a future happiness with the girl of my love.

Thurs. 17th April. We tracted in the rain between here and Kutenhausen. Three families promised to come. I read Papini's "Life of Christ" in the afternoon. . . .

Tues. April 22, 1930. I studied this morning, enjoying father's April article in the Era [number VI of a twelve-part series, "A Spiritual Philosophy of Life"]. We tracted between Minden and Stummer and collected some little black fleas that caused a busy evening and alcoholic spray. . . . I studied for Br. Dröscher's lesson on "the fullness of Life." The day was concluded by arranging our trip to the Passion play about July 9th.

Fri. [April] 25th. I just finished Price's "O. T. History" and enjoyed it immensely, especially the last part—history between Malachi and Christ. The lives and teachings of the prophets were indeed interesting. It gives one a more human point of view and after all we are people, not a race of Gods, and the Lord handles with us as we do with a group of children. . . .

Tues. May 6th. . . . I surely love Dröschers and their good clear spirit. Moral conditions in Germany are absolutely rotten in all classes. There are 100 girls to 70 men in Germany. It's get a Man whether you have to marry him or not. It will surely be a fight for the good life in the whole world. . . .

Wed. 14. We blessed sister (82 yr. old) Justinia Meierhoff at Dreisbach's. She is a peach. We had a fish dinner at Dröschers and an enjoyable supper and English class, followed by a good Mutual class on the priesthood. . . .

Montag. May 19th. . . . This afternoon we tracted . . . met our old American friend and best of all Herr Heinrich Tahe, a philosopher 37 yrs. old. . . . We sat in his living room and talked of philosophy. I told him incidentally that my father was a professor of philosophy. . . . We talked about Kant, Aristotle, Schopenhauer. I was lucky enough to not express my ignorance on the subject. I must read more of these fellows. I explained our idea of a personal God who was a being in the universe and under law of course but at the same time ruling the Universe, just as Burbank had different crosses in plants so in a larger sense can God rule the world. His God was nature, but that isn't anything, doesn't explain the philosophical "Ausgang"—outlet. I felt the need of a book in the church for such good honest philosophers as this fellow and some day, if no one will write such a tract, I'll try. We shall take him a Book of Mormon. . . .

Mon. May 26th. This morning Br. Kerksiek told me I was transferred to Switzerland to be district Pres. of Zurich. He said [Pres.] Tadje had me in mind for Cologne for a long time or Karlsruhe but thought I would like it better in Zurich. I surely feel humble, but very happy to get to work in Switzerland. . . .

Thurs. June 5, 1930. I was in Bielefeld . . . and ate dinner at Recksieks. I surely love that family. Sis. Recksiek dreamed I came and greeted them. Well, it was a sad parting. They think lots of me, for some unknown reason. We heard the old records again; she gave me bananas and we said goodby with wet eyes and a lump. It surely pays to make friends rather than see cities or accumulate wealth.

Sat. 7 June. [In Heidelberg on way to Zurich] I stayed at Hotel Schrieder. . . . At six I was out, hiking up to old Heidelberg Castle and U. The latter isn't so prominent but it certainly is a beautiful old castle—a reddish sandstone with green vines and crumbly walls. Göethe wrote there in the fall of 1814 & 1815. They have a monument to him. . . . My first hotel stay in Germany. Merle and I must spend an evening (if not a semester) in Heidelberg—Germany's oldest University, founded in 1338. . . .

Sunday June 8th. . . . In Zurich I stayed at Baumans' who have been treating me wonderfully well. . . . In the evening meeting . . . Br. Tadje announced Br. Cannon's leaving and he spoke. Then I spoke a few minutes poorly, but enjoyed it immensely. Br. Tadje spoke very feelingly at the close. . . . The Saints were very friendly and good to me and if I'm not happy here it will be my own fault.

Br. Tadje told me they needed a spiritual leader here, a preacher—said I was the man. He's certainly off. Br. Winfield Cannon is a very wonderful fellow and I'm afraid. But I'll live a humble, clean hard-working life and trust the Lord to help us out. We closed the day at Baumans', enjoying graham bread, milk and cake.

Sunday 15th. I caught a train at 6 A.M. for Glarus. These Swiss "Bumble" trains stop every five minutes. At last I arrived at 8:15 and met the Oertli kids. That was some family; seven kids and two Aunts and nearly all very odd. We held Sunday School, ate salad and an Italian rice, then I preached poorly—wasn't prepared for enough inspiration. . . . I have a lot to learn and do and hope with the coming week to start anew in humility, faith and diligence. . . .

Mon. 16th. . . . Well sir it looks to me as though everything here needs changing. The problem in life is not to choose between good and evil but to choose within the realm of righteousness. The Lord help us.

Sunday, 22nd. We left for Basel at 7 A.M. and enjoyed a wonderful conference. Pres. Gaeth spoke well on youth in the afternoon meeting. In the evening Pres. [J. Golden] Kimball and [John A.] Widtsoe spoke very well and inspiring; especially Pres. Kimball on testimony and things understood by the spirit. . . .

Tues. July 1. . . . Lad, By, and I visited all of the classes in Mutual. Afterwards we had the famous session to settle difficulties between Br. Bauman & Suter. It lasted till 12 P.M., didn't become hot and was very enjoyable and a fascinating study. With the Lord's help all was well at 12 P.M. I walked home with Br. Feh, who was greatly relieved. I certainly felt a good spirit, and as though I was really useful here. . . .

Sunday, [July 6]. Reports off; Sunday School was interesting. Br. Feh requires "the word I was thinking of"—a poor art of teaching. . . .

Wed. July 9. [In Munich on the way to the Passion Play.] We went to see Emil Jennings in the "Blue Angel." The play was very poorly produced, but the acting was supreme. I'm back to the old conclusion. On a mission I'd rather work than travel.

Fr. July 11th. [At Oberammergau.] . . . The house was packed—5,000 and the show started at 8:15. I'm sitting a long ways back at the right. The good woman on the left allows me to use her field-glasses to see the tableaus which are indeed beautiful. Not a finger is moved. I enjoyed Judas, Mary Magdelena, Kaiphas and Nicodemus very much. Christus is very good—but fails to touch me with the mildness of Christ. Petrus is smaller and not so wild as I had him planned.

The long chorus of 50 makes a forceful impression as they march in and out. I was certainly impressed with the proceedings of the Sanhedrin. It was the old hate and jealousy of the world made living through the old law of self-justification. Justice and right aren't as flexible and relative as one is often led to think. . . .

The show was really remarkable considering the little town which produced it. Only native-born Oberammergauers were permitted to take part. I doubt that the sincerity was there which might have been years ago. I'm sure our church could put on something better, but not perhaps in such a small group. . . .

Tues. July 22nd. . . . We ate dinner at Ringgers. He gave me the works of Kant, Schopenhauer, Buddha, and Mohammed—if I could only find time for them. Supper was had in a rush at Müllers, then M.I.A. Well, I was weary—no mail from Merle.

Thurs. July 24th. Reports off to Basel, after a strenuous day—forgot it was July 24th. I went to Priesthood meeting in Zurich—don't like Br. Feh's question answer—"That isn't the word I wanted."

Sunday, 27th. [At St. Gallen.] . . . We had chocolate at Häfens, hiked up the mts. and then talked with Billiters on Free Masons. Read "The Mysterious Preacher," Elder Ballard's Sermon on the Masons. "Paradise Lost" by Milton. In fact I must read more, exercise more faith, get my eyes well and happy and really enjoy life to its fullest. I am too often depressed of late—due to a realization of ignorance and the sad conditions one sees.

Sat. [Aug. 2]. I wrote letters and sent supplies out this morning. This afternoon I wrote long letters [and mailed them], came home, pressed my suit, ate carrots & a piece of bread & honey & settled down for a little bit of Buddha's philosophy. I found it to be very good and was deep in thought when Br. Meierhofer arrived and we went and blessed Sister Lauhe, who had broken her wrist. . . .

Sun. Aug. 17th. . . . In Zurich this evening, I made a fool of myself trying to talk about "false teaching of churches at the time of Jos. Smith." The people were tired & I was faint and the Lord left me very much alone. I guess I wasn't worthy of his spirit—anyway I felt like 2 cents afterwards. . . .

Monday [Aug. 26]. I went to St. Gallen, meeting an interesting old lady on the train, who had been in America four years. I shall send her a Book of Mormon. . . .

Sunday [Sep. 1]. Branch Conference in Zurich; the meetings were good and well attended. Br. Gunnel & I had dinner at Birkmeier's, after which I studied for the evening meeting. The Lord certainly helped me. I felt a wonderful spirit and a great deal of joy in speaking on faith & Christ's divinity and second coming. . . .

Sat. Sept. 6. This afternoon I read history and articles on "Current History." It was a good change. Tonight I'm writing letters and studying for tomorrow. I feel well, happy and full of faith.

Sunday [Sep. 7]. I went to Wäderswiel with Br. Suter to their Sunday School Conference. It was interesting. The saints have an inferiority complex. I gave a poor talk. Afterwards I went to Luzern. We enjoyed a good meeting in which Br. Bauman talked from Adam to Joseph Smith and I spoke 15 min. on the S. S. Afterwards brother Stewart baptized Minna Heine (twice) and I confirmed her. Perry and I went to bed at 11 together. At 2:15 I left him with mutual consent and slept much better on the floor.

Monday [Sep. 8]. We arose a bit late, went tracting in the country, enjoying a fruit lunch sitting on the banks of a creek. . . . Perry suggested that we would do better, have more success in bringing souls to the church, if we would go home and raise babies.

Thursday, Sept. 18, 1930. Two years ago this morning Merle and I got married. We were happy, in love, full of faith in each other and a supreme being. Here I am sitting in a train between Schoffhausen and Winterthur. My happiness is enriched with gratitude and appreciation, which could only come with the experience of the last two years. I certainly love Merle and imagine what a brave girl she has been these two years. Some day I hope to make it all good—but I believe she is already repaid. . . .

Mon. [Oct. 13]. This A.M. I wrote the [district elders] and arranged packages. In the afternoon I studied, chased costumes with Br. Suter, ate supper (a very dry one) at Weiersmüller's, and talked a little psychology, sang a song and got home at 11 P.M. Sometimes I feel much better than others, mentally. I still have a big fight on—sometime—somewhere.

Thurs. [Oct. 23]. . . . We had a good dinner at sister Schelble's and afterwards she told me her troubles from 20 years back. People enjoy heaping their troubles on me it seems, and I hear them gladly because I can understand their feelings and help them occasionally. Tonight I received a very sweet letter from her & shall answer the first chance. We were called to bless Sister Ringger. It fell my lot to seal the anointing and I enjoyed a sweet spirit, promising her health. Afterwards I rode to church with Br. Ringger on his motor—Boy what a thrill.

Friday. Sister Ringger feels better after the blessing last night. We had supper at Fehrs and oh my what a sad situation. They know less about raising kids than anyone I have ever seen. . . .

Sunday, Nov. 2nd. It is a funny feeling to have a conference in which you take charge. Ours started at 8:30, at which 105 were present. It was really very worthwhile—this separation into different classes. The only mistake was that we had 2 themes instead of just one. One must concentrate in such meetings. Sunday school . . . was very good. . . . 340 attended, a record for Zurich. . . .

Thurs. Nov. 13th. I was up early reading Faust, tracted with Br. Gunnel, hearing his troubles and ambitions. He's a good fellow, but doesn't receive the help and encouragement from his partner, that he should. . . .

Tues. 18th. . . . I enjoyed Schiller's "Thirty Year War" and the Book of Mormon. In fact I was so interested that my train left without me. Instead of becoming disgusted, I bought some hazel nuts and figs, my favorite lunch. . . .

Sat. Nov. 29th. Today was a full, enjoyable day. This morning I worked on the books, went to dinner at Benz's. After which I dug up their garden for 1 hour and perspired freely. It made me feel healthy and living again. She appreciated it too. I returned home at 4 P.M. and found letters from Merle and father. They were certainly good and interesting. Father & Merle had agreed that we should stay in Europe and study until I received a Ph.D. I was quite thrilled and stimulated with this thought—and really believe it the best thing to do. . . .

Sunday 30th. . . . The Relief Society evening & play in Zurich was wonderful. They played it very well. I enjoyed talking on the subject of Mother & purpose of Relief Soc. for a few minutes. I felt a sweet, determined spirit. . . . We blessed Br. Führer and Sister Urban. I like these folks better every day. Sister Thur said she had a wonderful dream about me. . . .

Tues. [Dec. 9]. Br. Führer was indeed happy to see us in the hospital. He is a dear Brother. I enjoyed reading III Nephi very much.

Thurs. [Dec. 11]. We walked and tracted to Hügglingen. . . . The most excitement came as a couple of fellows tried to take my tracts away. We refused them the privilege, and got away without being mobbed. . . .

Sat. [Dec. 20]. . . . From Meierhofers, we went to see Br. Führer, blessed him and promised him health and strength. I was chilly and not at all well until I felt that sweet spirit. I was indeed happy as we left his home. . . .

Thursday, Christmas 12:10 P.M. 1930. Since last Saturday I haven't had time to write, sleep or eat regularly. I worked on reports each night till 12-3 A.M. One of my joys has been the recovery of Br. Führer, for whom we fasted and prayed and blessed.

. . . I feel very responsible to other people and not quite as selfish as I used to. My heart really goes out to the poor and needy and sick. I hope the Lord will see fit to lead me in paths of enlightened service for my fellows. I wish I could increase the faith of other people in God. . . . I've enjoyed an unusual amount of eye strength in the last few days. I never dreamed they could stand the strain. I am very thankful for this blessing—it gives me new hope in future efforts. . . .

Sat. [Jan. 3, 1931]. I . . . went to Wehrli's for dinner, discussed geology with him and then left for ________, where the ________ family welcomed me. [Their daughter] confessed her sin to me and I did my best to comfort her & pleaded for a better life as her only means of receiving forgiveness. . . .

Thurs. [Jan. 8]. . . . A special delivery . . . announced the birth of a girl to [the ________ daughter] and the death of the same. I was asked to go or send someone. It was very saddening news, to have to bury a child under those conditions, illegitimate, well-known in a small village.

Friday. I arose early after a restless night and caught a 6:55 for ________, where I found things very dark. We held a funeral at 2 P.M., all 10 of us, on a cold day. . . .

Tues. Jan. 20. . . . I went to Eggenbergers where we discussed the Gospel until 2 A.M. At last I got to the grounds of his theory of immortality. I told him he was wrong, entirely so. . . .

Tues. Jan. 27th. . . . At 12:40 I arrived in Glorus and spent an enjoyable afternoon at the Jennys'. They fixed my old coat and new one too. Dinner and supper were very tasty. Coming home on the train an old beggar pleaded for 1 Fr. for food. I gave him a half of [my bread].

Fri. Jan. 30th. A long sweet letter from Merle quite thrilled me. She certainly nourishes a lovely spirit in life and love. . . .

Sunday [Feb. 8]. Today was enjoyable. In the officers' meeting I had fun asking the question, "What should be the first question in a class?" . . . In the evening meeting I enjoyed a helping spirit, speaking on [H. G. Wells's] "In the Country of the Blind." I tried and the Lord helped me cheer a great number up a little.

Wed. Feb. 25th. . . . [Went to] Dr. Strasser's concluding lecture on Mental Diseases and Criminology—affirming my old learning, that criminals aren't born.

Sunday, Mar. 8th. Br. Luter and I visited sister Jagger in Richterswil and tried to comfort her. In the meeting in Wädenswil we talked about her and certain higher principles of the Gospel rather earnestly. . . .

Monday [Mar. 9]. . . . We fasted today for Br. Anderson . . . I spent the afternoon writing a lesson for the city missionaries. . . .

Thurs. Mar. 19th. . . . I enjoyed a good day working on lessons, . . . reading a little on the Atom and Molecule. Life is a funny thing indeed but very interesting.

Saturday [Mar. 21]. . . . Br. & Sis. Schmid confided in me—saying that she was suffering from a form of insanity. Br. Schmid called it being possessed with the devil. I saw her condition as a result of her physical weakness. We blessed the poor soul. She hung on to me, to my embarrassment.

Wednesday, April 8th. Pres. Tadje wrote me assuring me of a prompt release, etc. My heart dropped about an inch. It will be hard to say goodbye to these dear old saints here. . . .

Friday, April 10th. We had a good missionary meeting, which proved to be a touchy affair. I certainly felt poor—broke down a little. Afterwards we saw Charlie Chaplin in "City Lights." I didn't care much for it. . . .

Sat. [April 11]. I spent the day [in the hospital] with Merrill Anderson, who was feeling very blue—a few pains etc. [after his emergency operation the day before]. I read "An American Idyll," which pepped me up some—as much as him. I translated until 10:30 P.M. I am very tired, very much lost in the schedule of things.

Wed [April 15]. We had real old American "mush" at Fehs, visited Br. Anderson with [Pres. and Sis.] Tadje, said goodbye to them and went to Suters, where we had a good dinner. To my surprise, Suters showed and expressed regret at my leaving. It was very comforting to me. . . . I rushed to Luzern and told them goodbye, promising, if possible, to return some day.

Fri. [Apr. 17.] . . . No mail from home—no time to write.

Saturday Morning, May 23rd. 8:45 A.M. A telegram from Spencers. "Merle on Train." Talk about your thrills and surprise. I am fairly shaking from emotions. Good old Spencers, always pulling off something original and unique.

3

The Place of a Liberal in Religion

Words change their meaning in time through usage. *Awful,* for example, once meant full of fear and awe; now it usually means bad or appalling. Likewise the word *radical* means literally "a person who gets at the root of things," but has come to mean one who is disruptive, if not destructive.

Words not only change in meaning through usage but they also mean different things to different people. This is particularly true of abstract, general terms that lack a concrete referent. The word *liberal,* the focus of our interest here today, is just such a woolly word. It has enjoyed a long and quite respectable history, but today a conservative Latter-day Saint may equate his liberal brother with a heretic or an apostate, while the [apostate] may refer to a liberal Mormon as a middle-of-the-roader unwilling to stand for anything.

The title of my talk today implies that there is room within religion for a liberal. And since we are meeting under the auspices of a Latter-day Saint Institute of Religion, my title also implies that the liberal has a respectable role to play in faith in The Church of Jesus Christ of Latter-day Saints.

The Meaning of Liberal

Let us first look into the derivation of the term. The word *liberal* has a Latin root *libera* from *liberare* and means to set free. A liberal means literally, "pertaining to a free man." From the *Oxford English Dictionary* we read such characterizations as these: "free from restraint," "free in speech or action," "free from narrow prejudice," "free from bigotry or unreasonable prejudice based on tradition and established institutions," "open-minded," "candid."

From Webster's unabridged dictionary we read that a liberal is a person who is "not confined nor restricted, open-minded, broad-

Dr. Bennion delivered this classic talk at a devotional of the LDS Student Association at the Salt Lake Institute of Religion on February 28, 1969.

minded, not bound by authoritarianism, orthodoxy, or established forms in action, attitude, or opinion," "tolerant of change," "not bound by dogma, tradition or convention."

One author summarizes these statements in one sentence: "The defining trait of the liberal character is a will to be liberated from the coercion of external controls."

The History of Liberalism

Liberalism as an outlook on life—a *Weltanschauung*—is a product of modern Western civilization, of Europe and America. It was a movement to set men free from the rigid authority, control, dogmas, and traditions of both political and religious institutions of the Middle Ages. The liberal spirit found expression in many facets of life—in economic and political changes as well as in philosophy and theology. John Milton, John Stewart Mill, John Locke, and Adam Smith in England; Descartes and Rousseau in France; Goethe, Schiller, Lessing, and Kant in Germany; and Channing and Emerson in America—to name but a few—were liberators of the human spirit. Liberalism had many roots: the Renaissance (which was to a great extent a restoration of Greek culture), the Reformation, Humanism, experimental science, but most of all man himself, a free agent seeking his own freedom. These are some of the roots, I think, of our liberal tradition.

With this all-too-sketchy effort to define the word *liberal* and to recount the origin of the liberal movement, let us turn to the role of the liberal in religion today. (I warn you at this point that I shall be developing my own conception of a liberal, so be critical. However, I think that what I am going to say is consistent with the traditional meaning of liberalism. It is not inconsistent with the historical usage of the term.)

1. The first characteristic of a liberal is that he thinks. This means that he does his own thinking. In fact, anyone who thinks must think his own thoughts. A parrot or a parakeet is not a thinker but a mimic.

A liberal recognizes that man is a rational creature—*homo sapiens,* which means literally man of wisdom or knowledge. Believing that "the glory of God is intelligence" and that man is a child of God and made of eternal intelligence, how natural for a Latter-day Saint to believe that the glory of man also lies in his intelligence.

To say that a man does his own thinking does not mean that he is self-sufficient, that he has no need of the thinking of fellowmen or God. Only a fool lives within the perimeter of his own self-generated thought. A liberal mind is simply an open mind, eager to learn from any man. If he is a religious liberal, he will also feel his dependence on God, walk with humility—seek, ask, and knock at His door.

A liberal can also even accept things on authority. This he must do or learn everything from scratch. But the liberal is careful in his choice of authorities; he follows those who have established themselves legitimately through their logical thought, experience, or intuition and revelation. And he will prove his authorities by the same methods by which they became such—by thinking, by experience, by inspiration. A liberal will test another man's thinking by his own thinking, another man's inspiration by his own quest for inspiration, another man's way of life by his own.

Religion, like music, philosophy, or science, has no meaning to a person until it becomes his own. And so a liberal in religion carries his own lantern, which he lighted by the flame of an Amos, Alma, Jesus, or Joseph Smith and which he tries to keep aglow by the Spirit of God.

(I remember a very vigorous discussion one summer with college students in a Sunday School class in the University Ward. A student from BYU answered a question by quoting her teacher in theology. The meaning of her quotation was not clear to the class and so we asked her what it meant. She said, "I don't know, but I believe it because Professor So-and-so said it." She was not a liberal.)

While the liberal in religion has a high regard for the use of his mind, his religious life is not limited to his thinking. He knows that religion's unique function in life is to help man face the unknown and his contingency and to find meaning in his total existence as part of his total being.

"Life," said Goethe, "divided by human reason leaves a remainder." Religion is one appropriate way of dealing with that remainder. Religion transcends knowledge. It is also deeply concerned with relationships—man to man and man to God—and with other ultimate values in life: freedom, integrity, love, hope. These basic values and relationships can never be known by reason alone but must be learned intuitively and experientially.

Yes, a liberal walks by faith and lives by hope. He has no other choice save despair. And he is too optimistic to succumb to despair and cynicism. His walking by faith may differ from that of some of his co-religionists in two ways. Like Paul of old, he realizes that now we "see through a glass, darkly." A liberal is not dogmatic but open-minded, eager to recheck his thinking, to change and enlarge his view of religion as he increases in experience. (He takes the ninth and thirteenth Articles of Faith literally.) He realizes that his own knowledge of even eternal truths—of God's nature, of love or any other principle of the gospel—his knowledge of these things is not absolute but relative to his capacity, experience, and position.

People talk of unchanging truths in the gospel, and they worry about anybody who talks about changing truths. Now I'm not denying that there are absolute truths in life, in the universe, in the mind of God. I think love is an absolute, universal value. The thing I'm trying to say is that *man's understanding of any of these absolutes, of any truth, is not absolute, is not eternal, and ought not to be unchanging.* Our own human understanding is relative to our ignorance and to our limited experience. This is a difference that some people don't seem to understand.

A liberal is willing to walk by faith, but not blindly, if and when he can see. And so he uses faith not as a blind substitute for knowledge but as a springboard or a flashlight by which to gain knowledge. He feels free to question interpretations of religion that run counter to his knowledge, experience, and inspiration. (I think it was John Taylor who said that he would not be a slave to God Almighty.)

The Latter-day Saint liberal sees in the spirit of the Mormon movement encouragement to use his mind freely. There is a strong rational emphasis running through the restored gospel—frequent reference to a law-abiding universe, encouragement to seek learning by study and by faith, the statement that "man cannot be saved in ignorance," the admonition to "be anxiously engaged" in a good cause because the power is in man wherein he is an agent unto himself. These things are said so often they become trite. But think about them; they encourage us to use reason, to think.

Mormonism, like all historical movements, is a vast and complex phenomenon, and it may appear to be eclectic, an anachronism, or a hodgepodge to the outsider looking in. But to some of us on the inside, it has an inner logic of its own. Religion is not all emotion and faith and grace, as important as these things are; it also has a rational structure growing out of faith. The Ten Commandments make a lot of sense; the Beatitudes build on each other step by step to form a remarkable set of values, which one author calls "a map of life." Faith, repentance, baptism by water, and the Holy Spirit lay a coherent foundation for the Christian life; the attributes of God—justice, love, freedom, creativity, intelligence, fatherhood—complement each other and together form an adequate conception of a personal being worthy of our full adoration and commitment. Free agency, eternal progression, the brotherhood of man, "man is in the image of God," "man is that he might have joy" are postulates of faith about the nature of man that challenge the mind as well as belief and feeling. The liberal Latter-day Saint has every reason to make thinking a cornerstone of his religious life.

We've been talking about a liberal as one who tries to think critically, thoughtfully—do his own thinking. A liberal does more than think.

II. Second, a liberal's religion has strong human interest. For him, theology, scriptures, ordinances, priesthood, and history are not ends in themselves but are sacred and important means of helping men to realize the purpose of their lives. Religion is purposeful, and its purpose is "to bring to pass the immortality and eternal [God-like] life of man." Jesus said, you recall, that man was not made for the sabbath but the sabbath was made for man. He might have said the same thing for each and all the principles of the gospel. Throughout the Gospels, Jesus is depicted as one who cared for men, who related the gospel to human needs, who told his disciples to do likewise: "Feed my sheep," "Feed my lambs." "By this shall all men know that ye are my disciples, if ye have love one to another." "Inasmuch as ye have done it unto one of the least of these my brethren, ye have done it unto me." A liberal does not reject theology or scripture; he simply believes that they must be interpreted and used in ways that will serve the divine purpose in human life.

One of my liberal friends called Mormonism "humanism in a context of faith." And I like that. Humanism in a context of faith—a humanism supported by faith and with divine goals and eternal perspective, if you will.

With his intense concern for man's welfare here and now, the liberal is not playing the role of the heretic but is walking in the tradition of the greatest of the prophets and of Jesus. The law of Moses was, despite its occasional lapses into harshness and particularism, humane and compassionate, remarkably so for the time in which it was written. The Hebrew prophets—Amos, Hosea, Micah, Isaiah, and Jeremiah—gave justice and mercy among men top priority in religion, in man's service to God. Paul said, "Though I have the gift of prophecy, and understand all mysteries, and all knowledge; and though I have all faith, so that I could remove mountains, and have not charity, I am nothing." (1 Corinthians 13:2.) And Joseph Smith tried desperately in many directions to transform the life of the individual and society through the medium of religion.

III. Third, a liberal emphasizes the ethical and moral aspects of religion. This follows naturally from his human concerns. Morality has to do with man's relationship to fellowman right now, in the present. This emphasis is also basic in our Judaeo-Christian faith. The prophets were harsh indeed on men who worshipped God with their lips while they were robbing the widow and orphan with their hands between sabbaths. Hear the words of Isaiah:

> To what purpose is the multitude of your sacrifices unto me? saith the Lord: I am full of the burnt offerings of rams, and the fat of fed beasts; and I delight not in the blood of bullocks, or of lambs, or of he goats.
>
> When ye come to appear before me, who hath required this at your hand, to tread my courts?
>
> Bring no more vain oblations; incense is an abomination unto me; the new moons and sabbaths, the calling of assemblies, I cannot away with; it is iniquity, even the solemn meeting. Your new moons and your appointed feasts my soul hateth; they are a trouble unto me; I am weary to bear them.
>
> And when ye spread forth your hands, I will hide mine eyes from you: yea, when ye make many prayers, I will not hear: your hands are full of blood. Wash you, make you clean; put away the evil of your doings from mine eyes; cease to do evil; learn to do well; seek judgment, relieve the oppressed, judge the fatherless, plead for the widow. (Isaiah 1:11-17.)

What Isaiah is saying, as you know, is that it doesn't matter what our prayer life is like or our temple work or the ordinances we've participated in or what sacred days and ceremonies we celebrate, if we do not practice justice; and if we do not relieve the oppressed and the widow and the orphan or the minority groups or anyone else in need, then our formal religious life is vain.

The liberal does not put man above God—far from it—but he recognizes God's deep concern for man, remembering that Christ lived, suffered, and died for man, and that he loved the poor, dined with sinners, and healed the afflicted. The liberal believes, with Jesus and the prophets, that nothing should stand in the way of justice and mercy among men, that everything written not only in "the law and the prophets" but in all of scripture depends on love of God and man.

Morality is not the most unique contribution of religion to life; faith is the more distinctive gift of religion to man. However, in the teaching and life of the Hebrew prophets and Jesus, morality had a certain primacy. Religious worship and belief that ignored or contradicted justice and mercy were condemned. Micah gives classic statement to the essence of religion and ends with what I think is the creed of a religious liberal, when he says: "Wherewith shall I come before the Lord, and bow myself before the high God? . . . He hath showed thee, O man, what is good; and what doth the Lord require of thee, but to do justly, and to love mercy, and to walk humbly with thy God?" (Micah 6:6, 8.)

IV. The liberal in religion feels a closer kinship to the prophetic than he does to the priestly role in religion.

Careful students of religious history have noted two types of religious leaders, particularly in Judaism and Christianity. Max Weber, a great German scholar, classified religious leaders as prophets and priests. And mind you, these are types and they are perhaps spoken of more in sociological than in religious terms.

Weber described prophets as men who spoke "as one having authority" out of their own calling. They broke with the existing order; they were critics of the immoralities and religious formalities of their people, such as I've illustrated with Isaiah and Micah. Like Jesus, they were revolutionary in their day: "It is written . . . but I say unto you." Jesus didn't reject the old, but he gave a new thrust and a different emphasis to that which had gone before: "Woe unto you, scribes and Pharisees, hypocrites! for ye pay tithe of mint and anise and cummin, and have omitted the weightier matters of the law, judgment, mercy, and faith: these ought ye to have done, and not to leave the other undone." (Matthew 23:23.)

Prophets try to get people to put religion in perspective, to see it in terms of great fundamentals and in terms of ethics as well as theology. Prophets have never been bound by the past. They speak for God afresh in the interest of man, in the light of the great ideals of religion, and in the light of God's purpose and character. The other type of religious leader, Weber calls a priest. By this he means a man in any faith whose primary concern is to conserve the religion of the founder—of a Moses or Christ, for example. The priest canonizes scripture, refines doctrine, establishes tradition, records history, performs sacred rites and sacraments. In this way he builds and maintains the church, welding the believers into a meaningful fellowship.

Religion wouldn't survive if we just had the prophetic word. It would die with the prophet. Religion needs an order of religious leaders who are concerned with conservation and preservation. And I have the greatest respect for men who have done and who do this for us. If we didn't come together and partake of the sacrament as a body of believers; if we didn't sing Mormon hymns together and pray together; if we didn't have traditions to inspire us, we wouldn't exist as a religious movement, and maybe our individual religious life would fade out.

Both the prophet and the priest have great roles to play in religion, the one to create and the other to preserve. Individual leaders and followers may be closer to one type or the other or may even combine both in their lives, as Ezekiel did. But I repeat that I think liberals are more caught up with the prophetic emphasis than with the priestly.

Conclusion

Now a word in conclusion. Let me recapitulate and bear my testimony. We have described the liberal as one who feels free to think about religion and make it his very own. We have noted that the liberal's first concern is "the worth of souls," of each human being here and now as well as in eternity. Therefore, the liberal is deeply committed to the moral requirements of the gospel—to justice and mercy—in the life of the individual and in the nature of society. He sees this as the main thrust of the prophets and Jesus.

The liberal in religion has great affection for the creative, idealistic, and fundamental character of the prophetic emphasis in religion, though he also respects and sees the need for the more institutional functions of religion—if these are used to build faith and righteousness and satisfy human needs and not to substitute for them.

I have an idea that all religious people have to have some way of knowing that they are being religious, that they are religious. There is a danger, I think, that people who are too wrapped up in theology may get their religious satisfaction out of theology; or if they are too wrapped up in institutional activity—church activity—they may equate religious living with church activity. I maintain that theology and church activity, and all the ordinances of the Church, ought to lead us somewhere. They ought to result in people learning to do justly and love mercy one to another. They ought to build faith and righteousness and not substitute for these things. And every ordinance of The Church of Jesus Christ of Latter-day Saints, if you look it up in the original, has this intention. It is a symbol of moral religious living, not an end in itself. (You're not baptized until you become a real Christian, if you read Doctrine and Covenants, section 20, verse 37.) Listen to the sacramental prayer next Sunday. We bear witness that we take upon us the name of Jesus Christ, and keep his commandments, and always remember him, that we might have his spirit to be with us. The sacrament is instrumental to the religious life, to the moral life; it is not an end in itself. We mustn't get caught up in theology and history as ends in themselves.

The liberal also sees more good than evil in human nature. As one of them, an interesting convert to the Church, said to me, "How can a person who is a child of God be more innately evil than good?" Despite man's terrible inhumanity to man, the liberal Mormon will not despair of human nature but will work for its self-fulfillment with Christ as the ideal.

A final word. There are many liberals in our society outside of the domain of religion who are highly critical of it, particularly in its institutionalized forms. I have friends who are highly critical of everything that goes on in the name of religion. Many of these liberals are not only free-thinking but also highly ethical, moral, and humane. I have great respect for them. But there are also liberal-minded people within religion—and many within the Latter-day Saint faith. Each is an individual with his own cherished faith and his own principles. It is a gross and shameful error to stereotype all Mormon liberals as heretics, apostates, hypocrites, or wolves in sheep's clothing. Many Mormon liberals—as I have tried to characterize them—share with their conservative brothers faith in God, faith in the Lord Jesus Christ, faith in personal immortality, and faith in the restoration of the gospel and Church of Christ.

In my judgment, a liberal Mormon can be just as orthodox as a conservative Latter-day Saint. Orthodox means to be true or sound in belief or opinion. A religious liberal may in one sense be more orthodox than his critics because of his thoughtful commitment to the great fundamentals of his theology and religious ethic. The liberal's faith may be stronger than that of others because he has not been afraid to test it in the arena of thought and in the crucible of man's total living.

It is my hope and prayer that so-called conservative Latter-day Saints may learn to respect the so-called liberals in the Church and that liberal Mormons will respect and value the role of the conservative. After all, these terms are but labels imposed on people who are unique and human. Surely the gospel of Jesus Christ is big enough to accommodate more than one emphasis within its framework. Consider how the books of James, Romans, and 1 John differ from each other in emphasis, and yet each contributes so richly to the fullness of our Christian faith. Martin Luther called the epistle of James an epistle of straw and preferred Romans and all the epistles of Paul.

Well, I like James too, and Romans, and I appreciate John's great emphasis on love. And these books represent phases: three facets, three dimensions of the Christian life. May we who profess discipleship of Jesus Christ cooperate in building his kingdom, and, in the process, may we be willing to hear one another and then to either respect or hammer out our differences, I pray in Jesus' name. Amen.

4

The Things That Matter Most

I've been well repaid for coming here, after that long ride from Salt Lake. I've enjoyed the lectures and the music. Mormons can shift moods faster than anyone I know. But it has been a very rich educational week and enjoyable for me. I have also been pleased to meet former students here, and new acquaintances, and have enjoyed the hospitality of your stake people and the Lythgoes [Dennis and Marti]. You have received so much that I think your glass is full, but I'm going to chat with you a little bit tonight. If I see you dozing off, I think I'll turn it into a discussion. I'd rather teach than preach anyway.

I have also decided to talk off the cuff rather than to read a scholarly paper, though I certainly respect the scholarly papers that have been read.

We all think we live in two worlds. One is the world of reality, the objective world, the total world and universe in which we live. That is the world of nature and her laws; the world of human nature, of nations of people with all their problems and all their conflicts. And in the world of God the Creator, his ways are mysterious at times and not fully known to man. We live in this total reality, this total objective reality. When I think of this, I don't feel very important; I don't feel very powerful. I have to adapt to nature. I have to adjust the best I can to the laws and forces of nature. I don't have a lot of influence with my fellowmen. I can't do much about China and Russia and other nations. I can't even do much about American politics.

Man in his total existence is quite powerless and quite contingent. That is to say, he is dependent on forces beyond his control. I didn't used to think that when I was young, but I know it now. Somebody said years ago that man is an infinitesimal bit of nothingness standing on the brink of eternity. That is a special definition of man. That is

In 1977 Dr. Bennion was invited to give this address for the Education Week in the Boston Stake; it was published as a book under the same title but in a modified form, by Bookcraft in 1978.

even a kind of biological definition. In the face of war, cancer, and pollution, I feel quite helpless.

We are living in this larger world of what I call reality, this objective world. We also live in a subjective world that is part of the larger world, but each of us, I think, has this faith: Each of us can carve out of the larger world a life of our own. We prefer some things to others. We have desires, strong desires that we can pursue. We call these preferences values. I prefer Beethoven to rock music. You may prefer rock music. I prefer orange juice to beer. Some prefer beer—not here, but I know people who do.

When we find our values in life, things that are most worthwhile, things of greatest worth to us, then we begin to feel our individuality, our creativity, our freedom, our strength. We begin to get possession of life when we concentrate not on the whole of reality in which we feel insignificant, but when we select certain things we are determined to live for; it seems to me that's when we get hold of life again. I have here just a sentence from Plato that says the same thing: "The free individual is one who can direct his energies and labor to purposes of his own choosing." I believe that.

This world of values that you and I have built for ourselves is a very personal world, a very subjective world. The objective world out there is the same for all of us. Cancer, the law of gravitation, whatever—it treats us all alike. But you and I choose to value certain things, and we have the right to do so. Your values may not be mine. I do have the feeling, though, that since mankind has so much in common, many values are really the best values for all of us. I believe that the values of life are grounded in life, in human nature. There is a certain objectivity about them, but I respect anybody who prefers one kind of value to my value.

I am going to talk vigorously tonight, as vigorously as I can at this hour and this time of the week. I am going to honor certain values that I have found, that I cherish, that I believe in, that make my life meaningful and give me a sense of creativity and excitement about life. You can take them or leave them. All I say is that you ought to find yourself, you ought to feel like an individual, free and creative, excited about life. You need to find your values and live for them.

Now, the supreme value of life, to me, is life itself. That seems so obvious. I think of life as a gift. The gift of grace, the gift of God, the gift of my mother and father to me. And since I've thought of life as a gift, it is all the more precious to me. Life itself is the supreme gift. We have an obligation to ourselves to cherish that gift, to make the most of it, to realize it for ourselves—because it is the very substance of our being here.

Elder [Paul H.] Dunn last night very effectively told us that people count. I want to emphasize in addition what happens if people count most. It's not just enough to serve people. Elder Dunn talked about spiritual growth. What is important is this self-realization, this self-fulfillment that a person can experience as a human being. What is important in life is being or becoming what God and nature made us to be. Often our values or our goals are somewhere out there. Maybe it's position, maybe it's money, maybe it's exaltation, maybe it's getting someplace. I'd like to stress that the important thing is not getting somewhere, but being something, fulfilling one's nature, realizing the potential we have as human beings and as children of God.

The enrichment of life, the enhancement of life, growth in life, satisfying one's very basic nature: that's what I think life is all about. To me, salvation is more a process than an end. You have heard that before, I'm sure, but what is happening to us along the way is what really matters. We take so much of our salvation with us into eternity. Then God can give us new opportunities to express our being. It's not as if we earn money and get a check sometime in eternity. I asked my Sunday School class the other day what would they do, how would they live if they lost their faith in immortality. And my dear eighty-six-year-old neighbor said, "I'd have a bash." She was half-joking. "I'd have a bash."

There are people who think that religion is the price you pay—here—in restraint, in dull living, so that you might be rewarded hereafter. Latter-day Saints know that the same principles that make life good and exciting here (and I'm going to try to illustrate that) are the very principles we take with us into eternity and that will make for excitement there.

Somebody said life's only goal is infinite and unending increase—enrichment, enhancement, and expansion of life through the values we choose and live by.

The apostle Paul says over and over again that we should grow up in the likeness of Jesus, Christ Jesus. We should increase in love and abound in love. If you read his epistles in Sunday School with this idea in mind, you will find Paul excited about learning to increase growth and virtue in the gospel of Christ.

Now what are some of the values we might pursue to realize the full and good life? I can't reveal any new ones to you—mankind had thought of all of them before I came along— but maybe I can drop an idea about some of them, or maybe our total view will have some meaning for you.

Visualize in your mind a pyramid, and underneath, the ground we call footings in a building. I would suggest that two basic values I would call footings are health and economic adequacy. President [Richard] Bushman mentioned the one, economic adequacy. I don't believe in economic security. It just isn't there.

I think health, both physical and mental, emotional, is a tremendous value we ought to cherish. It is kind of an instrumental value. It is very difficult to enjoy what I might call the higher values of life—spiritual, ethical, social values of life—if we don't have good mental health. And we are greatly handicapped with poor physical health. Young people are so wasteful of life, so careless of life, what you eat and what you sleep. You have lots of accidents, more so in the teen years and early twenties than later. Guard your health; take pride in that body. I think the Word of Wisdom is a remarkable document. You know a lot of the details in that so I won't go into it except to say that we Mormons haven't learned the principle of moderation. We work ourselves to death.

Another principle I just love in the Word of Wisdom says to enjoy all these things with prudence (that is, moderation) and thanksgiving. I decided, brother and sisters, that much of our health depends upon an attitude of cheerfulness, of gratitude, of thanksgiving. Call it sane optimism. If you're grateful for food, grateful for life, grateful for everything pertaining to your body and state of mind, you will enjoy much better health.

Somebody asked me what my state of mind in my old age is. I refuse to be a cynic. I refuse to be a pessimist. I want to be a sane optimist. I want to have hope, courage. I want to endure. I'm determined to endure, determined to enjoy the battle of life. It makes for good health.

Economic adequacy: I think that the economic side of life is for life what grammar is for language. If you don't learn grammar reasonably well, it is an impediment to communication. On the other hand, if you are forever conscious of grammar, which some of us are, then it inhibits the free flow of talk, conversation. The best thing to do with grammar is to learn it and then use it spontaneously. The best thing to do with our economic adequacy, I believe, is to learn a skill, gain the ability to earn your way—preferably a skill that is within you, within your own power. Good economic virtue, habits of thrift, economy, self-control, that sort of thing. And then live for other things.

What a tragedy to make material values the supreme value of life, when the kingdom of God is not on the outside but within. We Americans are greatly blessed and can spend most of our energies in living for things other than economic survival.

Okay, health and economic adequacy are below the surface of my pyramid. Now let's go up one side. Another value is what I would call sensuous satisfactions. There are two words here that are sometimes confused: sensual and sensuous. Sensual has negative connotations. It means maybe lustful, carnal. On the other hand, sensuous simply means pertaining to the senses—to the eye, the ear, the nose, the smell, the taste, the touch. We have two ways to communicate with the world. One is verbal, through words, a beautiful way. The other way is nonverbal—through our bodies, through our senses. They support each other, they relate. In this modern urban asphalt society in which we live, I have a feeling that our senses are dull.

I took a hearing test today and was grateful to find I am within the normal range. My wife thought I was hard of hearing and the doctor said, "Tell her you have selective hearing." But you know people in simpler societies, closer to nature, I think, who enjoy sensory experience more than we do. City folk go for days without looking at mountains or the ocean. Out where I live in Salt Lake, I look at Mount Olympus. I used to milk a cow night and morning. I would go out there and feast on Mount Olympus. I'd sing "Hills of Home," "For the Strength of the Hills," and "O Ye Mountains High." I made up hymns to what my eyes beheld. I have a little ranch in the Teton country of Idaho, and it is a different life up there for a few weeks in the summertime, looking at those peaks, with the sun coming up behind them and the reflection on them in the evening, or the thunder and lightning, the changing color, and the touch of rain and the sound of the thunder. I've even walked around in lightning and thunder to get the thrill of being part of nature.

Touch. What you can't do with your hands. You know, newborn babies have to feel their mothers and their fathers. They have to have that body contact, that warmth, that closeness, nearness. We have one daughter and four sons. This last child, this daughter, I used to walk out to the swing. I liked to interlock my fingers with hers when she was young. Oh, that was fun for me to hug her, to feel her hand. I like to interlock my fingers with my wife's. I like to shake hands, firmly, with brothers, even with sisters. You have to be careful with this touch business; use a little discretion—with students.

I work with boys in the summertime. How they love to have you put your arm around them, pat them on the back, push them on their shoulders. Touch, touch, touch. We have overdone individualism. We've neglected the social aspect of man. Men belong to one another. We need each other. We need to feel of each other through sensory experience. Husband and wife have beautiful opportunities to be one, to express their love in nonverbal communications.

We lived in Europe for two years, going to school and on a mission. Europeans take two hours to eat lunch. They take an hour to sip a glass of wine. I wish I could take an hour to sip a glass of orange juice. I gulp it down, more or less. Europeans taste flavor more than we do. Good German cooks take a thin piece of round steak and wrap the onion and cabbage in it and bake it, and it is absolutely delicious. Vegetables flavor the meat, the meat flavors the vegetables. Sounds like a whole other talk, doesn't it?

Another great value in life—and some of you know much more about it than I—is what we call an aesthetic feeling. It's different from just ordinary sensory experience. Aesthetic feeling is the feeling that is aroused in us by a work of art, or sometimes nature, or something in even a human relationship. In ordinary emotions, for instance, if you witnessed a murder, it would just tear you to pieces that murder should occur. If someone were to shoot a gun at me, it would cause an emotional response that would be devastating to you—I hope. Yet you go to a Shakespearean tragedy, where there is murder all over the place, and it doesn't destroy. You come out feeling refreshed, renewed, cleansed from within, elevated, because of that make-believe situation and because of the concentration on certain feelings and senses. In aesthetic feeling, you identify with the object. You lose yourself, become one and whole, and are tremendously recreated.

I think each of us, we Latter-day Saints, ought to learn to enjoy at least one of the arts. Music is usually the easiest for many of us. Poetry or great prose, architecture, painting, sculpture: we need that each day to renew ourselves, to find a wholeness in life, I believe.

Another value that I think is tremendously important is—I don't know what to call it exactly, but maybe I would call it learning, exercising the mind. The supreme thing about man is his brain or his spirit. Animals excel us in many ways. Deer go traipsing through my ranch with more grace and speed and jumping ability than I've ever had. My pigs eat and sleep much better than I do (I'm not a good sleeper). Some sniff better, such as dogs. Birds fly. The unique thing about man, the essence of man, the glory of man, is his mind or his brain. Not only is the glory of God intelligence, it is the glory of man. And man does not fulfill his nature unless he gets excited about ideas, about learning; unless he reads books, unless he talks ideas, not just the weather and people, but ideas.

I had a father who was the seventh son, the last son of his mother. His older brothers were all farmers, and when this boy came along, his pioneer father said, we would like one scholar in the family, so they named him Milton and it inspired my father at least to go to school to become an educator, become a philosopher. And all his life he read, and wrote, and thought. One of my early recollections is of sitting at his feet and cutting open the magazine pages that didn't come uncut then, while he read the magazine. Well, my father got diabetes at forty-five. This was way back before insulin. He had his left leg amputated below the knee at sixty-nine and his right foot, part of it, amputated at seventy-three. He suffered agony. He lived to be eighty-three. The last five years of his life he went from the bed to the wheelchair and back to the bed, in pain a great deal. But you know, my father, whose life was in his mind and in his heart, never lost his sense of humor, kept that mind working. He was fascinating to talk with. I've never known a person with a vigorous mind who couldn't stand up under the difficulties of life.

There is a doctor in Salt Lake who will only take patients over sixty-five. One time when I was teaching college students, he said, "Bennion, the saddest patients I have are not the poor and not the physically disabled, but those who didn't use their minds when they were young." He said the body breaks down, but the mind only *slows* down. It gets richer as you go through life and you have more things to relate to one another, more memories, if you keep it alive, like a muscle. Don't spend all your time socializing, working, eating, sleeping. Get something intellectual in your life. Get excited about some intellectual dimension of life. Read, read, read, and think, think, think, and be creative in that role. And you will find life taking on an increasing interest even when the old body breaks down, practically, as my back is.

Another value that I have touched on, that I have come to cherish greatly, is what I would call human relationships, human ties. When you think of all the wonderful potential possibilities we have in our human relationships, life gets extremely exciting. For instance, friendship. I have a few friends that I am completely open and completely frank with, and they understand me and accept me and forgive me. We talk to each other, we are loyal to each other, we accept each other for what we are. We feel creative together when we are together. We stimulate each other's minds. Spirit touches spirit. Build good friendships; don't neglect them. They have to be cultivated like a garden, or they are lost. But friendship is a wonderful dimension of life. Think of others—father and son. If I had known nobody but my father, I'd be grateful to have lived. Here I am a father, a grandfather, and a son and a grandson, and a brother, and an uncle, and a husband. All these human relationships grow; each is a precious thing to me.

In the past few years, more than ever before, I have been grateful for being a man among men and women, a human being among other human beings.

In my work in Salt Lake now I have a lot to do with Blacks, with Chicanos, with American Indians. I am on committees with them—Chinese, Japanese, Polynesians, common folk, poor folk, big shots. I have dealings with all kinds of people in my daily work, and it is fascinating, it's interesting. We live and move and have our being in each other as well as in God, and I think the most important thing in life—if I dare say this, on earth—is the quality of our human relationships, not only in the intimate family circle and friendship circle, but in relationships with all men.

I just have two or three more values. I think, brothers and sisters, that all the virtues of life, the ethical, religious virtues of life, come under two categories or are summarized under two basic ethical values. The one is integrity and the other is love.

If you want to simplify your moral life, your ethical life, or even your religious life, concentrate on developing and maintaining integrity on the one hand and brotherly love on the other. Integrity means more than honesty, though that's a great part of it—more than paying your bills and speaking the truth. Integrity means oneness, wholeness. To integrate means to make one. It is the strong personal virtue. Integrity presupposes sincerity, humility, repentance, meekness, moral courage. All these strong personal virtues go to make up integrity.

I think that the essence of integrity, too, is to try to square our living with our convictions. It is important, for example, to be honest not because it is the best policy, but because we believe it is right to be honest. We shouldn't live the ethical life in order to get a reward. We ought to live the ethical life because we believe it is the right way to live. Rewards will follow.

Don't love me so you will get to heaven, please. You will love heaven. Love me because I am a human being or because it is your nature to love. I think God blesses us because he is a loving person.

The other great virtue, Christian love, I believe is the great mother virtue of all the *social* virtues of life. If we have love, then we are tolerant, patient, kind, forbearing, forgiving, empathetic, compassionate.

We sometimes have trouble with brotherly love because it is so very hard to love all men. Some just aren't very lovable. And I would like to make one or two suggestions on how we can love more easily all men or any man. You don't have to like a person to love him. A person can be obnoxious to you in a way and you can still love him, because love means that you treat another person in his interest or in her interest. It's not synonymous with liking. It is an unselfish interest in the welfare of another person. Some people get on my nerves, but I hope to discipline myself to work in their interest and not use them as a means to my ends, nor ignore them.

Another misconception, I believe, about brotherly love is that people think if you love somebody you have to do for that person what he or she wants you to do. I had a dear sister during the depression who was not married and was earning very well, and a man came to her and proposed marriage. He said he had had a revelation. And she felt an obligation. She came to me for advice. She felt an obligation to marry this man because he wanted her to, asked her to. She had no love for him and no particular respect for him. Listen, you can knock the man down if it is for his good, with love. You can take a man to court, I think, if need be, if you do it in his interest as well as yours.

A few times in my life, in my teaching career, I have said no to students. It is hard to do. It hurt, momentarily. But that kind of firmness in their interest, not out of anger but in their interest, turned out for their good and built a fine relationship between us. In other words, *you* determine how you express love. And you learn to experience the best way to do it.

I have two other quick values to mention. Let me review: We have health and economic adequacy under the ground. Up one column of the pyramid we have sensuous satisfaction, aesthetic feeling, and integrity. Up the other column we have learning, using the mind; we have building fine human relationships; and we have love. These all build up to the good life at the top.

Another value that I believe in earnestly is what we call creativity, running through *all* these other values. I believe that an individual should do these things in his own way, should express his own individuality. That's all creativity means. It means to do your own thinking, work with your own hands, your own imagination, and your own mind—just be yourself. Anybody who has the courage to be an individual, honest, daring—if you have these other values, you won't go wild. If you have love and integrity, I'm not afraid of what you might do creatively.

Man is a child of God and God is a creator. I think that when we were created in his image, we were born with a great need to be creative, to make things in our own image that reflect us, even as God makes things that reflect him.

I want to read a couple of quotations from a favorite book of mine. It is by Romain Rolland in *Jean Christof* (1913, p. 364). Romain Rolland was a great French writer at the turn of the century. He said:

> There is no joy but in creation. There are no living beings but those who create. All the rest are shadows, hovering over the earth, strangers to life. All the joys of life are joys of creation. Love, genius, action, quickened by flame issuing from one and the same fire. Even those who cannot find a place by the great fireside, the ambitious, the egoists, the sterile sensualists, value being warmed in the pale reflection of its light. To create in the region of the body or in the region of the mind is to issue from the prison of the body, from the prison of the mind, is to ride upon the storm of life, that is, to be he who is. To create is to triumph over death.
>
> Wretched is the sterile creature, that man or that woman who remains lost upon the earth, scanning their withered bodies, the side of themselves from which no flame of life will ever leave. Wretched is the soul that does not feel its own fruitfulness and know itself to be big with life and love as a tree with blossoms in the spring.

You don't have to be a mother to be creative (I mean a biological mother, although that's one way to be creative). I told my wife that one thing I envy her is that I can't bear a child. I wish I could. She said, "I wish you could too." But it must be quite an experience, quite an event, to play that large a role biologically. But we can all be creative in human relationships. Anytime you help a person to find his own worth, anytime you can convey love to another human being or spark his mind, you are playing a creative role in human relationships—more important, I think, than biologic.

You don't have to be a Beethoven or a Shakespeare to be creative. You just have to put trust in those hands. Learn to play the piano like *you* want to play it. I've taken to baking bread every Saturday when I'm home. My wife broke her hand. I can't stand Wonder Bread; I wonder what's in it. And I get a big thrill, since I live in an abstract world during the week, with a lot of problems, out of making dough and hammering it and molding it and throwing it around, putting different things in it every week. It comes out different and often very good. But it's *my* bread. I put just a little in one little pan, about that much dough. I put it in the oven until it's done at noon, and then I slice it down the middle and put a little butter and honey on both pieces, with a pint of cold milk, and that is my Saturday lunch. One of the best meals I've ever had in this world. But it's *mine,* all mine.

Make something, do something—with your hands, with your imagination, with your mind, with your soul, with your fellowman. Do something in their interest, something consistent with integrity and love and good reason, good sense. But, granted these other virtues, *cut loose.* Be yourself, be an individual, express yourself. Don't be a rubber stamp. God isn't that way. God is free, creator, full of love. We can be these too, I think, to satisfy our inner nature.

Another great value is faith or trust. As human beings we need a relationship to the whole. We need a relationship that is something of which we are only a part. In our Latter-day Saint faith, that relationship is mostly to God and to Christ, I believe. Joseph Smith entered the Sacred Grove and found his God, and built a very close and wonderful relationship with him through the years. Through Joseph Smith, we know *about* God, but each of us must also *find* him and find our relationship *to* him. We have to find our own Sacred Grove. And it's not easy. I confess that there are times when I have a hard time getting through to my Father in heaven. He leaves me to myself a great deal; he even left Jesus upon the cross. You remember, "My God, why hast thou *forsaken* me?"

I think that our relationship to him can be different from our relationships person to person. Let me mention one thing that has a lot of meaning for me in my relationship to Deity. I get this from a philosopher named Montague. He said, "Religion is the faith that the things that matter most in life are not ultimately at the mercy of the things that matter least." Think about that for a moment. The things that matter most in life—and I have named some of them tonight, beauty, truth, goodness, love, integrity—are not ultimately at the mercy of the grave. If there is no God in heaven, and man should destroy himself on earth, all the beautiful music, all the great ideas, all the aspirations of man, all the human relationships that we cherish, would perish with man.

Religion is the faith that God exists and is on the side supporting, giving cosmic support to, the things that we cherish most in human experience. I have that faith. I don't know absolutely, but I know for myself, and I have faith and trust that when I live by integrity—it's hard to do so always—and when I express Christian love, and when I stand up for freedom, and when I am creating human relationships, I have the faith that God is supporting me, that he is there, that he is on my side. Whether he answers my prayers or not, he is with me when I am with him, when I am working in his interest, in harmony with his attributes. And I get a lot of comfort out of that. It sustains me—that faith, that trust.

Of all the people who have ever lived, I admire and love and I would like to be a disciple of Jesus Christ. He understood life in its deepest, profoundest sense, and to make him an ideal of life, along with faith in his resurrection and redemption, is an anchor that gives meaning and strength to our existence.

Find some values to live by, to measure yourself to, and I promise you that life will be increasingly exciting for you. Not that you don't have them now, but *define* them and do it over and over again as you go through the different periods of life. You'll recover your individuality and your freedom, your sense of being.

5

A Final Tribute to T. Edgar Lyon

T. Edgar Lyon, a healthy and rugged man who had hardly known a sick day, died at age seventy-five after a short, losing battle with cancer. In his death, his wife, six sons, and thirty-two grandchildren lost a gentle, loving husband and father, and the Church a great historian and teacher.

Brother Lyon wrote courses of study for the priesthood, Relief Society, and institutes, and hundreds of articles and book reviews, but his major work—*The History of Nauvoo*—he left only half finished. This is an irreparable loss to scholars and the Church.

It was my privilege to be his colleague at the Institute of Religion, University of Utah, from 1939 to 1962. During the first half of this time he and I were the only faculty. We were together daily, evenings, and on Sundays. Several summers we worked together painting houses, digging out a basement, building an upstairs. With several couples, we formed a study group which has met for forty years. I could never get enough of his company. In those twenty-three years at the institute, and the sixteen which have followed, not an ill feeling or a derogatory remark has ever passed between us.

Those early years at the institute were the "golden days" of our youth. There was no established curriculum. We built courses around the needs and interests of students as well as on subject matter dictated by history and the nature of religion. With a remarkable group of students we laughed and danced, counseled and worshipped, taught each other, and created a fraternity—Lambda Delta Sigma—to meet their social needs and to provide leadership experience. The fraternity became our laboratory for the gospel we taught.

Ed Lyon was a real Latter-day Saint, a worthy disciple of Jesus Christ. In him was a total absence of pretense. He never sought the

---

This funeral tribute to "Ed" Lyon, Dr. Bennion's first colleague at the Salt Lake Institute, was given in September 1978 and published in the Winter 1978 issue of Dialogue: A Journal of Mormon Thought.

honors of men. He never took the chief seats. His only interest was to serve, to give of himself, to lose his life in the interest of others. I was younger than Brother Lyon and much less prepared to teach religion than he was. However, because I was appointed the first director of the institute, I remained in the position. Ed Lyon was not envious or resentful as my associate director, but wholly loyal and cooperative.

Ed exemplified the Beatitudes. He was humble, teachable, receptive of criticism without offense, meek, merciful, pure of heart, a peacemaker. I never saw him angry, deceitful, hypocritical, or selfish. In my memory, he will ever remain a saint of saints.

Brother Lyon was a fascinating teacher. He had a photographic, encyclopedic memory, a remarkable ability to retain even the minutest details if they were relevant. He was at his best teaching historical subjects or the Doctrine & Covenants and the New Testament, which he could make rich by feeding in historical background. A most delightful part of his teaching was his ability to relate stories and experiences apropos to the subject matter. His stock of tales seemed endless.

In our study group, if we were caught without a prepared lesson, we needed only to ask Ed a provocative question and he would entertain for the evening.

His teaching was informative and substantive. Ed Lyon never fed his students pablum, nor did he, as many religious teachers do, try to build faith on the esoteric and the unfounded myths and legends which grow up in any religious movement. He built faith on solid foundations, believing that the truth could stand the light of day. Ed's mother had been a bright, realistic woman who saw life as it really was, and her son appropriated this quality, which was strengthened by his studies at the University of Chicago and by his own integrity. T. Edgar Lyon was an honest man in whom I detected no guile.

He was also a man of deep faith. Much of this he acquired from his saintly father, Bishop David Lyon, whom he loved and admired so much. On his first mission in Holland, T. Edgar had the kind of spiritual experiences that only come to one who doesn't seek them but is ready to receive them.

His was not a simple faith. It had stood the test of the study of comparative religion, of extensive historical study, of sound scholarship. Ed was not ignorant of the human element in our history. He knew that a people as well as individuals can err. Church history presented him with problems as well as inspiration. He had great

admiration and love for Joseph Smith and for the Sa
150 years of history.

T. Edgar Lyon believed in Jesus Christ and in the et
man. He was as ready to meet his Maker as anyone I have eve
Therefore, we shall not say goodbye to our dear friend, but on
Wiedersehen.

Ed is gone, but his qualities of mind and character remain in our memory and in our lives, beckoning us to pursue them. And these same qualities bear witness to the intelligent, creative, loving God who created him. Surely a universe that can create the likes of T. Edgar Lyon has also the power to preserve him. This is my faith—which his life has strengthened.

6

... with Sociology

ity of Utah as a sophomore and ran m graduate work at the University of Chicago in social ... Beeley, an Englishman by birth and early training, fluent, articulate, and excited about scientific approaches to social issues, was a most stimulating professor. I took his classes in criminology and mental hygiene, and worked one summer on a "Survey of Boy Life" [a study of youth behavior in Salt Lake City] under his direction and enjoyed many personal conversations with him. He had come back to Zion with high hopes of helping to bring to pass the "Renaissance of Mormonism," by using scientific means of realizing the social idealism of religion.

Following graduation from the U., I went to the Swiss-German Mission for the LDS Church in the fall of 1928. In the spring of 1931, I entered the University of Erlangen, Germany, hence to Geneva to attend League of Nations meetings, then in the fall to the University of Vienna, where I intended to continue studies in political science.

University students in Germany and Austria are allowed much freedom in the selection of courses. So I attended classes in philosophy, economic theory, and jurisprudence, as well as political science and sociology. It was there that I was introduced by Eric Voegelin to the writings of Max Weber.

It was also in Vienna that I witnessed the rise and fanaticism of Naziism and had occasion to stand up for Jewish student friends. We loved Vienna and would have stayed there but we saw the handwriting on the wall with Hitler coming to power in Germany, so we went to Strasbourg, France.

At the November 1982 meetings of the Utah Sociological Society, held at Weber State University, Bennion was invited to relate his professional experience as it had involved sociology. He provides here an important perspective on his work as a sociologist, as well as an excellent summary of the thought of Max Weber, who greatly influenced his ideas and life.

Maurice Halbwachs, a disciple of Emile Durkheim, headed the sociology department and allowed me to matriculate and write a dissertation on "Max Weber's Methodology." He suggested that I write it in English, which I did. All my study of Weber was in German, which I had to translate into English with an inadequate vocabulary in sociology, and I eventually defended the dissertation in French.

Max Weber thoroughly captivated me. His intellectual appetite was insatiable and the breadth of his research seemingly without bounds. He made substantial contributions in both theory and methodology. As he developed his empirical studies, he quickly recognized the need for sound theory and methodology in social science. Initially, he had little respect for the sociology of his day. It was not until he had himself placed sociology on a firm theoretical and methodological footing that he acknowledged the legitimacy of the field.

Weber had a nervous breakdown in 1897, which took him out of the classroom until 1920. He spent the intervening years in research and writing. His studies are far-ranging and diversified, substantive and creative, complex and not well organized. They read almost as dictation from a brilliant mind that is anxious to move on. I will mention a few of his concepts that excited me and have been part of my life ever since.

Value-free Sociology

One of Weber's earliest and most persistent aims was to establish sociology—and related social sciences—as an empirical science. He eliminated metaphysical considerations, reform aspirations, prophetic predictions, and political decisions from the province of sociology. As in the natural and biological sciences, the task of social science, he believed, was to describe aspects of reality as they are. Difficult as it is, he insisted on objectivity, on establishing causal relationships among social phenomena, on the necessity of verification. There are marked differences in the techniques and procedures between the social and the natural sciences, which will be illustrated later, but there should be no difference in the basic spirit and purpose of all the sciences. Each is a rational, methodical, objective, descriptive, and verifiable effort to bring order into some aspect of reality by establishing meaningful relationships within it.

Weber called his scientific sociology *wertfrei*, or value-free. To this day sociologists are debating his position, some holding that it is impossible for a sociologist to be value-free in his work, while others argue that he should not even try, that he has an obligation to confess his values to his audience and to work for his values in his research.

Critics of Weber's value-free sociology often misinterpret his position. He did not believe that sociologists should be disinterested in values. For him, the very essence of culture is value-related. A sociologist without an interest in human values would have no subject matter. Likewise the sociologist himself, like any other human being, must have his own values and be committed to them passionately if his life is to have significance.

What Weber tried to eliminate from sociology were value judgments *(Werturteile)*. For him, empirical sciences could not be normative, stating what ought or ought not to be, what is good or evil, what is beautiful or ugly. Sociology, like any other science, has simply to describe what is or is not, what was, or what may be under given circumstances. It can never define for men what should be, and it should not attempt to do so.

Weber wrote a good deal about value-relationship or value-reference *(Wertbeziehung)*. He was most interested in the values and postulates of faith that people held. He studied religious values, for example, as objective data, and observed their influence on other aspects of culture, notably economic life. But he never made value judgments concerning the various ultimate value positions entertained by Calvinism, Lutheranism, the Hebrew prophets, or Buddhism.

Weber does make one exception to his strict value position. The scientist must be committed to truth, to a tough-minded effort to understand aspects of reality, and he must believe that his scientific efforts are worthwhile. Beyond this, Weber believed that all values are subjective, born of the culture in which one is socialized and the "daemon" [unique creative spirit] within one. Unlike some of his contemporaries, he did not accept any objective or universal order of values. There is just no rational or empirical way, he believed, to decide between the merits of ultimate value positions.

Following Kant, who distinguished between the natural world, which lent itself to rational analysis, and the inner world, the world of freedom and faith, Weber recognized a similar dualism in man's approaches to reality—the empirical and the evaluative. Facts and values for him were independent types of meaning—intimately interrelated in human experience, but to be distinguished clearly in the mind and method of the social scientist.

Weber recognized how difficult it is for a student of culture, being personally involved in the value aspects of his study and being in the habit of making value judgments continuously, to free himself from this practice. The scientist's values determine his interests, his point of departure, but in his methodology he can refrain from evaluation and remain descriptive. Thus, Weber insisted that the social scientist strive for objectivity even though he dealt with the subjective and value-dimensions of human experience.

Distinction Between the Natural and the Social Sciences

Since the social sciences developed late in modern times, it was only natural that they should ape the methodology of the natural sciences, which were already well established. A number of German thinkers before Weber recognized that both the purpose and the object of the social sciences differed radically from those of chemistry and biology.

Reality—everything that exists—is chaos in and of itself. Truth does not adhere to reality but [consists] in men's judgments of reality. Man gives order and structure to the universe, to human relationships, and to the world within himself. Man constructs his historical and social reality. Truth does not exist "out there" but in the minds of men.

The natural scientist, while recognizing that his science has given conceptual order and meaning to some aspect of reality, generally believes that there is an order in nature that he has simply discovered and has learned by ascribing names to it to communicate this order to others.

By contrast, Weber recognized that the historian and the sociologist are dealing with a reality that is truly chaotic in its complexity and infinity, and that any history or social science is not a discovery of an order that already exists. It is rather the construction of an order in the mind of the scholar, one that does not represent reality as it is, but enables the scholar to understand some very limited aspects of it. The historian could write any number of histories of an epoch of equal validity, depending on the values that determine his interests.

The natural sciences generalize, subsume phenomena under general concepts and universal laws, whereas history is interested in the uniqueness of events and their distinctive meaning. In studying the death of John F. Kennedy, for example, the physical scientist considers the cause of death in terms of forces and factors that apply to the death of all men in similar circumstances. By contrast, the historian is interested in those aspects of Kennedy's death that are unique—its effect on American history, legislation, the careers of his brothers, and so forth.

The sociologist, like the historian, is not concerned with all aspects of social action, but only with those which bear a relationship to his particular social values. For Weber, all values are relative to individuals and their respective cultures. These can be identified but not established scientifically. A scientific philosophy of life, a scientific *Weltanschauung,* was nonsense for Weber.

Weber was content to do particular empirical studies, which give insight into limited aspects of reality. It is not given to man, he thought, to understand the whole of social reality or to subsume it under general laws.

Weber's Ideal Type

Weber's major interest was to develop a methodology in social science that would be scientifically sound—empirical, objective, verifiable—and at the same time deal with the subjective, qualitative, and meaningful aspects of human action. To achieve his purpose, he created an original concept called the Ideal Type *(Idealtypus).* In some respects, the name is a misnomer because his types are not ideals to be emulated but simple logical constructs that give perspectives on social and historical reality.

Weber was a nominalist. His concepts are not[, he believed,] identical with reality. They are simply the means of giving logical or rational perspective in what is otherwise the bewildering chaos of social reality.

How did Weber build his ideal type? This can be best understood with an example of one of his historical types—modern industrial capitalism. He was a student of economics and of economic history. He had a vast knowledge of economic enterprises in various cultures and epochs. Like Karl Marx, he recognized the dominant influence of modern industrial capitalism in Western civilization. He studied this phenomenon in various countries, including Germany, in which capitalism developed so rapidly. From examining free enterprise in various circumstances, he singled out the elements of this economic form that were theoretically essential and congenial to its fullest functioning.

Thus the elements of the ideal type are drawn from empirical reality. The essence of industrial capitalism for Weber is its rational, methodical, disciplined way of gaining profit. Nearly all of the components of his ideal type of capitalism are *reckonable* factors. They are: (1) access to the goods of production, (2) a free market, (3) a rational technique for the means of production and exchange, (4) rational, dependable law, (5) free labor—that is, the existence of workers legally authorized and economically compelled to contract their labor on the open market, (6) the commercialization of business, (7) the separation of business from the household, and (8) bookkeeping and accounting systems. In addition, men must be of a reckoning disposition; they must have motivation and inclination to put value on work for work's sake, on calculation for profit, on self-discipline. Weber called this the *spirit of capitalism,* which he found to be closely akin to the Protestant ethic inspired by John Calvin's theology and social philosophy.

After the elements of the ideal type are found in history and in society, they are tested for their logical consistency with each other. Are they free of contradiction? Do they form a logical whole? They are thus integrated into a unified construct from what had been separate aspects of reality. These elements making up modern capitalism are now thought of as a single historical phenomenon. The elements and the whole are then accentuated, or "idealized," into a logical model more perfect than any existing form of capitalism.

This process of conceptualization, called the ideal type formulation, takes real factors from history and society and transforms them into logical constructs, called *Gedankenbilder* (thought-pictures), which are purposely made unreal. Standing on the edge of reality, they are rational possibilities that enable one to understand and to see, in perspective, real situations. They are not the goal of research but a means of gaining perspective, of building bridges across gulfs in reality. Weber called them utopias, constructions of the imagination, fictions, pure thought, or ideal (logically speaking) constructs.

I could go on and illustrate Weber's use of ideal types in his efforts to understand the subjective meaning of social action in various cultures, but enough is enough, and I shall return briefly to my personal saga.

In relative innocence, I received a doctorate from the University of Strasbourg in December of 1933. Returning home during the depression, I became an educational adviser in a CCC Camp (Civilian Conservation Corps) for nine months. Then John A. Widtsoe invited me to open an Institute of Religion at the University of Utah, which I did, expecting to remain a few years. I stayed twenty-six, interrupted by two years at the University of Arizona, 1937-39. These were fulfilling years. I was glad that I was not an expert in theology, Church history, or archaeology. I became interested in students—their thinking, their intellectual, social, ethical, and spiritual needs. In the beginning, we had no established curriculum. I developed courses in a personal philosophy of life, leadership, world religions, courtship and marriage, marriage and family life, along with the traditional studies in scripture. I was free to relate my studies in philosophy and social science to what was being studied on campus. The institute afforded me the most complete relationship I have ever had with students. I taught, counseled, dined and danced, worshipped, and served with them—with thousands of them.

In 1962, the LDS Department of Education decided to relieve me of my duties as director of the institute. I was invited to write courses of study, but I decided to leave the system and took a job at the University of Utah working in the dean of students' office and half-time under the leadership of Ray Canning on a study of juvenile delinquency.

When the latter project terminated, I became full-time associate dean of students. Henry Frost, then head of the sociology department, invited me to teach a graduate seminar on Max Weber. When Tom O'Dea left the University of Utah to go to Santa Barbara, I took over his class on the sociology of religion, which I particularly enjoyed, drawing heavily on Troeltsch, Weber, and O'Dea.

In 1972, I left the halls of ivy for the real world. The Community Services Council, a private, nonprofit social agency of agencies, needed a director. The council's financial situation frightened several very able candidates away. I accepted a draft to become the director. We proceeded to make a comprehensive study of the human service needs of the community and the present services available to meet those needs. United Way, our major funding source, wanted to do its own planning and evaluating and would no longer fund the council for these and related services. So, after losing the battle to keep them, we quite happily moved to provide direct services to agencies and individuals in the community. We now operate a food bank, do chore services for elderly and handicapped, make function-fashionable clothing for the handicapped, train quadriplegics in independent living, recruit thousands of volunteers, maintain an information and referral center, and enable senior citizens to obtain dentures and eyeglasses at greatly reduced cost and pay for them at five to ten dollars per month.

I have been involved in one other social experiment. Each summer,

I take two groups of about thirty-five city boys each to my ranch in Teton country and try to raise their self-esteem through work, recreational skills, discussions, and relationships.

I have found life to be adventurous, even exciting, all the way. I am grateful to have touched base here and there with both religion and social science. In my experience, they complement each other in human experience.

I haven't decided how I shall spend the rest of my days.

II

A Rational Theology

In a classroom at the Salt Lake Institute of Religion, about 1957

7

Joseph Smith: His Creative Role in Religion

Over a century ago a boy had a question. He found an answer, organized a church, published a book. He gathered in our fathers from the nations of the earth and imbued them with the faith to build a Zion in their own peculiar way. This Institute of Religion is a part of Zion which they built. It is indeed fitting that we here today honor the memory of this boy, who, in the last analysis, built this institution. We have heard beautiful singing, and reading, and inspiring prayer this morning, and now it is my turn to say what is in my heart to the memory of Joseph Smith. I want you to know that I am honored and feel humbly grateful for this opportunity.

My debt to Joseph Smith is great and manifold in its source, but today I would talk to only one quality of his which I love very much. My theme is also inspired by reflection upon this audience. Most of you people are of the same approximate age as Joseph Smith was when he dreamed his dreams, had his visions, thought his thoughts, and did his work. Moreover, you are associated here together in an institution where you are admonished to seek learning by study and also by faith, which he did and which he said for us to do. In evaluating the work of Joseph Smith, one may stand at a distance, as it were, and see him organizing a church, translating a book, and building Nauvoo. If we look at him in that way, we have no great part in his work. It was done before we were born. All we can do is to accept his work gratefully and carry on.

There is another way to pay tribute to the Prophet, I think, a way closer to our time—a contemporary way. That is to seek something in his life which we can appropriate even as he knew it, something

---

Dr. Bennion gave the annual Joseph Smith Memorial Lecture at the Logan (Utah) Institute of Religion in December 1948. The talk was subsequently published in the Logan Herald-Journal *on December 18, 1948.*

which we can share in common with him. This is our desire this morning, to call your attention to one of these things.

Joseph Smith was human even as you and I. He made mistakes and had his weaknesses. Many of his dreams and aspirations, he failed to achieve, just as you and I fail. He was martyred at the age of thirty-eight, without knowing the autumn harvest. Even as you and I, he only planted and tasted something of the summer fruit. The thing which inspires me about the Prophet, and it is something we can share with him, is this: He put his hand to the plow and did not look back. He kept his eye on the unplowed field ahead. He turned over virgin soil, again and again. One [question] led to another; one revelation called for another. Each day was a new day in the life of the Prophet.

It is this creative quality in his life, his teachings, and his work that we wish to pay tribute to today. You know, there is no joy in life, it seems to me, except the joy of creation. Creator is a name, an honored name, of Deity, and when God created man, he breathed into him part of his life, the urge to create, to build, to learn, to think, and to take old images and make them new. God has planted deeply in us the need to reproduce, to learn, and to build. When man is creative, he emerges from the prison of his own mind. He is no more a victim of circumstance, of the forces which are pressing upon him from all directions, but through the power of creation he builds his life anew, and the world in which he lives. Goethe, the German poet, says, "One sees what one carries in one's heart." The creative soul recreates life after the image he carries in his heart.

Too often religion has been taught us and accepted as a conservative force in life, as something which saves man from himself and from his sins. Religion is a conservative and a saving force, but it must be more than that. It is also a dynamic force in life in harmony with man's urge to create.

The Prophet Joseph Smith was creative. Everything he touched became a new thing. In him was something of the curiosity of a child, the imagination of an artist, the practical zeal of a reformer, the idealism of a utopian, and the fire of a prophet. His theology is dynamic. He used religion to remake life. He also assigned to each of us a tremendously creative role to play in religion. Let us illustrate his creativeness in certain fields of activity.

In June of 1830, he received a revelation describing a vision which Moses had from God. Moses was so overwhelmed by the creations of God that he said, "Now, for this cause, I know that man is nothing, which thing I never had supposed." Moses recovered from this momentary disillusionment to ask a question of God. "Tell me, I pray thee, why these things are so, and by what thou madest them?" In the answer he received, we get a vision of a God who is creatively at work in the universe, bringing about his great purpose. "Worlds without number have I created; and I also created them for mine own purpose; and by the Son I created them, which is mine Only Begotten. . . . The heavens, they are many, and they cannot be numbered unto man; but they are numbered unto me, for they are mine. And as one earth shall pass away and the heavens thereof even so shall another come, and there is no end to my works, neither to my words. For behold, this is my work and my glory—to bring to pass the immortality and eternal life of man." (See Moses 1.)

Revelation

This creative character of God is further reflected by the Prophet in his description of how God speaks to man. In the Book of Mormon we read, "Wo be unto him that shall say: We have received the word of God, and we need no more of the word of God, for we have enough! For behold, thus saith the Lord God: I will give unto the children of men line upon line, precept upon precept, here a little and there a little; and blessed are those who hearken unto my precepts, and lend an ear unto my counsel, for they shall learn wisdom; for unto him that receiveth I will give more; and from those that shall say, We have enough, from them shall be taken away even that which they have." (2 Nephi 28:30-31.)

"Know ye not that I, the Lord your God, have created all men, and that I remember those who are upon the isles of the sea; and that I rule in the heavens above and in the earth beneath; and I bring forth my word unto the children of men, yea, even upon all the nations of the earth? Wherefore murmur ye, because that ye shall receive more of my word? Know ye not that the testimony of two nations is a witness unto you that I am God, that I remember one nation like unto another? . . . And I do this that I may prove unto many that I am the same yesterday, today, and forever; and that I speak forth my words according to mine own pleasure. And because that I have spoken one word, ye need not suppose that I cannot speak another; for my work is not yet finished; neither shall it be until the end of man, neither from that time henceforth and forever." (2 Nephi 29:7-9.)

The revelations of God, according to the Prophet, were not to be confined to one man nor to one people. Men of all nations are inspired of God according to their need, their desire, and their ability to receive revelation.

"For behold," says Alma, "the Lord God doth grant unto all nations, of their own nation and tongue, to teach his word, yea, in wisdom, all that he seeth fit that they should have; therefore we see that the Lord doth counsel in wisdom, according to that which is just and true." (Alma 29:8.)

In 1842 the Prophet had reached, I think, the height of his mortal success. The Church had been established and the gospel in its main outlines had been restored. He had premonitions of the end of his own life. One might expect him to close revelation, to think of himself as the pinnacle of this great principle. It is interesting that he, at this time, set forth the Articles of Faith, indicating his great faith in the continuance of revelation. The ninth Article of Faith reads, "We believe all that God has revealed, all that he does now reveal, and we believe that He will yet reveal many great and important things pertaining to the Kingdom of God." And, as though this were not enough, the last and thirteenth Article of Faith opens the door wide to eternity and to the universe. "We believe in being honest, true, chaste, benevolent, virtuous, and in doing good to all men; indeed, we may say that we follow the admonition of Paul—We believe all things, we hope all things, we have endured many things, and hope to be able to endure all things. If there is anything virtuous, lovely, or of good report or praiseworthy, we seek after these things."

Surely this was no accident. The thirteenth Article of Faith is a natural and logical result of the dynamic theological concepts of the restored gospel of Jesus Christ.

There is scarcely any theology in the writings of the Prophet that is treated abstractly, as if apart from life. Everywhere theology is functional, related to man, beginning here and carrying into eternity. The creative role that the Prophet ascribes to man in the religious life is ever a source of wonder and amazement to me. We can only suggest and illustrate this in one or two ways here.

Man's Relationship to God

Man is not simply God's creature, according to the Prophet's words. There is something in man that is co-eternal with the Creator himself. Mark these words from the Doctrine and Covenants: "Man was also in the beginning with God. Intelligence, or the light of truth, was not created or made, neither indeed can be. All truth is independent in that sphere in which God has placed it, to act for itself, as all intelligence also; otherwise there is no existence. Behold, here is the agency of man, and here is the condemnation of man; because that which from the beginning is plainly manifest unto them, and they receive not the light." (D&C 93:29-31.)

These words, *intelligence, truth,* and *agency,* are not defined carefully in scripture, but it seems clear that the intelligent basis of man's life, including his capacity for creative and moral living, is uncreated, and co-eternal with God and with other aspects of the universe. If so, man's relationship with Deity, with his fellow intelligences, and with himself has been, is, and ever will be creative and dynamic.

I like these oft-quoted words the Prophet sent to the Saints who were trying to establish Zion in Jackson County, Missouri, in 1831. Evidently some of the Saints thought that God was to establish Zion without their help: "For behold, it is not meet that I should command in all things; for he that is compelled in all things, the same is a slothful and not a wise servant; wherefore he receiveth no reward. Verily I say, men should be anxiously engaged in a good cause, and do many things of their own free will, and bring to pass much righteousness; for the power is in them, wherein they are agents unto themselves. And inasmuch as men do good they shall, in no wise, lose their reward. But he that doeth not anything until he is commanded, and receiveth a commandment with a doubtful heart, and keepeth it with slothfulness, the same is damned." (D&C 58:26-29.)

Even in this great principle of revelation, God revealing himself to man, the Prophet has given man an active part. The finest statement we know in scripture on the meaning of revelation is in the first section of the Doctrine and Covenants: "Behold, I am God and have spoken it; and these commandments are of me." So far, in that passage, revelation seems to be all of God, his work alone. But, the scripture continues, " . . . and were given unto my servants in their weakness, after the manner of their language, that they might come to understanding. And inasmuch as they erred it might be made known; and inasmuch as they sought wisdom they might be instructed; and inasmuch as they sinned they might be chastened, that they might repent; and inasmuch as they were humble, they might be made strong and blessed from on high, and receive knowledge from time to time." (D&C 1:24-28.)

The Prophet's own experience with revelation had taught him that God speaks to man when there is a need, when man is aware of that need, and when man is seeking, learning, desiring, and pleading in humility and faith with an eye single to the glory of God and his work.

It is quite self-evident, I think, that when it comes to living the great principles of religion, faith, humility, and love, they have absolutely no meaning to man unless they are experienced and participated in creatively by man.

Joseph Smith also made of the religious life an everyday creative experience. The Book of Mormon, in particular, is filled with exhortations to us all to have love, charity, compassion, and tolerance for fellowmen.

King Benjamin links theology and religion beautifully when he says: "And behold, I tell you these things that ye may learn wisdom; that ye may learn that when ye are in the service of your fellow beings ye are only in the service of your God." (Mosiah 2:17.) A little further along in the same sermon he adds this note: "And now, if you believe these things see that ye do them." (Mosiah 4:10.)

In chapter 34 of Alma is an exhortation to us to pray—to pray over our flocks and herds and households, to pray for ourselves. Toward the end of it, however, we read this: "Yea, and when you do not cry unto the Lord, let your hearts be full, drawn out in prayer unto him continually for your welfare, and also for the welfare of those who are around you. And now behold, my beloved brethren, I say unto you, do not suppose that this is all; for after ye have done all these things, if ye turn away the needy, and the naked, and visit not the sick and afflicted, and impart of your substance, if ye have, to those who stand in need—I say unto you, if ye do not any of these things, behold, your prayer is vain, and availeth you nothing, and ye are as hypocrites who do deny the faith." (Alma 34:27-28.)

Most everyone knows that in the great principles of religion, life is a creative experience. People believe in the great principles. Most religions hold many of them in common, but there is a certain aspect of religion in which many people see no value. We refer to the ordinances, the rituals, and the ceremonies of a religion. Why should a man be baptized? Why should he partake of the sacrament? How can these things help a man to be a true disciple of Christ? Even in these sacramental aspects of religion, Joseph Smith gives man a creative part. There is not an ordinance mentioned in the Doctrine and Covenants or the Book of Mormon that is not inseparably aligned with a religious life. It is only efficacious as it prepares or inspires us to live righteously. We would like to illustrate this with one ordinance.

Nowhere in the Prophet's teachings is baptism taught as a means of bringing forgiveness of sin for which we are not responsible. Nor is baptism taught merely as a gift from God bringing us entrance into the Church and remission of sin, in exchange for passive obedience. The Book of Mormon teaches a wholly new emphasis in baptism that makes of it an exciting adventure.

Nephi, in discussing the baptism of Jesus, ignored the usual reasons for baptism when he raised this question: "Now, I would ask of you, my beloved brethren, wherein the Lamb of God did fulfil all righteousness in being baptized of water? Know ye not that he was holy? But notwithstanding he being holy, he showeth unto the children of men that, according to the flesh, he humbleth himself before the Father, and witnesseth unto the Father that he would be obedient unto him in keeping his commandments." (2 Nephi 31:6-7.)

We have been taught that Jesus was baptized merely to set us an example, to show us that we must also be obedient. But in this passage in Nephi, we find that Jesus' baptism meant something to him. He wanted to be baptized, to show to men and to his Father in heaven that he, too, humbled himself before God and took upon himself the will of God. And that, indeed, is to fulfill all righteousness.

In Mosiah, chapter 18, we have an account of Alma's baptizing several hundred people whom he had converted. Before doing so, he told them the meaning of the thing they were going to do. I think it the most beautiful of any scripture on baptism. Note man's part in this ordinance as I read this passage to you. "And now, as ye are desirous to come into the fold of God, and to be called his people, and are willing to bear one another's burdens, that they may be light; yea, and are willing to mourn with those that mourn; yea, and comfort those that stand in need of comfort, and to stand as witnesses of God at all times and in all things, and in all places that ye may be in, even unto death, that ye may be redeemed of God, and be numbered with those of the first resurrection, that ye may have eternal life—now, I say unto you, if this be the desire of your hearts, what have you against being baptized in the name of the Lord, as a witness before him that ye have entered into a covenant with him, that you will serve him and keep his commandments, that he may pour out his Spirit more abundantly upon you?" And, the record continues, "when the people had heard these words, they clapped their hands for joy, and exclaimed: This is the desire of our hearts." (Mosiah 18:8-11.)

Baptism is not simply an ordinance which brings salvation, it is the believer's joyous expression and witness that he is covenanting to be a true disciple of Jesus Christ. Even the baptismal prayer in this chapter of Mosiah brings out man's part in the covenant:

"And now it came to pass that Alma took Helam, he being one of the first, and went and stood forth in the water, and cried, saying: O Lord, pour out thy Spirit upon thy servant, that he may do this work with holiness of heart. And when he had said these words, the Spirit of the Lord was upon him, and he said: Helam, I baptize thee, having authority from the Almighty God, as a testimony that ye have entered into a covenant to serve him until you are dead as to the mortal body; and may the Spirit of the Lord be poured out upon you; and may he grant unto you eternal life." (Mosiah 18:12-13.)

Toward the end of the Book of Mormon, in Moroni, the subject comes up again. Here, again, it is man's creative part in baptism that is stressed. "And the first fruits of repentance is baptism; and baptism cometh by faith unto the fulfilling the commandments; and the fulfilling the commandments bringeth remission of sins; and the remission of sins bringeth meekness, and lowliness of heart; and because of meekness and lowliness of heart cometh the visitation of the Holy Ghost, which Comforter filleth with hope and perfect love, which love endureth by diligence unto prayer." (Moroni 8:25-26.)

This covenant, which we make in baptism, is renewed again in the sacramental prayer. Each week we have opportunity to witness to God that we are true disciples of Christ. And the words in the sacramental prayer are almost identical with the words Alma uses in his description of baptism. ". . . . and witness unto thee, O God, the Eternal Father, that they are willing to take upon them the name of thy Son, and always remember him, and keep his commandments which he hath given them, that they may always have his Spirit to be with them." (Moroni 4:3.)

I wish time permitted to show you that the priesthood, the gift of the Holy Ghost, temple marriage, as well as baptism and the sacrament, have no power or influence in our lives except as participation in them teaches us the true meaning of discipleship of Christ and inspires us to realize his kingdom. How I love this intimate marriage of the ordinances and ritual of religion with the moral life throughout the works of the Prophet Joseph Smith!

Religion and Life

Joseph Smith was consistent in his theology, creatively so, and likewise in his desire to apply theology and religion to life.

To borrow a figure from Amos, Joseph Smith stood upon a wall with a plumbline in his hand, and every important institution of life which was not in line with the fundamental principles and purposes of religion and human welfare must needs be made straight. Religion was not to be like a bottle of wine, placed in the cellar for safekeeping and aging, to be drunk one day in the celestial kingdom of God. No, it was to be a vine in the vineyard, ever producing its soul-refining juices. The vine would grow and expand over the wall, over every obstacle that stood in the way of Christian living.

I need only remind you that, in the Word of Wisdom, health was taught as a basis of intellectual and spiritual life; in the concept of the law of consecration, human values were placed above economic values. In his plan for the city of Zion, community welfare was far more significant than real estate values. In government, human rights arrived at through democratic processes were given divine sanction. Education in all things was encouraged as a means of establishing the Kingdom.

The Prophet did not live long enough nor receive enough cooperation to realize many of these dreams. His, however, was a creative spirit, expressing itself in fundamental principles. We have fallen heir to his unfinished work. We shall never accomplish it unless we keep alive in our own hearts something of the creative spirit of religion so characteristic of him. How can we be creative, even as he was, when his work was so well accomplished, when so much has been done, when the fullness of the gospel has been restored? Let me try, in conclusion, to suggest to you some ways in which we may emulate his creative spirit.

No less a mind than Goethe once said, "What from your father's heritage is lent, earn it anew to really possess it." Material things can be passed on from one generation to another, from one man to another. Sometimes the receiver appreciates them even more than the giver. But things of the spirit, of the heart and the mind, cannot be inherited, cannot be given from one to another. Religion is not like a cloak that one can receive and wrap around his shoulders, and in which he may feel secure, not for long.

I learned this truth anew one day last spring when some students took me up to Brighton to ski. It was the first time in [my] forty years that I had been on skis. Because I had at one time played other sports, I assumed I could learn to ski rather rapidly. For a half hour I tried to go fifty feet uphill; afterward I made a lunge for a hose which was to carry me up the lift. I caught hold all right, but my feet became involved with one another. It took many minutes to extricate them and resume my journey up the hill. Coming downhill, I spent the afternoon learning how to arise with greater facility.

On that majestic mountain slope, however, I learned something else with greater conviction than I had ever learned it before. My relationship to skiing was not unlike my relationship, and your relationship, to the gospel of Jesus Christ. Skiing is a well-accomplished art; there are thousands and perhaps millions of people in the world who can ski, but to me it is only an opportunity, a possibility; it was not mine. And so it is with the gospel of Jesus Christ. It was restored through the Prophet Joseph Smith. He went into the Sacred Grove and found God. He learned through faith and humility to commune with his Maker. He knew God lived; he loved him and served him with courage and faith. Because Joseph Smith went into the Sacred Grove, and loved God and knew him, doesn't mean that we Latter-day Saints know God. It only means, it seems to me, that we know *about* him. If ever you and I are to know God, it will be because we learn to pray and to commune; it will be because we find our way to love God with all our hearts and serve him. This is true of every principle of religion. Humility, faith, love, and repentance, the great concepts we have inherited as Christians and Latter-day Saints, are only words to us until we make them our own through our own creative living.

There is a great difference between a truth and our understanding of that truth. Jesus Christ's concept of love I accept as an eternal and universally applicable truth, but my conception of love is not eternal and is not universally applicable. My conception of love is no greater than my experience with love. I must forever grow and learn the larger meaning of love and of every principle of the gospel. God is that he is. But what God is, and my conception of what God is, are two different things. My knowledge of God is partial and limited, and so is yours. I like, again, the words of King Benjamin in Mosiah, when he said: " . . . believe that man doth not comprehend all the things which the Lord can comprehend." (Mosiah 4:9.) Or the words of Isaiah: "For my thoughts are not your thoughts, neither are your ways my ways, saith the Lord. For as the heavens are higher than the earth, so are my ways higher than your ways, and my thoughts than your thoughts." (Isaiah 55:8-9.)

To be creative in religion, brothers and sisters, we must not think we possess it; we must look upon it more as an opportunity, as something to be realized. May I illustrate that with a humble experience.

Some time ago, during the war, I had a cow which went "the way of all flesh." I went about looking for a new cow. Cows were in demand and no one would sell me one. One day a very fine Jersey cow strayed over from a neighbor. I looked at her and I admit that I coveted her, but finally my Christian faith got the upper hand and I returned the cow to her rightful owner. I said to him, "Brother, what do you do with all the milk from this cow?" He said, "My wife is so tired of straining, skimming, and bottling milk, I have taken to giving the morning milk to the pig." Whole jersey milk to a pig! I said to him, "How would it be if I came over every morning at seven o'clock and milked the cow and took the milk home. I'll be happy to pay for more than my share of the feed, if you'll think upon the cow at all other times. Think it over carefully," I told him. It's easy enough to love all men, and to cooperate with them—the difficulty comes when we specialize.

He and his wife thought it over and said they were willing to give it a try. That was two and a half years ago, and this morning, even before seven o'clock, I went over to my neighbors' and milked a cow.

Why do I tell you this experience? You know, I had always thought that we were free because we had free agency. It is one of the great doctrines of the Church. But I've discovered a new freedom in sharing a cow. And I would like to tell you about it. It saves me one hour a day not to have to go home at night and change clothes, usually twice, and milk that cow. Moreover, it is often a late hour and a very precious hour when sleep is needed. That is not all. When I am ill, or when we go on a vacation for a week, my good neighbor milks the cow and brings the milk over, or keeps it as we desire. My wife has freedom; she only strains and takes care of the milk once a day. We save money, and money may be an avenue to freedom. My neighbor has found freedom. Whenever he is ill, I milk his cow. When a relative dies in Ogden, he may go there while I take care of his cow. We have both gained a lot of freedom, but more than that, before we shared we were people who had a common property line between us, a fence. Now we are neighbors. Every morning we greet each other. In the wintertime he greets me through a kitchen window with the glow of a fire to his back. He is a man of seventy-four and suffers some from arthritis. It does my heart good to see him stay in the kitchen on a cold morning. In the summertime we exchange ideas, greetings, and build friendship. I found that I could help him with heavy jobs—put up his hay and the like. He has a wheelbarrow with a pneumatic tire which is at my disposal, and I did not know it until I went over to milk his cow. He has tools. More than that, we love each other; we have mercy for one another. Yesterday I administered to him in his illness and he thanked me with tears in his eyes. If sharing a cow can bring man freedom and cultivate mercy, understanding, and love, as I love him, what could we not do if we would look upon our religion as an opportunity to become true disciples of Christ rather than to take for granted that we are such, because the gospel has been restored.

You students have often been hiking in the mountains, tired and thirsty, and have come to a mountain spring. You know the joy of falling to the ground and of putting your face in the water and drinking that cold water. To me, the gospel of Jesus Christ might be likened to that mountain spring. It is there before we come to it and it is there, flowing, when we do not think of it, and it is there after we are gone. When we get thirsty, we kneel down and drink of the truths of the gospel. I pray that we may be humble more often and thirsty more often and desirous of partaking of something that is so much greater, in a sense, than we are. If we would adopt that attitude toward religion, we would carry on in the spirit and tradition of the Prophet Joseph Smith.

Faith

There is a second way to be creative in religion. It is the way of faith. We live in a world where many have been greatly disillusioned in their faith. There are intellectuals who prefer to live by knowledge and who distrust faith, especially the kind that is associated with religion. I, too, wish to live by knowledge whenever and wherever I may gain it. I would rather have knowledge of the character and cooking ability of a prospective wife than just faith in these things. But I have learned that knowledge is not sufficient to meet the demands of life. Knowledge we gain through past and verifiable experience. Life is dynamic and every day is a new day, and people who live by knowledge only often become cynical and conservative and afraid. Their hearts and minds are not equal to the creative possibilities of life. Faith is an attitude of mind by which we live as though the possibility were already a reality, and by that very process we create reality out of the things we carry in our hearts. Let us not live by a blind faith—a faith without works, one that is in contradiction to our knowledge and experience, or one that has no meaning or value because of the things in which we have faith. Let us be true to the first principle of the gospel, faith in the Lord Jesus Christ. Faith

in Christ means faith in his Beatitudes, in the tw
ments. It means faith in our Father which is in heave
in one's self and in every man who is our brother and a
Living by faith is a great and creative adventure, if we ha
the right things.

To the Prophet Joseph, as already indicated, religious faith
an instrument through which to realize Zion and the Kingdom. L
us keep it as such. Theology is not the end. Religion is not something
to be preserved. The Church is not something to serve simply as an organization. Life is the end: to bring to pass the immortality and God-like life of men. Self-realization toward a more Christ-like life for all men is our goal. Like the Prophet Joseph, let us keep people in mind, use our theology, live our religion, and serve our church, as great instruments through which, by faith, we may help to realize God's eternal purpose. Such a faith will bring its own reward and its own satisfaction. To be creative in religion, we must look upon it as an opportunity and not a possession. We must not be afraid to live by faith, faith in Christ that makes a difference in every walk of life, in our homes in our business, in government.

There is a third way in which we may be creative. No one is truly creative anywhere in life unless he loves that which he does. No one is creative in religion unless he rises above fear, duty, reward, and compulsion of every kind and lives his religion because he believes in it and loves it.

In the Bible we are told that "perfect love casteth out fear"; and Jesus and the author of Deuteronomy both said, "Thou shalt love the Lord, thy God, with all thy heart, and with all thy mind, and with all thy soul." This we cannot do if our religious life is impaired by the love of other things or by the love of ourselves.

There is one last passage I would like to read to you from the works of the Prophet Joseph, a little gem that many of us have passed over for decades without appreciating. In chapter 32 of Alma, Alma is speaking to some people who have been cast out of their synagogues because of their poverty, and do not know how to worship in their condition. In rather a direct and blunt way, Alma says to them, "I say unto you, it is well that ye are cast out of your synagogues, that ye may be humble, and that ye may learn wisdom; . . . for it is because that ye are cast out, that ye are despised of your brethren because of your exceeding poverty, that ye are brought to a lowliness of heart; for ye are necessarily brought to be humble.

"And now, because ye are compelled to be humble blessed are

compelled to be humble, seeketh
soever repenteth shall find mercy;
dureth to the end the same shall be

, that because you were compelled
ye not suppose that they are more
elves because of the word?
himself, and repenteth of his sins,
e shall be blessed—yea, much more
elled to be humble because of their
ther circumstance, we might add].
humble themselves without being
compelled to be humble; or rather, in other words, blessed is he that believeth in the word of God, and is baptized without stubbornness of heart, yea, without being brought to know the word, or even compelled to know, before they will believe." (Alma 32:12-16.)

It is only when we love humility and take delight in it that we have a chance to learn its deeper meaning. And this is true of every principle of religion.

I love the creative spirit and the creative way of the Prophet Joseph Smith. It is a divine way. I humbly pray that you and I may emulate that spirit by walking with humility and learning the gospel of Jesus Christ, by having faith in him, and by learning somehow to love every great principle the Master taught. If we will do this, we shall honor the memory of Joseph Smith, and we shall become worthy sons of God and true disciples of Jesus Christ. God help us to this end, I humbly pray in Jesus' name. Amen.

8

The Uses of the Mind in Religion

Since you have distinguished yourselves as thinkers and scholars and, by your very presence at Brigham Young University, bear witness of your commitment to religious faith, I thought it not inappropriate to talk with you this evening about the uses of the mind in our relationship to the restored gospel.

Living in these latter days, we are the recipients of many legacies from East and West, but the two that have been most influential in Western culture are doubtless the faith and morality of the Judeo-Christian tradition and the rational and aesthetic emphasis of the Greeks. These traditions are not wholly distinct. There is considerable rationality in the Law and the Prophets and Jesus' words, even as there is notable ethical reflection in Socrates, Plato, and Aristotle, but there is a difference in emphasis.

Both the religious and rational footings of our civilization are beyond price. For me, nothing in all the ethical thinking of mankind quite equals the combined ethic and morality of the Hebrew prophets and Jesus. The prophets taught justice and mercy in human relations and tied these principles to the ethical character of a living God. Scholars call this ethical monotheism. Jesus, respecting his prophetic forebears, stressed the worth of the individual and taught men to walk with humility, to act with love, and to trust in the Father. Both Jesus and the prophets exemplified moral courage as they attacked the superficialities and hypocrisies of their day. Greek philosophers delighted in man's capacity to create order out of mystery and chaos. They began to think about nature, how men think, and the rules of logical thought. They inquired into aesthetics and ethics, and the nature of society. They were not afraid—as were the Jews—to create works of art in sculpture and architecture, in addition to drama and

---

This essay, printed in Brigham Young University Studies, *Autumn 1973, was originally given that spring as an address to BYU faculty and graduating students who had received the Phi Kappa Phi award for academic achievement.*

literature. They laid the foundations not only for philosophy, but also for history, the natural and social sciences, medicine, and the arts. Most of all, they discovered and nurtured faith in man's capacity to think and to create.

I do not understand how a person who has come to know these two traditions, in any substantial manner, can turn his back on either one. I confess my profound respect for each of them and try in my own life to effect a marriage between them—a marriage that has all the tension, adjustments, frustration, joys, and ecstasy one finds in a marriage between man and woman. Even as I prefer marriage to living alone, so do I prefer to live in a world of both faith and rationality rather than in a world of either alone.

It is not my intent this evening to try to reconcile faith and reason—a task that has been tried over and over again. Rather, my purpose is to indicate the value of thinking within the gospel. Rationality not only has its place in fighting cancer and in getting man to the moon; it also has a place within the gospel. A quotation from Pascal triggered afresh my own interest in this theme. It reads: "If one subjects everything to reason our religion will lose its mystery and its supernatural character. If one offends the principles of reason our religion will be absurd and ridiculous. . . . There are two equally dangerous extremes—to shut out reason and to let nothing else in."

In the spirit of this quotation, let me hasten to make clear that religion is more than reason. Thinkers for centuries have noted that life and the meaning of things are greater than reason and objective study. Religion's first and unique mission is to transcend knowledge and to help man find meaning in this uncertain existence. If all were known, religion would disappear or change its meaning drastically. Religion enables us to take "the leap of faith," to rise above our contingency, to triumph over our tragic predicament as mortals conscious of our ultimate powerlessness. I am not suggesting that reason should displace faith, however, because man must transcend reason in order to face the future and his total existence.

Religion transcends reason also in the area of human values. I don't know how one can choose purely objectively among competing values. Our choice among value positions rests ultimately, I believe, on feeling, on intuition, on our total experience—not on the cold analysis of empirical evidence. I respect the inspiration of the prophets and of the religious sages of mankind in this field. Micah's words have the ring of truth: "What doth the Lord require of thee, but to do justly, and to love mercy, and to walk humbly with thy God?" (Micah 6:8), but I would not like to have to prove them to be true.

It is often said that the gospel—in contrast to the thinking and philosophies of men—is eternal, unchanging truth. No thinking person, including the scientist himself, would dispute the fact that all human efforts to know the truth are tentative, unfinished, and changing. A glance at textbooks over the years is evidence of this. The hard-won, laboriously acquired knowledge of the greatest of the scientists will be superseded one day by a larger, truer vision. Even the great artist is rarely satisfied with any of his creations. None fully expresses his felt impressions.

But the gospel—it is said by way of contrast—is divine, revealed of God, taught by the Christ, recorded in holy writ, and hence unchanging, eternal truth. From my limited experience, I believe that the gospel of Jesus Christ is eternal, universally valid, and true in the lives of men and Deity. But my understanding of the gospel, and dare I suggest yours too, is not eternal truth and ought not be unchanging truth.

In the mind of God and Christ, the gospel is known in its full beauty and actuality, but in your life and mine, the truths of the gospel are only partially known and are relative to our capacity, humility, and experience. Faith, repentance, love, God, atonement are but words in a book, symbols of attitudes and realities that we comprehend only in part. This we sometimes forget, but the prophets profess it in moments of profound humility and insight.

Isaiah said for the Lord: "For my thoughts are not your thoughts, neither are your ways my ways, saith the Lord. For as the heavens are higher than the earth, so are my ways higher than your ways, and my thoughts than your thoughts." (Isaiah 55:8-9.)

"Woe is me!" said Isaiah when he was called to the ministry, "for I am undone; because I am a man of unclean lips, and I dwell in the midst of a people of unclean lips: for mine eyes have seen the King, the Lord of hosts." (Isaiah 6:5.)

The apostle Paul, who was not lacking in testimony and assurance, said in his sublime eulogy on love: "For we know in part, and we prophesy in part. But when that which is perfect is come, then that which is in part shall be done away. . . . For now we see through a glass, darkly." (1 Corinthians 13:9-10, 12.)

Some of that same spirit of humility is found in latter-day scripture. Moses had a remarkable vision of God and some of His unending creations. The prophet's fascinating response to that overawing presence was: "Now . . . I know that man is nothing, which thing I never had supposed." Satan took advantage of Moses' humbled position and said to him, "Moses, son of man, worship me." To illustrate how relative man's view of the situation is, Moses recovered his perspective and answered, "Who art thou? For behold, I am a son of God, in the similitude of his Only Begotten; and where is thy glory that I should worship thee?" (Moses 1:10, 12-13.)

For a long time I have been grateful for and impressed by the Prophet Joseph's description of his remarkable vision of the Father and the Son, wherein he said, "I saw two Personages, whose brightness and glory defy all description." (Joseph Smith–History 1:17.) Revelation itself is not a one-way communication, but a teaching process dependent on the learner as well as on the teacher. It is so described in the preface to the Doctrine and Covenants: "Behold, I am God and have spoken it; these commandments are of me. . . ." This is the divine part of revelation. That which follows reveals the human limitations on the divine word to man: " . . . and were given unto my servants in their weakness, after the manner of their language, that they might come to an understanding. And inasmuch as they erred it might be made known; and inasmuch as they sought wisdom they might be instructed; . . . and inasmuch as they were humble they might be made strong, and blessed from on high, and receive knowledge from time to time." (Doctrine and Covenants 1:24-26, 28.)

Perhaps I have belabored this point, but I feel that many of us are too complacent. Because of the remarkable events and teachings associated with the Restoration, we assume to know all about God and his ways. When we act on that assumption, we reduce him to our image, and we lose our hunger and thirst for his truth and his righteousness. Jesus said, "And this is life eternal, that they might know thee the only true God, and Jesus Christ, whom thou hast sent."(John 17:3.) To know them, we must come to think as they think, feel as they feel, create as they create, love as they love. We must, as Christ did, receive grace for grace. This is an eternal quest.

I have tried to distinguish between the eternal truths of the gospel and our limited, human understanding of them. I like the way Yvor Winter puts it in his *In Defense of Reason:*

> The absolutist believes in the existence of absolute truths and values. Unless he is very foolish, he does not believe that he personally has free access to these absolutes and that his own judgments

> are final; but he does believe that such absolutes exist and that it is the duty of every man and of every society to endeavor as far as may be to approximate them. The relativist, on the other hand, believes that there are no absolute truths, that the judgment of every man is right for himself. (Swallow, 1947, p. 10.)

The gospel of Jesus Christ contains eternal truths, but our knowledge of them is relative to our humility, study, capacity, and experience.

If we recognize our limited understanding of the gospel, our next step is to study it earnestly, searchingly, and prayerfully. May I suggest too that the object of our major study ought to be simple, fundamental principles of the gospel. Too often these are taken for granted or passed over superficially, while we occupy ourselves with "things which lead not to edification" or we elaborate on the things the Lord has only touched on lightly.

What we need to understand more fully are the attributes of God—the meaning of integrity, creativity, intelligence, and love; the teachings of Christ that are iterated again and again—humility, meekness, love, trust in God. We need to grow within our understanding of each gospel principle.

A child in Primary is taught: "We believe in being honest. . . ." But honesty is one thing to a child, quite another to a thoughtful adult. The former thinks of honesty in terms of not lying and not stealing. The adult includes these in his conception of honesty, but he learns the difficult role of being honest in relationships and in being true to his own deepest convictions. He struggles between keeping his own integrity and his concern for the feelings of others and their well-being. Honesty must sometimes vie with mercy in the mind of the sensitive adult.

One of the rewards and joys of gospel teaching is what one learns from his students either directly or by the questions they raise. I remember a freshman in a large Book of Mormon class who, when the class was asked how the covenant of baptism differs from a marriage contract, replied, "In a marriage contract, either party may fail, but in the baptismal covenant, only man can fail. God will not." This was a new and beautiful insight to the teacher.

The restored gospel is a religion of action. It is not an end in itself, but was designed to bring about growth and fulfillment in man. To do so, it must penetrate the inner life of the individual and the social systems of society. To accomplish this goal, religion must be more than feeling, more than even faith and good will. The life of man, living in society, needs to be understood. There are factual and rational aspects to the economic, political, and social life of man. To have any impact on these, we must understand both the nature of society and gospel principles. This is a rationale, as well as a question, of value. For example, roughly twenty percent of our population in America live in poverty. They cannot succeed in our competitive, "free" society. The gospel teaches us to love those who have least, and that it is more blessed to give than to receive. How do we give love to the poor in ways that will build the freedom and respect of the individual? I submit to you that we have not begun to learn—on a large scale—how to live the principle of love in a modern, complex society. I think this could well be the subject matter of a priesthood or Sunday School course of study of a year, or a decade, and it would tax the mind as well as the heart to the limit. It calls for thinking to make the gospel viable in human relations.

One further example may illustrate the same point. We speak of free agency in sermon after sermon and in class after class. It is a beautiful and fundamental principle of the gospel, but too seldom do we recognize that we are not free. Every man has free agency—a desire and capacity to be free—but none of us are completely free. We fail to make the distinction between free agency and freedom. Some are not free to resist overeating, to communicate honestly with husband or wife, to forsake greed or lust, to acknowledge one's weakness or sin, to follow one's convictions of the right. Freedom is won with knowledge, with understanding, with wisdom, sometimes with love, and with cooperation from others. Here is another "commonly spoken principle" of the gospel a class could profitably study for a year or a decade.

I would like to suggest one more use of the mind in religion. Someone has said that there is nothing so lost as an isolated fact. In every field of study, facts are related to each other by hypotheses, by theories, by conceptual schemes.

This same learning process applies to the restored gospel. One needs to see it whole. It contains a basic framework of theology and an integrated ethical pattern for living. But the scriptures were not written by systematic theologians or moral philosophers—thank goodness—but have come to us as spontaneous records, quite miscellaneous in form, containing the experience, inspiration, and words of men as they have struggled with God and his people.

Without destroying the freshness of the scriptures, we need to look into them to find these fundamental, oft-repeated, and established truths which give the scriptures their great meaning and value. This is an intellectual and imaginative exercise as well as a spiritual search.

Not only does the gospel as a whole seem to hang together, as it were, but within it are several groups of beautifully integrated ideas. I can mention but two or three this evening.

Jesus and the prophets portray God the Father as a person of integrity and impartiality, love and mercy, and as a Father whose purpose it is to bring the abundant and eternal life to man. If we keep this character of God in mind, we shall not interpret his relationship to men in ways that contradict these divine attributes, even though isolated passages of scripture might give us license to do so. We will not believe him to be jealous, revengeful, and wrathful as we know these qualities of character in human experience.

The restored gospel teaches us also that the elements, some laws, the intelligence of man along with his capacity for freedom, are co-eternal with God. If we believe and understand this, we shall not ascribe the limitations of nature and human nature to him. Rather we shall be inclined to help him overcome evil and to realize the ideal.

The Beatitudes are another example of a beautiful, logical framework within the gospel. I commend to your reading a book by Henry Churchill King, called *The Ethics of Jesus,* in which the author describes the Beatitudes as Jesus' map of life. He shows how each builds on and presupposes those that have gone before. Dr. King gives new insight into the meaning of "blessed are they that mourn," which he calls "the penitent," and of "blessed are the meek," which he equates with self-control at its highest. The Book of Mormon, with the phrase "who come unto me" inserted in the Beatitudes, adds additional meaning to this map of life.

Finally, I am impressed by the remarkably intimate relationship of the first principles and ordinances of the gospel. Faith in Christ leads to, inspires, and gives direction to repentance. Baptism bears witness to a new beginning and of a bond with Christ and with each other. And, in the words of Mormon,"because of meekness, and lowliness of heart," which follows from faith in Christ and repentance, "cometh the visitation of the Holy Ghost, which Comforter filleth with hope and perfect love." (Moroni 8:26.) This whole process of becoming a disciple of Christ is renewed in the sacramental covenant.

One has every reason to be intellectually eager and alert as he relates to the gospel of Jesus Christ and seeks to apply its principles to the demands and privileges of living.

I must admit that the thoughtful way is not, in the short run, the easy way. It is less troublesome to be as sheep led or herded without thought, and with little sense of personal responsibility. Thinking is always critical. It means analyzing, taking apart, and synthesizing, or seeing things in new relationships. Thinking means questioning, even doubting, and trusting that the gospel can stand the test of thought. Thinking means carrying one's own lantern, living one's own testimony.

God himself does not seem to object to our questioning even him and his ways. Abraham persuaded the Lord to save Sodom if He could find ten righteous souls. Jacob wrestled with his heavenly antagonist until he got his way. And most impressive of all, Job challenged God's justice and compassion and stood by his own integrity through an extended debate. He learned that he had "darkened counsel by words without knowledge," but God did not condemn him for his honest thinking, whereas his complacent friends – Eliphaz, Bildad, and Zophar – who upheld the traditional, limited Hebrew view of the reason for suffering, received a judgment from God, for they had not spoken of him "the thing that is right."

The gospel of Jesus Christ was restored in response to a youth's search for truth. Throughout our history, prophets have asked questions and reasoned freely about truths of the gospel. I trust that you will bring your best thinking as well as your deepest feelings to bear on the gospel of our Lord Jesus Christ, and I hope that you will love the Lord thy God with all thy heart, and with all thy soul, and with all thy mind.

9

Three Loyalties in Religion

Being religious can mean many different things—like going to church, reading scripture, believing in God, keeping the commandments. In fact, religion embraces so much that one needs to cast his own religious beliefs and feelings into some kind of mold or framework that will bring simplicity out of complexity and order out of miscellany.

There is more than one acceptable way to integrate one's religious living into a meaningful whole. Tonight I wish to do so in terms of three basic loyalties. One reason for my choice is that the religious life means commitment, and so it appears logical to think of it in terms of loyalties. I shall speak in personal terms; I cannot speak for you, since I am not sure you share these same commitments in the order in which I do, or at all.

My first, central, and highest loyalty is to persons, both mortal and divine. Nothing else in religion, on earth, or in the universe is quite so important. Nothing matters ultimately except what happens to persons and relationships between persons.

Many experiences and ideas have led me to this conviction, including religion itself. Nothing inspires me more than the view of creation depicted in the first chapter of Moses (verse 39) in which the prophet is given a glimpse of some of the creations of God through the Son and is told, "Worlds without number have I created." Moses pressed his Creator to tell him the meaning of his endless, ongoing creations. Finally, the now well-known answer came: "For behold, this is my work and glory—to bring to pass the immortality and eternal life of man."

It would seem that "eternal" in this context has a qualitative connotation, meaning God-like, even as it does in the Gospel of John, wherein Christ said, "This is life eternal, that they might know thee the only true God, and Jesus Christ, whom thou hast sent." (John 17:3.) The very work of Deity is to bring man—all men—to a greater

---

This sacrament meeting talk appeared in Dialogue, *Spring 1974.*

realization of the life which God knows, to help men increase in integrity, love, freedom, and creativity, to achieve the full measure of their creation as sons of God. If this is the divine purpose, why should it not become yours and mine, if we are to do his will and love him with all our hearts, minds, and souls?

The Hebrew prophets have taught me in unforgettable language to care above all else for what happens to persons. In the days of Amos, ancient Israel was doing many things in the name of religion—keeping the sabbath and the new moon, offering sacrifices, uttering prayers, remembering their fathers, Abraham, Isaac, and Jacob. But they had forgotten one thing—God's concern for man. To paraphrase Amos, they were at ease in Zion, playing musical instruments, drinking wine out of bowls, stretching themselves in idle luxury as the chosen of God, but they were "not grieved for the affliction of Joseph." (Amos 6:6.) They gave no thought to the widow, the orphan, the poor, those who were hurting, except to sell them into slavery for the price of a pair of shoes or to take advantage of them in the court by bribes and deception.

Among the prophets, Micah defined religion most beautifully when he asked and then answered his own question: "Wherewith shall I come before the Lord, and bow myself before the high God?" Not, he continues, with sacrifices and rivers of oil and human sacrifice, for "he hath showed thee, O man, what is good; and what doth the Lord require of thee, but to do justly, and to love mercy, and to walk humbly with thy God?" (Micah 6:6-8.)

Here Micah is defining religion in terms of personal relationships between man and man (do justly and love mercy) and between man and God (walk humbly).

You are familiar with the Savior's concern for persons. He had, I believe, two supreme loyalties—to his Father and to his fellowmen. He began his ministry by quoting from Isaiah: "The Spirit of the Lord is upon me, because he hath anointed me to preach the gospel to the poor; he hath sent me to heal the broken-hearted, to preach deliverance to the captive, and recovering of sight to the blind, to set at liberty them that are bruised."

Follow the Christ through the Gospels and you will see how closely he kept to his original charge. "He went about doing good." Even "sinners drew near unto him." He sought out those who needed him, fed their hunger and stilled their thirst. Even the sacred law—the sabbath—in his eyes was made for man. "Is it lawful to do good, . . . or to do evil? to save life, or to kill?" (Mark 3:4) was the question that guided his actions.

Christ was as humane and man-centered as any humanist in his concern for persons, but he also loved God and shared with him his love for man.

And so my loyalty to persons includes man, every man, I hope, but also Deity—the Father and the Son. They too are persons. I don't know that they need my direct adoration and affection, but it is my simple faith that they suffer when men suffer and rejoice when men have cause to rejoice. So in a modest way, but with all my heart, I would diminish their suffering and enhance their joy.

My second loyalty in religion is to the principles of the Gospel, to faith, repentance, justice, freedom, the Beatitudes, love and its many expressions—empathy, mercy, and forgiveness. These have my loyalty because I have seen what they do for persons, how they help men to be whole, hopeful, self-controlled, and generous; how they refine and enrich human relationships and increase peace and good will among men.

I have seen these principles work in the lives of converts, countless students, and friends. There was the young man who confessed that he had committed every sin in the book: stealing, adultery, drunkenness, and hypocrisy. Then I saw him find faith in Christ and overcome greed and lust and regain self-respect, a self-respect chastened by "the furnace of affliction," mellowed and meek but not without strength and joy. There comes to mind also a young woman, single and alone, who was once steeped in fear and self-pity. I heard her say, "I used to be afraid of life and of myself, but I am no more. I can love and serve others. I have found joy in following the Master."

Gospel principles do not excite me in the abstract. They have meaning only in the life of the individual and in his relationship to fellowman and Deity. And so my second loyalty is intimately related to the first.

This, too, I have learned from Jesus. He was not committed to the law as an end, but used it to serve life. His entire mission was geared to human needs; he taught repentance not to the righteous but to sinners, gave hope to the poor, the healing power of faith to the afflicted, and forgiveness to sinners. Gospel principles and human need were inseparable in his mind.

To be a disciple of Christ, one doesn't have to always be turning the other cheek. Christ knocked over the tables of money changers, called Herod "that old fox," and told Peter, "Get thee behind me,

Satan." He called principles into play to effect change in human life and behavior, including honesty and moral courage. We can use gospel principles in business, in politics, in the courthouse, and in the classroom. There are those appropriate to every real situation.

My third loyalty in religion is to the Church. I place it third, not because it is unimportant, but because in my judgment it is instrumental to the other two loyalties already discussed. In the language of Paul, Christ "gave some, apostles; and some, prophets; . . . for the perfecting of the saints . . . till we all come in the unity of the faith, and of the knowledge of the Son of God, unto a perfect man, unto the measure of the stature of the fullness of Christ: that we . . . speaking the truth in love, may grow up into him in all things." (Ephesians 4:11-15.)

The Church is not an end to be served, but an instrument through which together we may serve God and man. It is a fellowship, called and ordained of the Lord, blessed and empowered from on high, to inculcate the principles and spirit of the gospel into the lives of men.

I am grateful to the Church, for within its fold I have begun to learn and experience the meaning of the gospel. There I have found a choice fellowship with co-believers; through it I have received faith, the gift of the Holy Spirit, the priesthood, and rich opportunities to serve and worship.

But again, one cannot serve the Church fruitfully without prior loyalties to God and man. There is always the danger in organized religion that institutional ends become the goals of religion. Meetings may be held as ends in themselves, missionary work measured in terms of baptismal quotas, and welfare projects evaluated in quantitative terms. When this happens, the religious life becomes idolatrous—serving false gods instead of God and his children. Whenever institutional goals are placed first, persons become means to these ends and integrity and love become secondary if not forgotten. The Church, though called of God, is made up of men like you and me among whom "many are called but few are chosen," and our human interests and ambitions becloud our vision of God's work and glory, to bring to pass the immortality and eternal life of man.

Yes, I have three basic loyalties in religion: to persons, to gospel principles, and to the Church. They are not in conflict with one another, but blend beautifully even as the moon, stars, and open sky, *if* I remember all three and serve them in proper conjunction with the others. I pray that we may always remember these commitments, in the name of one who did, even Jesus Christ. Amen.

10

Reflections on the Restoration

The world's living religions began with the lives and teachings of charismatic leaders such as Moses, Buddha, Confucius, Jesus, and Muhammad. Each won a following by the force of his character, the witness of his faith, and the humane content of his teaching. In the beginning these religions were relatively simple in their teaching, with limited ritual and organization and, of course, without tradition.

As they acquired a following and the founders died, their disciples, wishing to carry on the words and mission of their leaders, canonized their words, elaborated rituals and organization, and built material monuments to the faith—cathedrals, statues, temples, and historical markers. This process is called institutionalization, and it characterizes practically every ongoing movement, be it economic, educational, political, or religious in character.

Thomas O'Dea, insightful sociologist of religion, made a simple but profound statement when he said, "Religion *needs* most and *suffers* most from institutionalization." If religion were not institutionalized, it would likely die with the founder or with his immediate disciples. It would not be integrated into the social fabric of society. Religion is a social phenomenon. To be shared and preserved, it must have a body of beliefs and other ways of expressing feelings and aspirations by the group. Scriptures, rituals, and traditions fill this need.

On the other hand, religion may suffer from institutionalization because institutional practices and interests may increase dramatically and divert people from the original purposes and values of the founder. In my missionary days in Europe, I became aware of the dangers to religion found in the elaboration of church dogma, ritual, and organization that took place when the church of Christ became the

---

This summary of Lowell Bennion's convictions and insights concerning his own Mormon theology and its institutional form, the restored Church of Jesus Christ, appeared in Dialogue: A Journal of Mormon Thought, *Autumn 1985.*

church of the Roman Empire. Indeed, this was one explanation and evidence of the apostasy in early Christian history. It was not, however, until I began to study the process of institutionalization that I gained a fuller understanding of its meaning for religion.

In many well-established religions, ethically and spiritually sensitive members have felt burdened by the weight of their religious institutions. They have sensed that the purpose and spirit of the pristine faith have been weakened and impaired by the excessive or irrelevant accumulation of doctrine, ritual, authority. Nearly every reform movement in Christianity has been a search for the simplicity and authenticity of the Christian faith of the New Testament times. John Huss and Martin Luther attacked practices of the Catholic Church. John Wesley and George Fox, founders of Methodism and the Society of Friends, sought to recover the true spirit of Christianity within the Church of England. When their reform efforts failed, they established new religious movements. These new religions developed into institutionalized religions of their own. The Quakers are an exception. They have retained the simplicity of their original faith better than any group I know. In spite of (or because of) their success, they have remained a very small group.

The Church of Jesus Christ of Latter-day Saints represents another effort to restore the pristine gospel and church of Christ as it existed in apostolic times. It is by no means the only Christian movement of the nineteenth century that sought to do this. But in several ways, the concept of restoration in the LDS faith is distinctive.

First of all, the idea that this new religion was the restored church and gospel was made clear from the beginning. Joseph Smith was not trying to pour new wine into old bottles. For him, the divine church of Christ did not exist on earth. A fresh revelation and a new dispensation were needed to bring back the gospel and a church acceptable to Deity. Joseph was not learned in Christian history or dogma. Young, untutored, and unaffiliated, he sought not to reform existing churches but began anew to reestablish the true Christian faith. This was a bold undertaking that he did not claim to initiate himself, except through prayer. After his first vision, he felt, like Amos of old, called to speak for God.

The beginnings of Mormonism have inspired me from my youth. I was deeply moved by my belief in the reality of a personal God, the resurrected Christ, and the principle of revelation revealed through the experience of Joseph Smith. I resonated with the fact that Mormonism began in the inquiring mind of a youth who sought God on a spring morning in the springtime of his life. I have cherished the feeling all my life that this, my religion, was more like a free-flowing mountain spring than a lake filled with moss or covered with ice.

A second distinctive aspect of the restoration in the LDS faith is the concept of divine authority. Religious leaders have felt called of God and doubtless have been moved often by His inspiration in their search for the true Christian faith. Joseph Smith not only felt inspired but said that he received authority in a very real manner. He claimed that leaders of the original Christian movement—John the Baptist and Peter, James, and John—appeared to him and Oliver Cowdery, laid hands upon their heads, bestowed on them the priesthood of God, and commissioned them to organize the church of Christ, to perform the ordinances of the church, and to act for Deity in sacred matters. I am not aware of any other movement that, in its attempt to reestablish the true Christian faith, makes such a claim to divine authority. The priesthood exercised by most Christian leaders is an inner subjective calling felt by the individual and confirmed in the same way by his congregation. Lutherans call it the priesthood of all believers. The Catholic Church is an exception, claiming divine authority through apostolic succession from Peter.

A third remarkable element in the restoration of The Church of Jesus Christ of Latter-day Saints is the incorporation of much of the religion of the Old Testament. Inspired in part perhaps by the Apostle Paul's emphasis on the distinction between Judaism and the Christian faith, many Christian movements have made little room for the religion of Israel in their efforts to return to the pristine Christian faith. The faith of Jesus, Paul, and the other apostles, however, had much in common with the religion of Israel. All of them quoted the Old Testament repeatedly to justify and validate their new religion. For early Christians, Jesus was the fulfillment of Old Testament prophecy. His ethical teaching was in complete harmony with that of the prophets and some later teachers in Judaism. For them, pristine Christianity was Judaism plus the mission and life of Jesus Christ.

Like the founders of Christianity, Latter-day Saints have incorporated much of the religion of Israel into their own faith. They call themselves modern Israel and claim kinship with Joseph who was sold into Egypt. The Book of Mormon overlaps both the Old and the New Testament periods. The Book of Mormon quotes extensively from the Old Testament and also highlights the coming of Christ. In part, the Book of Mormon is a fusion of the Old Testament and the New Testament. Its authors call it a record of Joseph and declare that one of its purposes is to serve as a New World witness of the Bible. (The LDS Church itself now subtitles the book "Another Testament of Jesus Christ.") The forced exodus of the Mormons from Nauvoo, to a promised land to build a new Zion, had much the same meaning to the Mormons as the exodus from Egypt must have had for ancient Israel.

When Orson Pratt celebrated the arrival of the pioneers in the Salt Lake Valley, he identified their new home in the "tops of the mountains" with the Zion spoken of by the prophets. Indeed, the Saints saw themselves fulfilling Old Testament prophecy in this, their heroic adventure.

> But in the last days it shall come to pass, that the mountain of the house of the Lord shall be established in the top of the mountains, and it shall be exalted above the hills; and people shall flow unto it.
>
> And many nations shall come, and say, Come, and let us go up to the mountain of the Lord, and to the house of the God of Jacob; and he will teach us of his ways, and we will walk in his paths: for the law shall go forth of Zion, and the word of the Lord from Jerusalem.
>
> And he shall judge among many people, and rebuke strong nations afar off; and they shall beat their swords into plowshares, and their spears into pruninghooks: nation shall not lift up a sword against nation, neither shall they learn war any more.
>
> But they shall sit every man under his vine and under his fig tree; and none shall make them afraid: for the mouth of the Lord of hosts hath spoken it.
>
> For all people will walk every one in the name of his god, and we will walk in the name of the Lord our God for ever and ever. (Micah 4:1-5.)

Like ancient Israel, Latter-day Saints considered themselves a chosen people, called to establish Zion, a New Jerusalem. Their flight west was reminiscent of Israel's flight from Egypt. They named their river, which flowed from the fresh waters of Utah Lake to the Great Salt Lake, the Jordan. They constructed a defense of polygamy that included the lives of Old Testament patriarchs. Someday they would return to Missouri as the Jews would to Jerusalem.

A fourth important characteristic of the restoration was an attempt to establish a cohesive society based on Christian love. This intent is beautifully portrayed in Mosiah 18 in the Book of Mormon, where Alma teaches the meaning of baptism. "And now, as ye are desirous to come into the fold of God, and be called his people, and are willing to bear one another's burdens, that they may be light; yea, and are willing to mourn with those who mourn; yea, and comfort those that stand in need of comfort, and to stand as witnesses of God at all times and in all things, and in all places . . . what have you against being baptized?" (Mosiah 18:8-10.)

The rest of the chapter tells how their baptismal pledge became reality in their daily lives.

Early in Mormon history, valiant but unsuccessful attempts were made to establish a law of consecration that would have gone far to eliminate poverty and to enable the more capable to contribute richly to the common good. The Saints were told to "remember in all things the poor and the needy, the sick and afflicted, *for he that doeth not these things, the same is not my disciple.*" (D&C 52:40; italics added.)

Brigham Young made repeated attempts to achieve the same goal, as evidenced in *Building the City of God* by Leonard J. Arrington, Feramorz Y. Fox, and Dean L. May (Salt Lake City: Deseret Book, 1976). All of these socio-economic experiments in Missouri and the West failed for political, economic, and human reasons, but they illustrate how the restoration was more than theological and ecclesiastical. Sincere and sacrificial efforts were made to establish a Christian society.

The pristine gospel taught by Jesus had both institutional elements and profound religious and ethical principles. Jesus himself submitted to baptism, called the Twelve, and sent them to preach and baptize. To Peter, he gave authority to bind on earth and in heaven. His chief concerns, judging by his sayings and actions, however, were the will of his Father and the well-being of the human family. He said little about institutional matters and much about humility, faith in God, and love of neighbor: "By this shall all men know that ye are my disciples, if ye have love one to another." (John 13:35.)

Because of the fragmentary nature of the New Testament record and the possibility of more than one interpretation being placed on passages of scripture, it is difficult, if not impossible, to prove rationally and definitively that the LDS faith is a restoration of the primitive Christian church and gospel. Many fundamental aspects, however, support the claim: the lay character of the LDS Church; the assertion of divine authority; the simplicity and form of its ordinances (the blessing of children, the administration of the sick, baptism by immersion and of the spirit, the sacrament of the Lord's Supper); baptism for the dead; the presence of prophets, apostles, and other officers named in the New Testament; its emphasis on faith and repentance, the first principles and ordinances; its concept of Deity and man; and its many programs that promote the welfare and fellowship of its members.

The Church plays a very important, necessary role in the religious life and salvation of its members—teaching the gospel; performing essential, grace-bestowing ordinances; offering opportunities for corporate worship, fellowship, and service; and motivating people to live the gospel. However, the Church is not an end in itself. It is a means of developing true disciples of Christ—persons who have faith in him, who are learning to live the kind of life he would have them live, and who believe in and trust his grace.

Like pristine Christianity, Mormonism also has within it both institutional elements and gospel principles and ideals. Both derive their value from helping to "bring to pass the immortality and eternal life of man." Both are a means to an end, the end being the developing of Christian faith and living in the lives of God's children. As the Church ages and expands in size, territory, and functions, I am concerned that it continue to serve this, its primary purpose, rather than being diverted to institutional ends.

1. My first concern is that we do not equate the religious life with church activity. The Church is an essential part of the religious life. There we are taught the gospel, make sacred covenants, and have opportunities to serve one another. But the Church is not the end of the religious life. We are not here to serve the Church but rather to serve people through the Church. Men and women are not made for the Church, but the Church, like the Sabbath, is made for them. We do not teach lessons but people. Ultimately nothing matters in a class, a meeting, an interview, or a church activity except what people take away—ideally, increased hope, faith, knowledge, desire to serve, or resolution to live the teachings of Jesus.

2. My second, similar concern is that institutional goals do not become ends in themselves. When they do, they may violate gospel principles and inhibit spiritual growth in members. About twenty-five years ago, some ambitious, well-meaning mission presidents made baptisms their goal. They established baptismal quotas and pressured their missionaries to meet these goals. Selling techniques were introduced. Some children were baptized without fully understanding the meaning of the ordinance and without informed consent from their parents.

Some home teaching is done just to get it done, not to build caring and serving relationships with those visited. Just last week I heard two contrasting reports from people visited. In one instance, the brethren come faithfully and never fail to say, "If there is anything we can do, call us." The sister lives alone, is in frail health, cannot drive, and would very much like to be taken to church but is too proud to ask. Her teachers never offer her a ride. She stays home. The other elderly widow has a home teacher who keeps snow removed from her walks and makes minor, needed repairs on her house. He takes the initiative, sees what needs to be done, and does it.

3. My third concern is that we do not think that the ordinances of the Church have value in and of themselves apart from the quality of our lives. We must not be content because we were baptized, married in the temple, ordained to the priesthood, given the gift of the Holy Ghost, or made recipients of the sacrament or of temple ordinances. Church rituals and ordinances are not ends in themselves. They are linked with gospel living. If our baptism doesn't motivate us to bear one another's burdens, it is putting trust in dead works; if the priesthood doesn't make us better servants of Christ, amen to its value in our life; if temple marriage does not contribute to the Christian quality of our marriage, of what value is it?

4. I am concerned also lest the scriptures become an end in themselves. This happened in ancient Israel. The Mosaic law introduced a humane and ethical emphasis in religion, particularly in the teaching of Amos, Micah, Isaiah, and Jeremiah. But there developed in Israel the tendency to elaborate and worship the law irrespective of human values or consequences. A classic example was Jesus' conflict with Pharisees over keeping the Sabbath. Did man exist for the Sabbath or the Sabbath for man? Is it lawful to heal on the Sabbath, to save life or to lose it? (Luke 6:1-10.)

Latter-day Saints are taught to study and revere scriptures as the word of God, but they must not be interpreted apart from God's purpose in human life or the fundamentals of the gospel. Jesus made the scripture of his day—the Law and the Prophets—"hang" on the love of God and love of man. This principle still holds for scriptural interpretation today. The scriptures are not of one quality; they are not a legal document, equally binding in every book and on every line. As with the law of Moses, some of it was conditioned by the state of the times and is no longer valid today.

The principle of continuous revelation enables the prophetic leadership of the Church to relate the will of God to ongoing human needs and understanding that may, at times, change an earlier teaching or practice. Jesus, for example, did away with animal sacrifice among the Nephites and instead called for "a broken heart and a contrite spirit." (3 Nephi 9:19-20.) The 1978 revelation, giving worthy males of every race opportunity to hold the priesthood, is a classic example of a change in policy that is consistent with gospel fundamentals and human welfare and salvation. The divine will is not fully known. The work of the Church is not finished. We have yet to learn the full meaning of Christian discipleship. The salvation of men is still in the making, and every succeeding generation of Latter-day Saints must learn anew what it means to be a disciple of Christ. Goethe wisely said, "What from your father's heritage is lent, earn it anew to really possess it."

5. My fifth concern is that we may identify our being Latter-day Saints primarily with things peculiar and distinctive in our religion, such as the Word of Wisdom, welfare projects, temple work, missionary service, family home evening, and genealogy. These are valuable programs but again only means to an end. We are here [on earth] and in the Church to learn to become disciples of Christ—to learn the meaning of love, humility, faith in Deity, and to worship God and to remember his Son—to take his name upon us and have his spirit to be with us. I am deeply grateful for the Word of Wisdom. It is one of the reasons why I am grateful to have been reared a Latter-day Saint, but it must not be my chief interest in the gospel of Jesus Christ. The same goes for genealogy or keeping a journal.

6. My sixth concern is that we make our commitment to God and Christ and fellow human beings whole souled. We should make friends for the sake of friendship, not to gain converts to the Church. Friendship is not to be a means to an end, a technique of selling the gospel. I hear people say that they are living the gospel to receive blessings, to gain the celestial kingdom, or to earn exaltation. If that is their primary motive, I wonder if their goal doesn't detract from the quality of gospel living—if they are not serving two masters, the gospel and their own interests. I prefer the Savior's statement: "Thou shalt love the Lord thy God with all thy heart, and with all thy soul, and with all thy mind." (Matthew 22:37.) I believe we should love our neighbors because they need our love and because we need to learn to love. Love is its own reward.

7. We must teach people, not lessons. We must reach hearts, not statistical goals. Giving lessons is an institutional emphasis. Teaching individuals is a gospel emphasis. The purpose of Sunday School is not to teach the gospel, but *to teach individuals* the gospel. Nothing matters in a church class or activity in the last analysis except what

happens to the people involved. This is true of a sacrament meeting, a class, a social, a basketball game, or home teaching.

I remember asking an M-Men basketball coach what his purpose was in coaching his young men. His answer, "To win the stake—and if possible the Church—championship." I repeated the question with emphasis. He repeated the answer with emphasis. His objective was institutional. He did not see it in either gospel principles or the well-being of individual team members.

Similarly, in a leadership meeting, I asked scoutmasters what their purpose was in scouting. One answered, "To get every boy registered and in uniform." Another said, "To have at least 75 percent attain the rank of Eagle." These answers reminded me of an experience one of my students related years ago. He said that every boy in the troop in his ward but one had qualified for an award at a given Court of Honor night. Desiring 100 percent, the scoutmaster said to this boy, "If you will promise to complete your second-class work in the next thirty days, we will present you with a second-class award Friday evening at our Court of Honor." To the scoutmaster's shame and the boy's credit, the lad refused to accept "the honor." Institutional goals sometimes do violence to religious and ethical principles.

8. A final illustration of institutionalization that may divert effort from more genuine, religious goals is taking pride in materiality. Jesus had no place to lay his head. Churches, with worthy motives, build cathedrals, temples, meetinghouses, monuments, and historical sites to inspire members and to honor the founder of the faith. These are legitimate unless they become a source of pride or divert attention from true gospel living. Catholics have been criticized for building and decorating great cathedrals in the midst of poverty. Looking to our day, Moroni warned us, "Why do ye adorn yourselves with that which hath no life, and yet suffer the hungry, and the needy, and the naked, and the sick and afflicted to pass by you, and notice them not?" (Mormon 8:39.)

I like to think of the restoration of the pristine gospel of Christ not as a single event in the past, but as an ongoing effort on our part to make the things important to the Savior important to us. We have the authority and the teaching to accomplish the restoration, but each generation of Latter-day Saints must learn the meaning of Christian discipleship anew and realize it in their lives. Thus, we must not view the Church as an end in itself, but as an appropriate, wonderful means of helping people to become true disciples of Jesus Christ. Only in this way can we gain the values and avoid the limitations of institutionalization.

I feel the need to worship God more leisurely and more purely, to visit the sick and afflicted and lonely more often, to be more neighborly, to cultivate a broken heart and a contrite spirit, to be less busy in and out of church and to be more committed to Christ and his way of life. Never has the need to be true disciples of Christ been more urgent and perhaps more difficult. The world needs to witness a Christian society. This is our opportunity—not only to preach the Restoration but to realize it by choosing, in our personal and community life, to live by the weightier matters of the law, faith, justice, and mercy.

III
THE ATONEMENT OF

With Merle and their four sons, Ben, Doug, Steve, and Howard, at the Bennions' Millcreek home, 1947. A daughter, Laurel, was born in Paris in 1933 and died at six months; another daughter, Ellen, was born in 1952.

CHRIST

11

Salvation Through Jesus Christ

The Mission of Jesus Christ

To the men who wrote the New Testament, Jesus Christ was a singular person who had come into the world to bring salvation to mankind. He was more than a prophet, more than a teacher, more than a friend. In him was the very light and life of men, the hope of mankind. Note how overwhelming and consuming was their conviction that Jesus Christ was sent by God to all men, and that all men needed to have faith in him, to receive him in their hearts:

> And he said unto them, Go ye into all the world, and preach the gospel to every creature. He that believeth and is baptized shall be saved; but he that believeth not shall be damned. (Mark 16:15-16.)

> Then Peter, filled with the Holy Ghost, said unto them, Ye rulers of the people, and elders of Israel, if we this day be examined of the good deed done to the impotent man, by what means he is made whole; be it known unto you all, and to all the people of Israel, that by the name of Jesus Christ of Nazareth, whom ye crucified, whom God raised from the dead, even by him doth this man stand here before you whole. This is the stone which was set at nought of you builders, which is become the head of the corner. Neither is there salvation in any other: for there is none other name under heaven given among men, whereby we must be saved. (Acts 4:8-12.)

> And being made perfect, he became the author of eternal salvation unto all them that obey him. (Hebrews 5:9.)

An Introduction to the Gospel, *based partly on his text for LDS institutes,* The Religion of the Latter-day Saints, *is probably Lowell Bennion's best-known and most-read book. It was published continuously by the Church from 1955 to 1971, used in various Sunday School and other Church courses, and translated into fourteen languages, as well as Braille. Included here are parts of chapters 19, 23, and 26.*

Through the ages since biblical times, untold millions of men and women—the learned and the unlearned, clergy and laymen, sinners and saints, bond and free—have looked to Jesus Christ with hope, with faith, with wonder, and even with anxiety and bewilderment, trying to understand him and to come to terms with him. He has meant many different things to different individuals and groups of people. A Christian religion is naturally centered in the mission of Christ. The interpretation of this mission reveals the character of any religion that professes his name.

Latter-day Saints affirm in their hearts the beautiful words from John: "For God so loved the world, that he gave his only begotten Son, that whosoever believeth in him should not perish, but have everlasting life. For God sent not his Son into the world to condemn the world; but that the world through him might be saved." (John 3:16-18.) We believe . . . that Jesus Christ is the Son of God who came into the world to do things for all mankind. What did he come to do? What is his mission among the children of men? . . .

The Meaning of Salvation

The root of the word *salvation* means to save. The entire word means "the act of being saved." Taken in this literal sense, there are things in the lives of men from which they would be saved, evils or limitations that they desire and need to overcome. Christ came to save men from these things. We might well ask, What are the evils of life? What things do we need to overcome?

The evils or limitations of life that men need to overcome trace back to three basic characteristics of human life: (1) mortality, (2) ignorance, and (3) sin. All of man's suffering, frustration, and remorse come, we believe, from one of these causes. Stated positively, Christ came to bring us immortality, knowledge, and the power to conquer sin.

I. Mortality

There are many people among us who are half-starved, cruelly oppressed, or suffering from incurable diseases. To them, life may be a heavy burden and death often a blessing. There are others among us who have sufficient to eat, enjoy the comforts of life and medical care, have access to things of the spirit and rich human companionship. To them, life is not a burden. With William Corey, they may say,

> Sweet, sweet is this human life,
> So sweet, I fain would breathe it still.

But even for those who enjoy life richly, it is fraught with deep tragedy. The richer and fuller one's life, the greater, in a sense, is the tragedy of its ending in death. To know life in its abundance, in its joy and power, whether in ourselves or in other persons, and then to see it end in death would be tragic indeed if death held final victory over life.

Christ died that men might conquer death and life. He came to save us from death. This was his own witness and the triumphant and exultant theme of his disciples. Jesus took the occasion of the raising of Lazarus from the dead to tell us of his power to raise all men from the grave. He said to Martha, "I am the resurrection, and the life: he that believeth in me, though he were dead, yet shall he live: and whosoever liveth and believeth in me shall never die. Believest thou this?" (John 11:25-26.)

Paul is assured of Christ's victory over death. He describes Christ as the first fruits of them that slept and declares that through him all shall be raised from the dead: "O death, where is thy sting? O grave, where is thy victory?" (1 Corinthians 15:55.)

II. Ignorance

A second great limitation of man's life is his ignorance, his lack of awareness of the nature of life. Buddha is reported to have said, "Long is the night to him who is awake, long is the mile to him who is tired, long is life to him who does not know the truth." Where there is ignorance, there is fear, superstition, and frustration. Man's progress in all fields has come largely through the discovery and right use of knowledge. This is as true in the social, moral, and spiritual life of man as it is in engineering or medicine.

Christ came to lead us out of spiritual darkness, to free us from ignorance. He taught us the truths and values of life, the will of God. These he also exemplified. He came to save us from ignorance.

"Then said Jesus to those Jews which believed on him, If ye continue in my word, then are ye my disciples indeed; and ye shall know the truth, and the truth shall make you free." (John 8:31-32.)

III. Sin

The third limitation of life is sin. To sin is to knowingly and willfully act contrary to that which one knows to be right. To act knowingly contrary to our own convictions is to sin against ourselves. To act knowingly contrary to that which we know to be for the well-being of society is to sin against society. To act knowingly contrary to that which God has declared to be right is to sin against God. Sin is moral wrongdoing.

Sin divides the self, brings evil into the lives of our fellowmen, and pits us against God and his purpose. It is a most destructive force in life, more so than ignorance, for when we sin we are out of harmony with the laws of God and we also know it. Hence we suffer the evils which come from violating laws, even as we would if we were acting in ignorance. In addition, we suffer all the damage wrought by man working against himself.

Christ came to save man from sin, to inspire him to rise above it, and to bring him forgiveness. To understand Christ's relationship to man's sins is a vital part of Christian theology. Salvation in its literal sense means the act of being saved from death, ignorance, and sin. This is the mission of Jesus Christ—to save men, or at least participate in the salvation of men, from these three limitations and evils of life.

The Fall of Man

Christian churches generally, while they give God full credit for the creation of man and his life on earth, believe that things got off to a bad start. It is believed that Adam and Eve, though originally created in a state of grace and divine favor, committed some grave sin and fell from grace. With their "fall," they plunged all mankind into death, sin, and damnation. Both Catholic and the major Protestant movements of Lutheranism, Zwingliism, and Calvinism have looked upon human nature as being depraved, having inherited original sin from Adam. According to this view, man is wholly evil by nature until God, through Christ, lifts him again into a state of divine grace or favor and redeems him from death and sin.

Latter-day Saints hold quite a different concept of the Fall from this traditional point of view briefly described above. In our belief, the "fall of man" was not a misfortune. God's plan did not go awry in the beginning. Adam was not a sinner who plunged mankind into a depraved and utterly helpless condition.

We believe that men lived a meaningful, spiritual life as children of God before they were born in the flesh. Earth life was planned by God and Jesus Christ as a necessary and valuable stage in the eternal progression of men. Men knew of the plan before they were born, and looked forward to coming to the earth to gain the experiences of mortality.

Adam and Eve were two of the noblest children of God. For this reason they were chosen to come to earth and to initiate mortal life for others of God's children. Just *how* God brought about man's life on earth, we do not know. The Bible is a deeply religious account of creation, not a scientific record. The story of the fall of man in scripture is an effort to explain the divine origin and purpose of life and should be read with this thought in mind. The story is brief and somewhat figurative and symbolic in language, but from it we can glean a few fundamental religious convictions. Latter-day Saint scriptures have thrown additional light on the creation story.

Adam and Eve were not sinners in the traditional sense of the word. We believe God gave them a choice of remaining in their premortal state or of taking on mortality with its attendant opportunities and suffering. They were given a choice between two conditions. They could obey the laws of their premortal natures and remain free from death and moral responsibility associated with mortality, or they could become mortal and subject to death and learn the hard lessons of life.

Adam and Eve chose the courageous role, the one God wanted them to choose. They "broke" the law of their premortal life, becoming mortal, or subject to death. The Bible says they partook of the fruit of the tree, of which God had said, "Ye shall not eat of it, neither shall ye touch it, lest ye die." (Genesis 3:3.)

Just how they became mortal, we do not know. But of one thing we are sure: they were not sinners. They chose to leave the presence of God and walk by faith, to learn to cope with the laws and forces characteristic of earth life. They "fell" in the sense that they left the presence of God and became subject to the limitations of mortality, including death, ignorance, and sin.

Adam's first choice, as we have seen, was to become mortal or to remain immortal. His second choice was either to remain in ignorance or to receive knowledge and thus become a moral, responsible son of God. He chose the latter alternative. As Latter-day Saints, we honor Adam and Eve because they had the courage and faith to become mortal and also to assume moral responsibility. We believe that in making these two choices, they were doing God's will and initiating the same two great experiences for us, their posterity.

The Book of Mormon adds a purposeful, optimistic, and new reference to the Fall:

> And now, behold, if Adam had not transgressed he would not have fallen, but he would have remained in the garden of Eden.

> And all things which were created must have remained in the same state in which they were after they were created; and they must have remained forever, and had no end.
>
> And they would have had no children; wherefore they would have remained in a state of innocence, having no joy, for they knew no misery; doing no good, for they knew no sin.
>
> But behold, all things have been done in the wisdom of him who knoweth all things.
>
> Adam fell that men might be; and men are, that they might have joy. (2 Nephi 2:22-25.)

The Doctrine and Covenants, in harmony with the teaching of the Book of Mormon, rejects the whole idea of original sin. "Every spirit of man was innocent in the beginning; and God having redeemed man from the fall, men became again, in their infant state, innocent before God." (D&C 93:38.)

Men are not born in sin, nor do they inherit the sin of Adam. From Adam we inherit mortality and death. As the Apostle Paul said, "By man came death," and "in Adam all die." (1 Corinthians 15:21-22.) From Adam we have inherited a knowledge of good and evil, the opportunity to become truly moral and spiritual beings. With him we share human nature with its potentiality for life and death, righteousness and sin. Adam was no different in his mortal life from us. He simply had the privilege and honor of initiating life on earth as a full, responsible child of God.

Another interesting passage from the Book of Mormon throws light on the Fall. Speaking of little children, we read, "Behold, *as in Adam, or by nature, they fall.*" (Mosiah 3:16; emphasis added.) The Fall simply means that we became mortal and may rise or fall in our mortal probation.

While Latter-day Saints reject the traditional views of the Fall and the nature of man held in Christendom, this does not mean that we in any sense reject the mission of Christ. Man is subject to death. Man is ignorant and needs divine guidance to find the truth, and man does sin. In his choice between good and evil, he inevitably sometimes chooses evil as well as good. He needs salvation from sin. In the wisdom and love of God and Christ, the latter was chosen to be a Savior to mankind, to help man rise above death, ignorance, and sin.

Christ—and the Purpose of Life

Christ's mission may be thought of not only in negative terms—in salvation from death, ignorance, and sin—but also in positive terms.

He lived and died to help men gain immortality and eternal life. He came to earth to help each of us realize the very purpose of life. What is that purpose?

Men are that they might have joy—that joy which is the fruit of self-realization of persons who are eternally free and also children of God. Men's destiny is to grow in the likeness of their Eternal Father as manifest in the life of his Son, Jesus Christ. "And this is life eternal, that they might know thee the only true God, and Jesus Christ, whom thou hast sent." (John 17:3.)

The mission of Christ may be summarized in one word—the Atonement. The word *atonement* means, literally, at-one-ment. Christ's mission was to bring about a state of at-one-ment, agreement or harmony, between God and man. Man, dwelling on the earth, subject to the limitations of mortal existence—to death, ignorance, and sin—is estranged from his Father in heaven. He needs to be one with his Maker, to know him, and to be worthy to return to him. Christ, the Son of God, is the great Mediator between the Father and his children. His role is to help us effect an at-one-ment between him and us. He accepted the responsibility of overcoming the estrangement between Deity and man. On this point all interpreters of the Atonement probably agree. The important question is: How is it to be done?

Some theologians in Christendom have thought of the Atonement in this way: When Adam fell, through sin, as they believe, all mankind was lost. God, in his anger, became estranged from men and, as it were, turned his back on them. Christ, by dying for the sins of men, restored men to favor in the eye of God, bringing about an at-onement between the Creator and his creatures. In other words, according to this view, Christ's mission was *to reconcile God to fallen humanity.*

As Latter-day Saints, we believe God to be the living Father of all men. Never has he turned his back on them. He is not estranged from men. The opposite is true. Men frequently estrange themselves from God. Men leave God, the fountain and source of their lives, and, like the Prodigal Son, go into a far country to spend their lives in riotous living. God, like the father in the parable, is waiting for his children to return and is ready to run to meet them.

If we may carry the analogy one step further, we may add that the Father has sent Jesus Christ, his Only Begotten Son, to bring man back to him. Christ lived and died not to reconcile God to man, but to reconcile man to God. It is man who must have a new vision, a change of heart, and be born again if he is to be one with God. This is clearly indicated in scripture as well as dictated by reason. In speaking of his death on the cross, Jesus said, "And I, if I be lifted up from the earth, will draw all men unto me." (John 12:32.) And again, he said, "I am come a light into the world, that whosoever believeth on me should not abide in darkness." (John 12:46.)

Christ's love for mankind and his great desire and effort to bring them unto God are also forcefully stated in the Book of Mormon: "For behold, my beloved brethren, I say unto you that the Lord God worketh not in darkness. He doeth not anything save it be for the benefit of the world; for he loveth the world, even that he layeth down his own life that he may draw all men unto him. Wherefore, he commandeth none that they shall not partake of his salvation." (2 Nephi 26:23-24.)

The Atonement can be suggested in a chart, which may help us to visualize the mission of Christ:

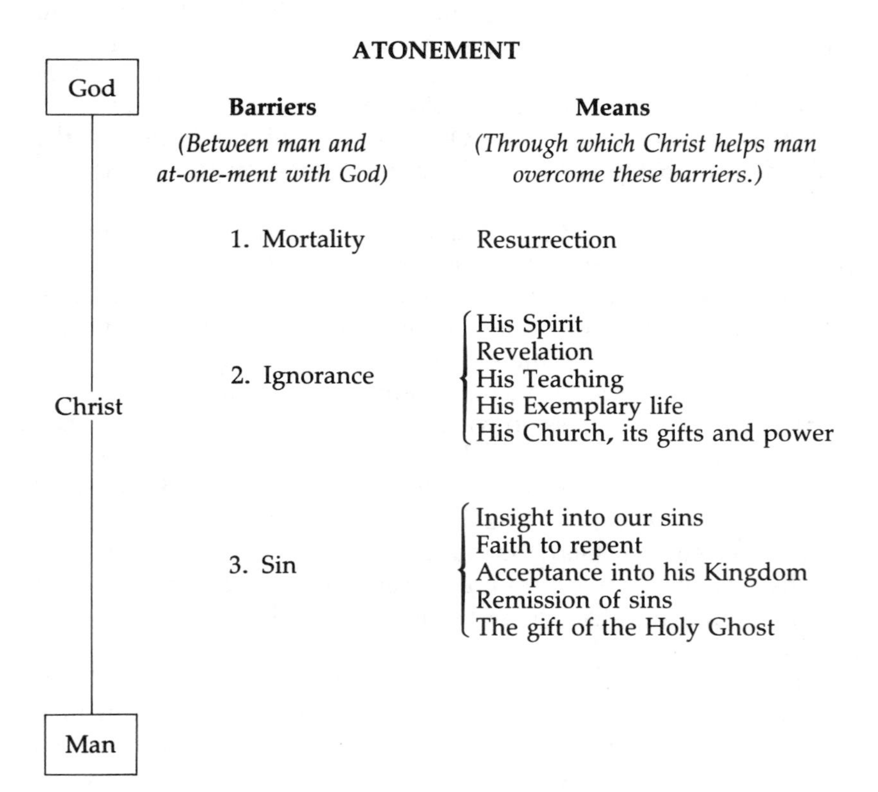

Man's Moral Nature

Man is moral by nature and by nurture. He has the capacity to make choices, to choose between things good and things evil. He must come to terms with himself, justifying his every act.

At times, man's moral nature brings him feelings of joy and strength. He feels free and creative in giving direction to his own life. He feels whole and strong when mind and heart are harnessed in pursuit of self-chosen goals. Man's moral agency can be a source of deep satisfaction.

Man's moral nature is not only a source of strength, but also makes him aware of his weakness and failure. Try as he will, it seems to be the fate of man to fall short of his ideal. He finds himself, in moments of weakness, acting upon impulses and out of motives not in harmony with his higher desires. Shakespeare describes this human trait:

> If to do were as easy as to know what were good to do, chapels had been churches, and poor men's cottages princes' palaces. It is a good divine that follows his own instructions: I can easier teach twenty what were good to be done, than be one of the twenty to follow mine own teaching. The brain may devise laws for the blood; but a hot temper leaps o'er a cold decree. (Portia to Nerissa in *The Merchant of Venice,* Act I, scene 2.)

The Apostle Paul likewise recognized this tendency in man to believe in the ideal and then act contrary to it. This he called sin:

> For we know that the law is spiritual: but I am carnal, sold under sin. For that which I do I allow not: for what I would, that do I not; but what I hate, that do I. . . .
>
> For I know that in me (that is, in my flesh,) dwelleth no good thing: for to will is present with me; but how to perform that which is good I find not. For the good that I would I do not: but the evil which I would not, that I do.
>
> Now if I do that I would not, it is no more I that do it, but sin that dwelleth in me. I find then a law, that, when I would do good, evil is present with me. For I delight in the law of God after the inward man: but I see another law in my members, warring against the law of my mind, and bringing me into captivity to the law of sin which is in my members.
>
> O wretched man that I am! who shall deliver me from the body of this death? (Romans 7:14-15, 18-24.)

We all fail to measure up to our ideals in one particular or another.

We are all sinners, though in various ways. The only person who will not acknowledge this is probably the self-righteous person who, in fact, is the greatest sinner of all because his self-righteousness blinds him to all his other sins.

Man not only suffers a sense of failure in particular things, but his life as a whole never quite measures up to that which he wants it to be and which he believes it should be. For the reflective person, his life is never fulfilled; it never attains the ideal to which he aspires.

The gospel of Jesus Christ offers to man the means whereby he can overcome his individual sins and also his sense of failure and inadequacy about his life as a whole. The first step in the plan is faith in the Lord Jesus Christ, which culminates in true repentance. We shall first discuss the meaning of repentance and then indicate how faith in Christ can give us the power to repent.

Two Paths Open

It is a law of life that man be whole, that conviction and action, the ideal and the real, be one. Man is ever striving to bridge the gap between his ideal of what he should be and the reality of what he is. There are two ways to do this that are well known to students of human nature. They may be illustrated in a diagram:

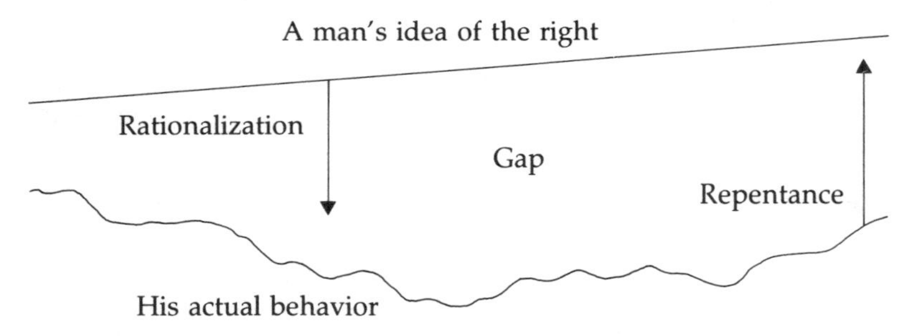

The upper line represents a man's idea of the right, his standard of behavior. It is made with an upward reach to indicate a growing conception of the right. The lower line, man's actual behavior, is likely to be irregular in its deviations from the right. There will always be some gap between the ideal and the real, but when the gap becomes too great, the mind is compelled to act to close it.

One method of accomplishing oneness is called rationalization, self-justification, or self-deceit. It is a process by which man, in search of unity and comfort, lowers his ideals to coincide with his actual behavior. It is embarrassing and humiliating to confess one's sins even to oneself. It is much easier to pull a blind over the mind. Some of us, although slow and sluggish and unimaginative in many ways, become highly ingenious and imaginative in our own self-deception. One can avoid some of the consequences of sin through self-deceit. But at what price? At the cost of lowering one's behavior to a point that is out of harmony with the constructive principles of one's life. If one is to change his standard of conduct, let it be because that standard is no longer valid, or because he has found something better or higher, and not merely because he wishes to be comfortable in wrongdoing. The truth seems to be that no one is completely successful in his self-deception. In more reflective and objective moments the wrongdoer becomes aware of his own effort at rationalization. He remembers also his conception of the right and secretly wishes he were capable of living in harmony with it. . . .

Repentance is the achievement of unity in life by lifting one's behavior to the level of one's ideal. It is a constructive principle by which man overcomes a sense of failure and inner frustration and works toward self-fulfillment. Repentance has been the watchword of the prophets throughout history.

> The time is fulfilled, and the kingdom of God is at hand: repent ye, and believe the gospel. (Mark 1:15.)

> Bring forth therefore fruits meet for repentance. And think not to say within yourselves, We have Abraham to our father; for I say unto you, that God is able of these stones to raise up children unto Abraham. (Matthew 3:8-9.)

> Repent ye therefore, and be converted, that your sins may be blotted out, when the times of refreshing shall come from the presence of the Lord. (Acts 3:19; read Isaiah 1, Amos 5, or Jeremiah 6, Alma 5, Acts 2.)

The Meaning of Repentance

Repentance has several related meanings in scripture. Most often it means to have "a change of mind," or to have "another mind." It calls for a new outlook on life, a "turning back" on old ways, freeing oneself of desires no longer deemed worthy to entertain. Repentance means action. Error, wrongdoing, and shallow living give place to truth, right-doing, and wholesome living. The old gives way to the new. Life is lived on a higher plane. Belief and action become identical. The exact steps in repentance may vary somewhat from person to person and from time to time, but they usually include the following:

1. *A recognition or recollection of the right and the wrong.* The evil we do is usually brought forcibly to our attention when we gain a vision of the good, of something better. Shadows are recognized most clearly in the full light of day. Sometimes our shallow living reveals its own emptiness to us; more often than not it is made evident to us by some higher revelation of life. Repentance begins when we acknowledge the wrong we have done.

2. *Feelings of regret and genuine sorrow for the wrong done, the life lived.* This does not mean that to repent we must sink into the depths of despair and pine away our lives in remorse. It does mean that we have "a broken heart and a contrite spirit," that we feel our spiritual need and have a sense of obligation toward those whom we have wronged, both God and man. David's plea to the Lord following a realization of his gross sinfulness expresses this feeling of regret and of a broken heart but in a constructive way.

"Create in me a clean heart, O God; and renew a right spirit within me. Cast me not away from thy presence; and take not thy holy spirit from me. Restore unto me the joy of thy salvation; and uphold me with thy free spirit." (Psalm 51:10-12.)

3. *Regret is followed by a firm resolution to forsake sin.* Action begins in desire and is fortified in thought. A firm resolve is an essential step in repentance. Ezekiel makes a plea for such a change of heart: "Therefore I will judge you, O house of Israel, every one according to his ways, saith the Lord God. Repent, and turn yourselves from all your transgressions; so iniquity shall not be your ruin. Cast away from you all your transgressions, whereby ye have transgressed; and make you a new heart and a new spirit; for why will ye die, O house of Israel? For I have no pleasure in the death of him that dieth, saith the Lord God: wherefore turn yourselves and live ye." (Ezekiel 18:30-32.)

4. *Whenever possible, amends are made for the wrong done.* Repentance is not complete if we have not tried to make good the wrong done. Stolen goods are returned; lies are acknowledged to those concerned; confession is made to those whom we have wronged and who will be helped by it.

5. *Finally, the wrongdoing is done no more but is replaced with right-doing, bad habits with good habits, good habits with better habits, culminating in a whole-souled devotion to one's new conception of the right.* Repentance takes time. To Latter-day Saints there is no such thing as death-bed repentance. There can be death-bed confession, but this is only one step in repentance and leaves the principle incomplete and unfulfilled.

No Other Way

Repentance is not an arbitrary commandment of God. It is a law of life which has been revealed to us for our own good, the means by which we may improve and gain increased integrity and freedom. In our belief there is no other way to free oneself from sin and its consequences, from evil, failure, and frustration, except through repentance. It is the second step in Christ's plan of salvation. Without repentance we cannot see the kingdom of God. Scriptures are emphatic on this point.

> And the times of this ignorance God winked at; but now commandeth all men everywhere to repent. (Acts 17:30.)
>
> The Lord is not slack concerning his promise, as some men count slackness; but is longsuffering to us-ward, not willing that any should perish, but that all should come to repentance. (2 Peter 3:9.)
>
> I tell you, Nay: but, except ye repent, ye shall all likewise perish. (Luke 13:5; see vv. 1-5.)
>
> But wo, wo unto him who knoweth that he rebelleth against God! For salvation cometh to none such except it be through repentance and faith on the Lord Jesus Christ. (Mosiah 3:12.)

The Strength to Repent

Repentance is not easy. Often in life we take the first few steps; we recognize our wrongdoing, feel remorse, resolve to do right, and then fail to do the right. Our need is to find genuine motivation which will give us the power to repent wholly of single evils and which will help us to increase in the fine quality of our total living. Where is such strength to be found? The strength to repent does not come from the evil done. There is no positive strength in evil. To preoccupy oneself with wrongdoing is to succumb to it more often than not. A person whose sin is covetousness does not surmount it while preoccupied with desire for other men's goods.

Repentance is more than a rational consideration. It is good to look at our mistakes and shortcomings with the cold, appraising eye of reason. Often help comes from a knowledge of habit-formation, from a vision of the consequences of behavior, and from other reasonable means of understanding ourselves. But reason alone is an inadequate weapon against the strength of such powerful forces as habit and desire. Reason is a necessary and essential guide in life, but by itself it is not the best source of motivation to act.

Jesus Christ came to earth to bring about "means unto men that they may have faith unto repentance," and "only unto him that has faith unto repentance is brought about the great and eternal plan of redemption." (Alma 34:15, 16.) Faith in the Lord Jesus Christ can bring us both the desire and the power to overcome our sins and our sense of failure. He can inspire us to overcome that which is evil and shallow and mean in life.

1. *Christ gives us a vision of what life can be.* In him is revealed the character of God, both in his teaching and in his living. In the light of his life, we can measure our own. We become aware of our sins. If we have faith in him, we shall be humble and contrite and shall be moved to change our lives and make them more like his.

2. *Christ taught us how to live.* As we learn and practice the positive ideals he taught, such as sincerity, humility, respect for each human being, and a love of fellowmen, we gain a feeling of satisfaction and strength which enables us to forsake wrongdoing. Paul said, "Be not overcome of evil, but overcome evil with good." (Romans 12:21.) To fill our lives with the good things Jesus taught is to crowd evil out, to leave it no room. Right is a shield against evil, as Paul well knew:

"Finally, my brethren, be strong in the Lord, and in the power of his might. Put on the whole armour of God, that ye may be able to stand against the wiles of the devil." (Ephesians 6:10-11.)

The same idea is taught by Alma, a Book of Mormon prophet:

"Preach unto them repentance, and faith on the Lord Jesus Christ; teach them to humble themselves and to be meek and lowly in heart; *teach them to withstand every temptation of the devil, with their faith on the Lord Jesus Christ.* Teach them to never be weary of good works, but to be meek and lowly in heart; for such shall find rest to their souls." (Alma 37:33-34; emphasis added.)

A man went to his bishop one day and confessed that in childhood and youth he had learned to lie to achieve his ends. Now in his full adulthood he was continually plagued with the same desire and tendency. The bishop asked him what he had done to try to break the habit, and the man replied that he had fought it. The bishop knew a better way. They knelt together in prayer. The bishop assured the brother of his moral support and of the help he would receive from God and Christ if he would try to live as they wanted him to live. The bishop gave him a good book to read, a fine service to render in the Church, the responsibility of speaking in meeting. In short, the understanding bishop helped his brother to so fill his life with the things of God and Christ that the need to lie gradually went away. The man became a new person through a living faith in Christ.

3. *The Spirit of Christ will be and will abide with us.* Whenever we

practice Christian principles, and particularly with faith in the Savior, his Spirit comes into our lives. It is a Latter-day Saint teaching that the light of Christ is given to every person as he enters the world. As we are responsive to it, through faith and Christian living, the Spirit of Christ will play an ever larger role in our feeling and action, lifting us above our limitations.

4. *Christ has promised us complete forgiveness on condition of repentance.* As we read the life of Christ in the New Testament and in Third Nephi in the Book of Mormon, we are impressed with the Savior's love for the sinner. In Luke, chapter 15, are recorded three beautiful parables which bear witness to this love. If we only knew how much Christ loves us, even in our weakness and sin, and how much he suffers because of our wrongdoings, we would be moved to repent and thereby give joy to him.

Christ's love for us is expressed in his willingness to forgive. Even on the cross, he said of those who had so unmercifully nailed him there, "Father, forgive them, for they know not what they do." The meaning of forgiveness and the conditions under which we may receive it will be developed in a subsequent chapter. Let it be noted here that the assurance of complete forgiveness gives us faith to repent. That assurance has been proclaimed again and again.

> Seek ye the Lord while he may be found, call ye upon him while he is near: let the wicked forsake his way, and the unrighteous man his thoughts: and let him return unto the Lord, and he will have mercy upon him; and to our God, for he will abundantly pardon. (Isaiah 55:6-7.)

> But if the wicked will turn from all his sins that he hath committed, and keep all my statutes, and do that which is lawful and right, he shall surely live, he shall not die. All his transgressions that he hath committed, they shall not be mentioned unto him: in his righteousness that he hath done he shall live. Have I any pleasure at all that the wicked should die? saith the Lord God: and not that he should return from his ways, and live? (Ezekiel 18:21-23.)

> For I the Lord cannot look upon sin with the least degree of allowance; nevertheless, he that repents and does the commandments of the Lord shall be forgiven. (D&C 1:31-32.)

The Remission of Sins

On the day of Pentecost when Peter and the other apostles were preaching the gospel with power from the Holy Ghost, thousands believed and asked Peter what they should do. He answered, "Repent, and be baptized every one of you in the name of Jesus Christ *for the remission of sins,* and ye shall receive the gift of the Holy Ghost." (Acts 2:38.)

Sin is any willful, conscious transgression of the laws of God. Sin is moral failure. When we fail to do that which we know we ought to do, or do that which we ought not to do, we are sinning. Some wrongdoings are far more serious than others, to be sure, but in all instances, the process remains the same: we are knowingly acting contrary to God's will and to our own better judgment.

Justice

We live in a world of law and order. This is immediately plain in our relationship to nature. The farmer who understands and obeys the principles pertaining to good soil management produces the best crops. A man who ignorantly or willfully ignores the laws of health will pay the price of ill-health sooner or later. There is a law of compensation operative in nature. As we sow, so do we reap.

Law and order prevail in the moral and spiritual life of man just as they do in the world of nature. Here, too, we suffer from both our ignorant and a willful neglect of the moral laws of life. The Apostle Paul expressed it this way: "Be not deceived; God is not mocked: for whatsoever a man soweth, that shall he also reap. For he that soweth to his flesh shall of the flesh reap corruption; but he that soweth to the Spirit shall of the Spirit reap life everlasting." (Galatians 6:7-8.)

The Lord inspired Jeremiah with the same idea: "Hear, O earth: behold, I will bring evil upon this people, even the fruit of their thoughts, because they have not hearkened unto my words, nor to my law, but rejected it." (Jeremiah 6:19.)

"Do they provoke me to anger? saith the Lord: do they not provoke themselves to the confusion of their own faces?" (Jeremiah 7:19.)

Sin has far-reaching consequences. When we are selfish, for example, we do injury to ourselves and to others; we are out of harmony with God and with his laws. Our behavior sets in motion consequences which are beyond our power to recall, control, or make good. Sometimes in our sin we do evil beyond our capacity to repair. If justice were the only principle of life, we would be forever in debt to those whom we wronged—to God, to fellowmen, and even to ourselves.

Fortunately, justice is not the only principle which governs the lives of men. If it were, some of us might be hopelessly obligated to others. But there are other principles of life, each with its contribution to make. Justice is one law, and very essential and beneficial too; but mercy is another, equally valid in its place, and more gentle.

Forgiveness

God is a Father. He loves his children. Even when we do wrong, he still loves us as any good earthly parent loves his child no matter what he has done. Our Father's work and glory is "to bring to pass the immortality and eternal life of man." (Moses 1:39.) He is more interested in persons than he is in impersonal laws. Our sins are important to him because of what they do to ourselves and to others. We cannot do evil without hurting others and without bringing injury to our own character and personality. Therefore, God hates sin but still loves the sinner whom he is trying to help. . . .

God's love for sinners was taught effectively by the Savior both in word and deed. Often he singled them out for special consideration. When Pharisees murmured against the Savior's disciples because they ate with publicans and sinners, Jesus said, "They that are whole need not a physician; but they that are sick. I came not to call the righteous, but sinners to repentance." (Luke 5:30-32.) Is it not remarkable that he who was without sin should draw "near unto him all the publicans and sinners for to hear him"? (Luke 15:1.) How else could this have been accomplished save through understanding and love?

When they came to him, he gave them hope and comfort. He taught three simple beautiful parables to help them feel and remember how God is reaching out, searching for the sinner, and rejoicing when he is found and turns home toward his father's house. Whenever the Savior meets with sinners who are aware of their sins and are responsive to his loving appeal to them to "sin no more," there we find him talking of mercy and forgiveness. (Read Luke 15 and John 8:1-11.)

Remission of sins means forgiveness of sins. God will freely forgive or pardon the moral failures of those who truly repent. This follows naturally from his loving nature. He is not interested in our condemnation but in our joy and salvation. The prophets of old, as well as Jesus, make this abundantly clear. Isaiah, after giving his people a sound tongue lashing for their iniquities, said,

> Wash you, make you clean; put away the evil of your doings from before mine eyes; cease to do evil; learn to do well; seek judgment, relieve the oppressed, judge the fatherless, plead for the widow. Come now, and let us reason together, saith the Lord: though

your sins be as scarlet, they shall be as white as snow; though they be red like crimson, they shall be as wool. (Isaiah 1:16-18.)

> Seek ye the Lord while he may be found, call ye upon him while he is near: Let the wicked forsake his way, and the unrighteous man his thoughts: and let him return unto the Lord, and he will have mercy upon him; and to our God, for he will abundantly pardon. (Isaiah 55:6-7.)

Ezekiel portrays the Father's real interest in man and his willingness to forgive and forget the sins of the truly repentant:

> But if the wicked will turn from all his sins that he hath committed, and keep all my statutes, and do that which is lawful and right, he shall surely live, he shall not die. All his transgressions that he hath committed, they shall not be mentioned unto him: in his righteousness that he hath done he shall live. Have I any pleasure at all that the wicked should die? saith the Lord God: and not that he should return from his ways, and live? (Ezekiel 18:21-23.)

"Mercy Claimeth the Penitent"

It is evident from the above scripture and numerous other passages that remission of sins comes only to those who are repentant. Until a sinner repents, he is subject to the law of justice. His wrongdoing condemns him. He is in no condition of mind or heart to receive forgiveness or pardon. His sense of guilt estranges him from his own best self, from other men against whom he has sinned, and from God, whom he knows to be a person of righteousness and truth. In his sin, he is in no position to be reconciled to himself, to others, or to God. His very sins reproach him and keep him in bondage to their influence on himself and others. Mercy cannot enter his life to counter the laws of justice. As long as he remains unrepentant, he suffers all the consequences of his wrongdoing. This is a law of life—the law of justice. We reap what we sow.

But when a person humbles himself, sees the evil of his ways, and effects a genuine change of mind and heart; when his repentance is successful, other forces become operative in his spiritual life and in his relationship to others and to God. Justice is not obliterated, but a new power is felt which enables him to find his way out of the meshwork of sin in which he had previously been entangled. When man invented the airplane, he did not do away with the law of gravitation which pulls everything toward the earth, but he introduced other factors which enabled him to leave the earth and remain aloft in the air. Repentance does not do away with justice, but it does invoke mercy. And mercy as well as justice can do things for man, under certain conditions, as the Book of Mormon states so effectively.

> But there is a law given, and a punishment affixed, and a repentance granted; which repentance mercy claimeth; otherwise, justice claimeth the creature and executeth the law, and the law inflicteth the punishment; if not so, the works of justice would be destroyed, and God would cease to be God.
>
> But God ceaseth not to be God, *and mercy claimeth the penitent,* and mercy cometh because of the atonement; and the atonement bringeth to pass the resurrection of the dead; and the resurrection of the dead bringeth back men into the presence of God; and thus they are restored into his presence, to be judged according to their works, according to the law and justice.
>
> *For behold, justice exerciseth all his demands, and also mercy claimeth all which is her own; and thus, none but the truly penitent are saved.* (Alma 42:22-24; emphasis added.)

Baptism—a Witness of Forgiveness

As we noted in previous chapters, baptism is a witness of a covenant between Deity and man. It is man's witness to God that he has faith in the Lord Jesus Christ, the faith that has given him power to repent of his un-Christian acts. In his baptism he promises "to be a witness of God at all times and in all things, and in all places," to take upon him the name of Christ, and always remember him, and keep his commandments, that he may have his Spirit to be with him. (See Mosiah 18:8-11; Moroni 4 and 5; D&C 20:37.) Baptism is also the witness on the part of Deity that man's sins are remitted, pardoned, and forgiven. Before God, he is clean again, born again, ready to begin a new spiritual life. His sins will not be mentioned unto him again as long as he refrains from sinning.

Baptism means forgiveness of past sins on condition of repentance. It also means forgiveness of sins in the future on condition of repentance. This point needs clarification. There is no perfection in human nature. And though a man has corrected mistakes of the past and is committed in faith to Christ, he is bound to err and fail in the future. Repentance, like learning, is a constant need of man. Therefore, baptism is both retroactive and operative in relation to the future. It is the divine assurance that the earnest, repentant disciple of Christ will be forgiven the sins which he will no doubt commit in his progress toward perfection in Jesus Christ.

The promise of forgiveness, both in relationship to the past and the future, must not be taken as license to sin. Moral failure brings with it sorrow and suffering for ourselves and for others. And though, through repentance and baptism, we attain a remission of sins, we will have already suffered considerable loss and have done harm to others. Foolish is the man who toys with sin through confidence in forgiveness. Such an attitude ignores the law of justice in his own life and the principle of mercy toward others, and may make it much more difficult to gain mercy for himself. A man does not know his own strength. By dallying with temptation and sin, he may readily succumb to them and find repentance beyond his power.

Forgiveness and Punishment

A question often asked is this: Though we be forgiven of our sins, will we not have to pay the full price of our sins—either here or in the hereafter? It is true that no one can do wrong without suffering a loss. Forgiveness does not mean that no damage has been done. In our wrongdoing we suffer pain and forgo all the rich experience and development which would have come had we been spending our strength in worthwhile pursuits. Even the repentant sinner will have suffered certain losses through his wrongdoing. There is no question about that. His sinful deeds in the past, with their effect on himself and others, are not undone by repentance and forgiveness. But this does not mean that a person must pay the full price of justice for his sins.

There is an element of grace in forgiveness. If a person had to pay the uttermost farthing for his wrongdoing, or, in other words, if justice alone prevailed, then forgiveness would have no meaning. Neither would love or mercy have place or meaning. Forgiveness implies that there is something to forgive, some unfulfilled obligation that is pardoned and erased. Let us illustrate.

A father had a son to whom he lent $5,000 at a low rate of interest. The son signed a note—a promise to pay. He began to repay the note faithfully; then misfortune overtook him. His wife's ill health and his own failure in a business venture ruined him financially. His intentions were good. He tried honestly to fulfill his obligation to his father. Time and again, the son sacrificed his own comfort to make a small payment to his father.

One day the father said to his son, "My boy, despite your misfortune and the prolonged and expensive illness of your wife, you have made every effort to repay me the loan. I am going to forgive you the rest of the note. Here it is, torn to bits."

The father was happy to forgive his son because the latter had done his part as well as he could. The father truly forgave because there was something to forgive. Most of the original loan had not been paid. It was to be cancelled. Had the father said, "Son, I forgive you the loan, but you must still pay it back with interest," what meaning would forgiveness have?

Forgiveness comes immediately with full repentance. There is no concept of purgatory in our theology—no place after death where men will be punished to satisfy divine justice for sins committed in the flesh of which man has repented fully. The repentant sinner pays a price for his wrongdoing; he knows sorrow and remorse and the digression or delay his wrongdoing has brought into his life. He can know also, however, that God's interest is in helping him attain unto godlike living, not in punishing him for the sake of justice, revenge, or glory. Therefore, *to the repentant sinner* the Lord will not add his own punishment to that which is the natural consequence of sin.

Forgiveness is complete and final if our repentance is also complete and permanent. God has no interest in punishment for punishment's sake. His greater interest is in the sinner, not the sin. As the late Matthew Cowley (a beloved apostle in the LDS church) said, in our hearing, "A sinner is greater than all his sins." This is illustrated in Jesus' parable of the Prodigal Son. When the Prodigal Son returned home, having "come unto himself," "when he was yet a great way off, his father had compassion, and ran, and fell on his neck, and kissed him." Then the father put a robe on him, put a ring on his finger and shoes on his feet, and killed the fatted calf and made merry. Why? Because his son who was dead "is alive again; and was lost and is found." The lad's repentance had begun; therefore, the father could rejoice. The boy's spiritual recovery was his father's whole concern. Such is God's love for the sinner, his willingness to forgive him fully and completely. Of course, the son must do his part. His repentance must also be complete or he cannot accept his father's forgiveness; his life cannot again become whole and increase in righteousness as God would have it increase. This is made amply clear in a passage in the Book of Mormon, which states that Jesus Christ lived and died to bring about "means unto men that they may have faith unto repentance. And thus mercy can satisfy the demands of justice, and encircles them in the arms of safety, while he that exercises no faith unto repentance is exposed to the whole law of the demands of justice; therefore only unto him that has faith unto repentance is brought about the great and eternal plan of redemption." (Alma 34:16.)

12

"For by Grace Are Ye Saved"

Years ago, when I was a Mormon missionary, I became anxious when a Protestant minister quoted these words of Paul: "For by grace are ye saved through faith; and that not of yourselves: it is the gift of God: not of works, lest any man should boast." (Ephesians 2:8-9.) And I quickly countered with a familiar text from James, the book which Luther called an epistle of straw: "Faith without works is dead."

For a number of years I continued to teach, as the Latter-day Saint way of salvation, individual merit and works in contrast to the emphasis on grace in Protestantism and sacramentalism in Catholicism, both of which rely upon the grace of Deity almost entirely. With co-religionists, I prided myself on a faith which stressed individual agency and responsibility, struggle and conquest, works and achievement. The only act of grace usually emphasized in the Mormon church (in my experience) was the crucifixion of Christ, through which man would partake of the resurrection and receive forgiveness. But even here, grace was qualified because one's status in the resurrection had to be merited and forgiveness fully earned, I thought, through repentance.

The years have brought a change of heart. I am as committed as ever to man's responsibility for his own welfare and salvation and that of his fellowmen as viewed in the restored gospel. Man is not helpless nor depraved nor wholly at the mercy of an omnipotent Deity. The finest goals of life and eternal life will not and cannot be attained without maximum human effort. I am not retreating on any of the basic Mormon doctrines of man and their implications for life: man's eternal intelligence of which free agency is a part, man's inherent capacity for good and evil action—for eternal progression or regression. But what I am coming to see, as never before, is how much grace there is in the restored gospel.

This special Christmas sermon was prepared for the fourth issue (Winter 1966) of the independent periodical, Dialogue: A Journal of Mormon Thought, *for which Lowell Bennion was serving as an advisory editor.*

And, on this eve before Christmas, it is my desire to bring to your attention some of the grace of Christ which is implied in that beautiful declaration of John, "For God so loved the world, that he gave his only begotten Son, that whosoever believeth in him should not perish, but have everlasting life. For God sent not his Son into the world to condemn the world; but that the world through him might be saved." (John 3:16-17.)

In the Mormon view of eternal life, grace precedes, accompanies, and completes individual effort and merit. And by grace we mean the unmerited gifts of Deity to man given freely out of Divine love.

According to Mormon doctrine, life as we know it is the creative work of God. In our pre-earth or pre-existent state, he took the eternal, uncreated, self-existent intelligence of man and gave it a spiritual birth, through which man in a very real sense became a child of God (a divinity in embryo), partaking of God's spiritual nature, hungering and thirsting to realize the attributes received of his Maker. This pre-earth, spiritual creation—belief in which is unique (in Christian circles) to Latter-day Saints—is, as far as we know, the gift of God, born of his love and his desire to share with others his own spiritual life.

Our faith is that mortal life also comes by the grace of the Father and the Son. We Latter-day Saints have been taught that we were permitted to come to earth as a reward for keeping our first estate, and by implication we have sometimes felt that we earned mortality. There is some truth here, but too often that truth is shallow and distorted. It is more accurate to say that we were, at best, prepared to profit from an experience in mortality. How does one earn the precious gift of life? As surely as there is a Creator in the universe, creation is an act of grace. Who knows what suffering, what effort, what powers of mind, what love went into the creation of man? How could man obligate his Maker to acts of creation?

I sense a lack of gratitude for life among countless human beings in our culture. Saddened by war and catastrophe, crime and delinquency, old age and cancer, and restless in our quest for material goods and entertainment, all too seldom do we look inside ourselves to discover what wondrous things God has made: eyes with which to see, ears to hear, hands to touch, hearts to feel, an imagination with which to create and reshape life (in some measure) to our taste.

I am not with this emphasis overlooking the stark tragedy of life. With many men in our century, I am saddened by the whole reality of human life, but I can also rejoice in man's capacity to bear suffering, to share its burden, and in some measure to alleviate pain. In the beauty and wonder of nature and in the presence of fellowmen and all that they are and have created, I feel to thank my Savior for the gift of life and I acknowledge it as his grace.

I had a brother who always thanked the Lord for the gifts and blessings of the gospel. The full impact of that statement is just beginning to dawn on me. In good Mormon tradition, I had been taught that each gift of the gospel had to be earned: the Holy Ghost, through faith, repentance, and baptism; the priesthood, by a worthy life and a willingness to serve; an answer to prayer, by faith and worthiness; and revelation, by diligent search, honest inquiry, and faith. This emphasis on my "rights" through good works had blurred my vision of God's grace that comes through the gifts of the gospel.

Now I realize that what we do by our own effort is to prepare ourselves to receive the gifts of Deity. Christ is under no obligation to send the Comforter. This divine influence is given freely to those who will be sufficiently humble and penitent to be capable of accepting it. And why should God delegate his priesthood—the very power of God, to man? How does man earn the right to divine power? Surely one cannot speak of divine obligation here.

For years I have taught that revelation usually, if not always, comes to the mind of the prophet and through him to mankind when man is aware of his need, when he thinks, struggles, searches, and somehow turns to God for help. This I still believe. Revelation is a teaching process, and an unwilling or deaf and blind student cannot be taught. But what I have neither taught nor heard sufficiently is that God's response to man—his revelation of himself, his Spirit, his mind and will—is not really earned but is born of love, of grace. Why else should he be concerned with man, to hear his plea, to touch his heart, to illuminate his mind?

Gospel teaching itself, through the Spirit of Christ and particularly that by the Master himself, is a manifestation of divine grace. When a man is paid for his teaching and goes about it in routine fashion, it may be called void of grace. But Christ taught voluntarily and with artistry and extraordinary intellectual, ethical, and spiritual insights; surely his teaching is one of his greatest gifts to man. I am grateful to have been born after him. How less rich life would be without his words.

There was a day when the resurrection was mainly a doctrine to me. But as the years pass and my days become numbered, I can no longer relegate the subject to theological discussion. I love life and would gladly continue living beyond the grave. Without the Christ,

I must confess I would probably be agnostic about personal immortality. Through him I entertain a hope and a joyful strong trust in the reality of the resurrection. He is in very deed my present Savior from death. How mortal man can earn immortal life as a resurrected, tangible, spiritual being, I know not. I accept it on faith as the greatest gift of God to man, and it comes through His Son.

No longer do I believe that a person must earn forgiveness. If he had to, then only justice and reciprocity would prevail in relationships between man and man and man and God. But "give" is the main root of the word forgiveness. And there is grace operating whenever anyone is forgiven.

Man is asked to repent to receive forgiveness, I believe, not because the Lord is not forgiving whether we repent or not, but because he knows that man cannot accept forgiveness and renew his life without himself taking some steps to change it.

And Christ is not only forgiving, but he is a source of strength to those who would change their lives so they can be forgiven, not least of all by themselves. I met a man years ago in another land who was in great turmoil because of his shallow and evil life (as he described and judged it). He had tried for years to create a new mind within him—but in vain. I asked him to render a particular service to Christ each Sunday morning. It was a simple and rather ordinary task in the eyes of most. He was to set the Lord's table with a cloth and trays of bread and water. Mark you, he was not privileged to offer prayers, just to set the Lord's table.

He came to me one evening after church and said, "I'm a new man. I have found my integrity again." Service to Christ, thinking about him, giving to him and "to the least of [his] brethren" in a very simple way led to better things and to a change of mind to repentance and forgiveness.

I suppose the greatest gift we have received from the Christ is the gift of himself. He lived among men. He revealed to us in word and deed the meaning of humility, meekness, mercy, love, and moral courage. In our doctrine, God sent his Only Begotten Son into the world because that son had already offered to come—to live and die for men, to give life "and to give it more abundantly" in those dimensions of life most worthy of man.

Christmas is a time of giving in honor of the Christ-child. One of the most obvious evidences of grace in his gospel is that he asked nothing for himself: "Simon, son of Jonas, lovest thou me? . . . Yea,

Lord; thou knowest that I love thee. He saith to him, Feed my sheep." (John 21:16.)

What gift can we bring to him this Christmas season? What need does he have of us? He asks just one thing: "Feed my sheep."

He is asking us also to believe in grace, to learn in our dealing with fellowmen to rid ourselves of prejudice, intolerance, covetousness, and hate, and even to rise above justice and to live life on the plane of grace.

In our homes, neighborhoods, communities, the nation and among nations, men need to learn to treat each other with profound respect and with mercy and this without regard to merit or reward. This, I believe, is the Spirit of Christ and the meaning of Christmas.

13

Overcoming Our Mistakes

Somebody has said that the purpose of religion is to comfort the afflicted and to afflict the comfortable, and I debated for a day or two which stance to take here. I decided to try to comfort the afflicted, and, as I talk about a certain affliction, those of you who are not afflicted may leave. This is a devotional, and I have chosen a personal topic in the gospel.

I had a friend who not long ago spent an hour and a half telling me about his wife, who, a few years back, made a big mistake in her life and who does nothing now but brood over it. She has lost her purpose and joy in living and has even threatened to commit suicide. All of her wonderful potential as a human being has come to the point of arrest, and this is tragic for him and his family. Furthermore, because she is so unhappy within herself, she makes life almost unbearable for her friends and her husband. She harasses them continually.

Historians have said you can't wage a war on two fronts; if you do, you generally lose. And the Germans have lost two wars fighting on the eastern and western fronts. (There may be other reasons too.) I find too that you can't carry on personally two battles in life—one the outside battle and the other the battle within yourself. And he who fights himself least is better prepared, I think, to fight the outside battle best. In fact, the outside battle is always there. The way I've learned to enjoy life is to not expect the ideal or the perfect. I look to it and work toward it, but the way to enjoy life is to acknowledge that it is a battle and there'll always be problems. There'll always be disappointments, and one must learn to relish the battle rather than the successful outcome of it.

All of us make mistakes in life, and some of us very serious ones. Any thoughtful person has a sense of failure because of his sins or

---

This devotional address was given at the Salt Lake Institute of Religion on April 14, 1972, and published in the New Era *in November 1972.*

his moral failures. If there are any sinners in the audience besides myself, I am talking to you, and I'd like to suggest what we might do about coping with our failures of the past so that they don't immobilize us for life today and for fighting the outside battle. Shakespeare once said, "Canst thou not minister to a mind diseas'd, pluck from the memory a rooted sorrow, raze out the written troubles of the brain, and with some sweet oblivious antidote cleanse the stuff'd bosom of the perilous stuff which weighs upon the human heart?" (*Macbeth*, Act V, scene iii.)

But if we're not all sinners by commission, I think we are all sinners by omission. The longer I live, the more I regret not my sins of commission but my sins of omission. We can go through life so indifferent to the things around us and so unaware of our calling, if you will, of our ethical demands, that all of us ought to suffer from neglect and from our omissions.

Just a few suggestions on what we might do to overcome our sense of failure, our sense of wrongdoing, and to learn to live with all our power in the present without dragging the corpses of the past with us. The simple solution is to say "Repent and you'll be forgiven," but I find repentance not easy. And even if we repent, sometimes memories cast a shadow on us, so I'd like to be more specific.

Aldous Huxley, in his introduction to *Brave New World,* said something like this: that "one doesn't get clean by rolling in the mire." One doesn't get clean and whole by brooding over the past and by reliving his mistakes. I've learned that there's no strength in weakness; there's no strength in sin; and we can't overcome our mistakes and our sins by fighting them directly. I think we succumb to them if we dwell upon them. I agree with Huxley that we ought not to roll in the mire and rehearse and rehash our past mistakes.

The second suggestion I have is that we ought to realize that no matter what we've done in life, no matter what we do, God and Christ still love us just as much as they did before we failed. God and Christ do not separate themselves from the sinner, from the wrongdoer. I'm speaking boldly—I shouldn't speak for God or for Christ, but I feel to do it on the basis of scripture. . . . In the Prodigal Son, the father expressed the feelings which Jesus felt our Heavenly Father has toward one who does wrong. You will remember that when the Prodigal Son remembered his home and turned back again, the father ran out to meet him. He didn't wait for him to get home and exercise full repentance, proven repentance, but ran out to meet him and fell on his neck and kissed him, and said two or three times in the parable,

"This my son was dead and is alive again, and was lost and is found." And that seemed to be all that really mattered to the earthly father.

I remember a returned missionary who dropped into the institute when I was here, down on University Street. He was just freshly returned from the mission field three weeks, and he had committed a grave mistake that caused him to think that his life was ruined forever. I said to him, "God loves you just as much today as he did last Thursday," and he couldn't believe it. The thought had never occurred to him. He wept like a child. You know, sometimes we think that God loves us to the extent that we please him, to the extent that we're good boys and girls, good men and women. Love is not earned. Love is not merited. If it is, it's justice and reciprocity and reward. Love comes from a loving heart, and God's love is unconditional. And he loves the worst of us and the best of us equally, I believe. We cause him to suffer when we do wrong, when he sees us live our lives in ways which destroy us, if you will, and when he sees us hurting other people—this must cause him pain. Christ suffers *because* of our sins, I think, perhaps more than *for* our sins, because he loves us.

I can understand this, being a father. I have good boys and a good girl. And, you know, when you're worried about your sons, you don't love them less, and when they're in trouble, you're not less anxious. You really love them more. I can understand why Jesus said that when the shepherd went after the lost sheep and brought him home, there was more rejoicing in heaven over one that was lost than over the ninety and nine that were safe in the fold. That used to tempt me to "make whoopee," so somebody would rejoice when I returned, but I find that not necessary to try.

We once had a child who was very, very ill and on the borderline of possible death. Our other children were well at the time. We loved the child who was ill, and we rejoiced at the time of his recovery more than over the others who were well. At the moment nothing else mattered. And I think that's the way Christ and God must feel about the person who's done wrong and who comes back. Even before he comes back. I think God is forgiving whether we repent or not. He asks us to forgive. He doesn't say forgive when people repent. He says forgive them seven times seventy. I don't think God would ask me to be forgiving when he is not. I think somehow that the principles of the gospel are his principles, too, don't you? Therefore, the reason we have to repent is to be able to forgive ourselves and to be able to get in harmony again with the principles and laws of good living, of life. We don't have to repent to earn God's love, even though some scriptures portray him as being pretty angry with the sinner. Others portray him as angry with the sin, not with the sinner.

Another thing we can do to overcome the past is to make amends. We know when we've done wrong, but sometimes we're afraid to go to those whom we've wronged. We are too proud. I've been too proud to admit my failures, my wrongdoing. When I've had the courage to do it, I find that great reconciliation has taken place. And if it doesn't, I've done my part. It's the offended person's responsibility to react to my efforts to be reconciled. Sometimes it's impossible to right wrongs that we've done with the person whom we've wronged. It's also impossible to pay those who've done good for us. I shall never be able to compensate my father and mother for what they've done for me. Never! I have friends of the same stripe; they've enriched my life to the point that I could never possibly repay them. And when you can't compensate a person for a wrong, when it's too late or impossible, then you can bless other people. We all belong together in this world. We're brothers and sisters with the same Eternal Father; we belong to the same human community. There are others we can bless, though we can't repair the damage we may have done to others of his children.

A fourth suggestion I would make is that the past, which some of us regret at certain points, is not as fixed and rigid as we ordinarily think it is. If you have shameful moments in your past, you're prone to isolate them, to rigidify them and think of them as being fixed. You've heard the saying that you cannot change your past—but you can. You can! You can't change single events in the past, but you can change the past as a whole—your past—and when you change your past as a whole, the meaning of every part of it changes. The significance, the value, the importance of every event in one's past is constantly changing by reason of the kind of past we're building. I'll tell you where I came onto this idea.

In Germany, years and years ago, a young girl confessed to my wife a very tragic period of her life, and she said, "Please tell Brother Bennion about it." So she came and told me. I won't go into her life, but it was a tragic life, and I've never seen a girl with sadder, darker, bigger brown eyes than this lovely girl of eighteen. And in trying to give her some comfort and hope for the future, it dawned on me that we're adding to our past, we're building onto it each day we live. Life is not a rigid, fixed, quantitative kind of thing. It's a growing, qualitative, whole thing. And a whole is greater than any of its parts, and the whole gives meaning to its parts. My arm by itself hung on the wall is one thing; my arm as a part of my body and servant of my mind is another thing. An event in that girl's past or even ten events were one thing at eighteen, when she was in the depths of despair. And then she came into the fold, was baptized into the Church, found some faith in Christ, converted her husband, reared a fine family, and her life has been going like this ever since. This valley of failure in her life is one thing by itself; it's another thing when it's one dip in a long, beautiful life. This may not appeal to you, but it surely does to me. This idea makes life dynamic. It's comforting and exciting to know that you can climb out of any low, just as you can fall from any high if you become complacent, self-righteous, and indifferent to life.

I think God feels this way about our lives. I want to read to you a familiar verse from Ezekiel. He says, "If the wicked will turn from all his sins that he has committed, and keep all my statutes, and do that which is lawful and right, he shall surely live, he shall not die. All his transgressions that he hath committed, they shall not be mentioned unto him." I don't believe that the books are going to be opened, literally, in heaven someday, and all the red marks weighed against the black marks. If any book's going to be opened, I believe (I'm just giving my opinion), it will be the book of life, *what you are* on judgment day. What I am. And the past is only significant in terms of what it has made me become. Ezekiel says, "All his transgressions that he has committed, they shall not be mentioned unto him. In his righteousness that he hath done, he shall live. Have I any pleasure at all if the wicked shall die? saith the Lord God: and not that he should return from his ways, and live?" (Ezekiel 18:21-23.) And Isaiah said, "Though your sins be as scarlet, they shall be as white as snow; though they be red like crimson, they shall be as wool." (Isaiah 1:18.)

This I believe. If God loves us, his only interest is in us. "Let no one till his death be called unhappy. Measure not the work until the day is out and the labor's done." I would say, don't measure life ever—even into eternity. We're still building on it; we're changing it.

I have two other suggestions. One is, I think we ought to be aggressive in our idealism, in our desire and effort to do what is right. I am the adviser to the Student Behavior Committee on campus and have been for eleven years. It was kind of painful when I started out; I wondered why I'd left this beautiful institute program to deal with students in serious trouble with the university. Then I found out that they were about like you and me; most were careless or frustrated in their families or in their personal lives and did foolish things in that mood. Many of us do wrong and get in trouble because we're not thinking of the right. Our concept of the gospel is very general. We feel good about it; we have a testimony; but we don't sharpen what we believe in. We can't say I'm going to be honest, and what does honesty mean? And what does it mean in this circumstance and in that circumstance? Or, I believe in chastity, and what does it mean and what is the spirit of it, and what is the nature of it? I think we get caught offguard when we don't define for ourselves repeatedly what we stand for, what values we hold to. And we don't tell ourselves why we believe in these values so that they become our very own—internalized. They're not God's laws only, they're our laws too, because we've come to test them and to believe in them. I'm very much impressed by basketball players who are trained to do very specific things, such as to retrieve the ball, to get the rebound. And they count how many you get in a game—anywhere from none to eighteen. Players are aggressive. In football you outcharge the other line—that's half the game. You don't sit back apathetically and see what happens to you. You outcharge your opponent.

Now why not be aggressive—and I don't mean with the mouth, I don't mean to boast or to be loud—but why not clarify what values we believe in? This applies to you whether you're a believer or a nonbeliever—Latter-day Saint, Catholic, Jew, Protestant, atheist, or anything else. Every man has to be whole within himself. He has to have integrity. You can't have integrity without clarifying your convictions or values or goals. You can change them, but you must always have some, I believe. And so you clarify your ideals and you determine to live up to them. If you're going to work in a bank and handle money, don't decide while you're handling money whether or not you'll be honest. Make up your mind before you go into the bank, before you accept the job. Say in your morning prayer, "Lord, help me not to take money today." Money is such a temptation when your wife needs so many things. It is so easy to replace, we think. This is the way we get caught in dishonest actions. The Apostle Paul said, "Wherefore take unto you the whole armour of God. . . . Stand therefore, having your loins girt about with truth, and having on the breastplate of righteousness; and your feet shod with the preparation of the gospel of peace." (Ephesians 6:13-15.) These words don't ring much of a bell to us as symbols in this day, but "put on the armour of God" and face life with whatever ideals you believe in, and shadows will disappear.

My final point is to make a friend of Jesus Christ. In the sacramental prayer each Sabbath day we hear and we say (I think rather routinely) that we bear witness to the Father that we take upon us the name of Jesus Christ and always remember him and keep him commandments, that we might have his spirit to be with us. Now, what does it mean to take upon us the name of Christ? What does it mean to always remember him? How many of us make him part of our daily life without being fanatical, without being "other-worldly," still living in the world? How do we draw upon the strength that comes with fellowship with our Savior? Do we leave it to Protestants to talk about fellowship with Christ?

I had an experience in the mission field that is very memorable to me. A man came to me after church—he was twice my age, a very unhappy person—and told me that he had committed a grave sin before he joined the Church; that his wife would not forgive him, would not divorce him, and constantly reminded him of his good-for-nothingness. He said, "I've come to think of myself at her estimate. How can I be whole again and pure of heart, clean in my thoughts?" I said, "What have your tried to do for this problem?" He said, "I've fought it. I've fought it." I'd had a class in psychology before I went on a mission, and I told him there must be a better way than to fight sin. We knelt in prayer together, and afterwards I gave him a book to read—*As a Man Thinketh in His Heart, So Is He*—and then I put my arm around him (he was shorter than I) and gave him a firm handclasp and told him that he could overcome his problem. And then, by inspiration or coincidence, I said to him, "How would you like to prepare the Lord's supper for Sunday School?" (He was a teacher in the Aaronic Priesthood.) He said, "Do you think I'm worthy to do this?" I said, "No, I don't think any of us are. But I think Jesus would be pleased if you would render him this service." And so he proceeded to set the Lord's table each Sunday morning. After about six weeks I met him coming up the aisle before Sunday School one morning. I put out my hand to reassure him. He put his hand behind his back and said nothing. I said, "Have I offended you?" He said, "Oh, no. I've just washed my hands with soap and hot water, and I can't shake hands with you or any person until I've set the Lord's table." That's the most beautiful reverence I've seen in that simple act of setting the Lord's table.

In another six weeks he came to me after church again and said, "I'm a new man. I'm a new man." Then I asked him to give a talk in church on some principle of the gospel of Christ that he really believed in and why. I kept him thinking about the Savior. Well, through serving the Savior in a simple way and thinking about him during the week, this man became a new creature. It was beautiful. And I realized that I'd never used the Savior in my own life in the same way. I don't mind telling you that I did after that. I had the wonderful thrill of overcoming what I thought was a weakness in me by thinking of him and making him the center of my prayers and my life.

The biggest tragedy of life is not to live—not to function with your full soul, with your whole life, with enthusiasm, with spirit, with faith, with love. And so, I humbly pray that none of you and none of us will be so burdened by mistakes and by failures and by sins that we won't have the courage and the wisdom to turn to the ideals of the gospel, to the wonderful Son of God, and to each other to find the strength to live life as it is meant to be lived. It's a beautiful existence we have, and it is not too late for any of us to enjoy it to the full. God help us keep faith with life, I humbly pray in the name of Jesus Christ. Amen.

IV

PRACTICAL RELIGION

At his Teton Valley Boys Ranch, about 1962

14

The Fruits of Religious Living in This Life

Ye shall know them by their fruits. Do men gather grapes of thorns, or figs of thistles?" Each tree produces its own kind. What fruits may one hope to pick if one plants a tree in the garden of religion? This question demands an answer for all those who would judge religion by its earthly harvest.

A short time ago a Gleaner girl made this confession: "Two months ago I had faith; I was happy in my religion. Everything seemed just right to me. Then my father became ill and died, leaving my mother and several small children. We had prayed for him: we needed him, but he went. And now, something has gone out of my life. I have lost the strong testimony that was mine."

A young man recently made this statement: "My father had worked all his life for the Church. He is as honest as any man who ever lived. In fact, he is too honest. Men have taken advantage of him. During the last few years he has lost the little bit that he did have. I can't see where his religion has helped him any."

We meet people of all ages and various experiences who have become disillusioned about religion. Among them are sons of pioneers, converts from the old country, young people who have been reared in the organizations of the Church—good, sincere individuals who feel that they have been deceived, that religion is not what it is purported to be. The difficulty sometimes lies in the fact that religion has been misrepresented to them, leading them to expect the wrong thing from religious living.

The two stories related above represent the two most common

In April 1941 Lowell Bennion published this as the first of his many essays in the Church's major official magazine, the Improvement Era. *It was republished as part of a series of classic* Era *reprints, in the November 1970 issue, and appeared in somewhat altered form as chapter 41 in* Teachings of the New Testament *(1953).*

misconceptions of the fruits of religious living. The first is *that religion will save men from all suffering, sorrow, and disappointment in life.* Religion, thus conceived, is a guardian angel who steers life's ship over smooth seas. But religious history and teaching prove that life is not that, and that religion makes no such promise.

The book of Job has a moral that man should not deny God even though he suffer loss of family, of property, and be sorely afflicted. One hundred thousand Jews died in defense of things sacred to them, as Syrians and Romans desecrated their sanctuaries. Early Christians suffered repeated persecutions unto death because of their faithfulness to the Cross. John Huss, Savonarola, and men of their type lost their lives in defense of religious truth. The Huguenots in France, the Puritans in England, the Jews the world over have suffered because of religious conviction.

No Latter-day Saint should forget the lives that Mormonism has cost to date. In the history of the Mormon church, men have endured almost every form of persecution and privation that man and the elements can impose. Joseph Smith experienced this both in life and in death, giving fervid expression to it in his prayer recorded in section 121 of the Doctrine and Covenants.

Religion literally leads men to places where sorrow, suffering, and difficulties abound. Jesus came to share the burden of the sinner, to minister unto the sick and afflicted, to comfort those who mourn, which means in effect to share the burdens of life, and he said unto his disciples, "Go thou and do likewise" . . . "Feed my sheep."

The religious life is not a fairyland existence which promises escape from the realities of life, but rather a life that shares responsibilities in the most vital of life's processes. It is not a flight from the world either in thought or in deed.

Jesus makes this clear in his Sermon on the Mount: "Therefore whosoever heareth these sayings of mine, and doeth them, I will liken him unto a wise man, which built his house upon a rock: and the rain descended, and the floods came, and the winds blew, and beat upon that house; and it fell not: for it was founded upon a rock. And every one that heareth these sayings of mine, and doeth them not, shall be likened unto a foolish man, which built his house upon the sand: and the rains descended, and the floods came, and the winds blew, and beat upon that house; and it fell, and great was the fall of it." (Matthew 7:24-27.)

All those who base their lives on the teaching of Jesus build their house upon a rock. Those who do not, build their house upon the sand. Note this, that both houses receive the same punishment. The rains descend, floods come, and winds blow and beat upon both houses. The difference is that one withstands the onslaught, the other does not.

The Master said to his beloved disciples: "I send ye forth as sheep in the midst of wolves." (Matthew 10:16.) And they found out that his words were true as they laid down their lives for him. To Ananias, who objected to the baptism of Saul of Tarsus, the word came: "Go thy way: for he is a chosen vessel unto me. . . . *For I will shew him how great things he must suffer for my name's sake.*" (Acts 9:15; emphasis added.)

No, religious living does not insure us against all tragic experiences in life. Religious people die like everyone else. They become involved in accidents not of their own volition or fault. Sometimes they suffer things that the carefree escape. But religion does spare one from much suffering. The keeping of the Word of Wisdom in its fullest sense will help to keep one physically fit and better able to resist disease and physical and mental strain. In prayer, faith, and administrations to the sick, religion offers one unique aid to health.

Most of the suffering and sorrow man experiences is not physical, but mental and spiritual. It is here that religion makes perhaps its finest contribution. The enemies of good mental health are based largely on a wrong conception of the place of self in the world. The religion of Jesus gives man the true conception of self in relation to other selves. The religious man is spared the life-destroying attitudes of envy and jealousy which result from selfishness; the hatred and licentiousness which follow from a want of sympathy and reverence for life; and the fear, worry, and anxiety which spring from ignorance, wrongdoing, and a lack of proper perspective.

The second misconception, illustrated by the statement of the young man, is *that religious living will make one prosperous.* There is justification and evidence for this point of view. It is a belief held by the Hebrews, Book of Mormon people, the Puritans, and Latter-day Saints.

History has vindicated this belief in certain religious groups. Book of Mormon history repeatedly testifies to the prosperity that followed righteous living. The followers of John Calvin, particularly the Puritans of Holland, England, and America, who were the preeminent creators of our modern industrial order, were greatly inspired by religious beliefs and practices. The Jains and Parsis, two small sects of India, are the most prosperous of the native people of India. Their prosperity is attributed in large measure to their religious way of life. The religious influence on the economic status of Latter-day Saints is apparent from the earliest beginnings of their history.

The gospel of Jesus Christ does and should produce prosperity in two ways: First, by developing the well-named "economic virtues"—industry, honesty, integrity, punctuality, thrift, and frugality. These inevitably lead to financial success, other things being equal. Second, a religious philosophy of life gives good direction to one's expenditures. Earnings are invested in the home, educational and cultural advantages for children, and physical, mental, and social health, and are not dissipated in channels that are destructive of or indifferent to man's truest needs.

But people will be disappointed in religion if they think that it guarantees one a rich share in the material goods of the earth, that one of the chief functions of religion is to make people wealthy. The fruits of religion cannot be measured in material terms. History records the ironical paradox that even when religion led to prosperity, this, in turn, tended to undermine the religious spirit. This was true of Puritan and Nephite history. It is also evidenced in the lives of many individuals.

It was certainly not the primary purpose of God to make the Latter-day Saints prosperous when he directed them to leave the fertile lands of Ohio and Illinois, potential commercial and manufacturing centers of great magnitude, to struggle with the physical hardships of the Rocky Mountain country and its more restricted types of economic endeavor compared with the East, the Pacific Coast, and the Great Lakes regions.

Motives more important than material interest led Brigham Young to develop agriculture rather than mining in the West, resulting in the acquisition of great sources of wealth here by non-Mormons. Then, too, much of the wealth produced by the Latter-day Saints goes into economically speaking nonproductive channels such as missionary work, temple work, the erection and maintenance of beautiful houses of worship, recreation halls, charity, and religious education.

There are a dozen better reasons for paying tithing than the hope of material blessings in return, in the spirit of making a trade with the Lord. Love of God, a sense of sharing in his work and purposes, loyalty to his church, love of service to fellowmen, the love of giving, the joy of practicing unselfishness are more noble and more blessed.

Yes, religion reaches down and permeates our material well-being, and indirectly leads to happiness and success in this important phase of life. Yet, let it be remembered that the Lord "maketh his sun to rise on the evil and on the good, and sendeth rain on the just and on the unjust." (Matthew 5:45.) Let no one measure the fruits of religious living primarily in dollars. It is not fair to the purposes of religion.

In one of the most beautiful chapters in sacred literature (Alma 32), Alma pleads with his people to plant the seed of faith with this promise:

> Behold, it will begin to swell within your breasts; and when you feel these swelling motions, ye will begin to say within yourselves—It must needs be that this is a good seed, or that the word is good, for it beginneth to *enlarge my soul*; yea, it beginneth *to enlighten my understanding*, yea, it beginneth *to be delicious* to me. (Alma 32:28; emphasis added.)

Then, comparing the religious life with a tree, Alma writes:

> But if ye will nourish the word, yea, nourish the tree as it beginneth to grow, by your faith with great diligence, and with patience, looking forward to the fruit thereof, it shall take root; and behold it shall be a tree springing up unto everlasting life . . .
>
> Behold, *by and by ye shall pluck the fruit thereof, which is most precious, which is sweet above all that is sweet, and which is white above all that is white, yea, and pure above all that is pure; and ye shall feast upon this fruit even until ye are filled, that ye hunger not, neither shall ye thirst.* (Alma 32:41-42.)

Second Peter 1:5-8 reads:

> Giving all diligence, add to your faith virtue, and to virtue knowledge; and to knowledge temperance; and to temperance patience; and to patience godliness; and to godliness brotherly kindness; and to brotherly kindness charity. For if these things be in you, and abound, *they make you that ye shall neither be barren nor unfruitful in the knowledge of our Lord Jesus Christ*. (Emphasis added.)

Paul enumerates the fruits of religion in Galatians 5:22-23:

> But the fruit of the Spirit is love, joy, peace, longsuffering, gentleness, goodness, faith, meekness, temperance: against such there is no law.

Among the most delicious fruits of religious living are things spiritual, as these writings testify. They relate to the mental and moral life of man; and where is life with its possibilities of either joy or misery, if not in the mind?

Religion, like music, opens up a new world to man. The truly religious person becomes identified with law. He learns to thrill in the satisfaction that comes from freely living in harmony with God's laws. To love fellowmen, to hold life in reverence, is no more a duty, but a passion that needs to be satisfied. And such a man, hungering and thirsting after righteousness, will surely be filled.

Religion will not preserve man from all sorrow and suffering, nor necessarily make him prosperous, but it does promise him the precious fruits of the spirit—peace, joy, love, and a meaningful life. And that promise holds for today, as well as for tomorrow: these fruits of the spirit are to be tasted and enjoyed in this life as well as in eternity.

15

An Attitude of Joyful Acceptance Toward Life

When life is threatened by ill health or danger, it assumes great value to all of us. We go to great lengths to save it. Strange how little we cherish it sometimes in routine living, in our days of safety and health. Our ardor for living is lost in a maze of petty concerns. We become apathetic and bored. Monotony and self-pity set in.

Let each one ask himself a few questions: How long has it been since I arose with a thrill to greet the dawn? When did I last kneel in prayer overwhelmed with gratitude for the gift of life? How much of my life passes in discouragement, remorse, and self-pity?

Let each of us discipline his mind and heart to accept life and to develop faith in it and to live it hopefully and joyfully. Even in moments of sorrow, danger, and failure, let us remember that life is good and worth the living. Such an attitude, we believe, is a worthy goal to seek and to develop.

Life's Reality

Question: What are some of the things which cause people to lose faith in life?

Lest you think us unduly optimistic and sentimental about our existence on earth, we would like to make a confession before trying to convince you that life merits our faith. We have lived long enough to know some of the realities about us. Ours is not a blind, irrational faith in living.

Surely, life is heavy-laden with tragedy. Death, which is no respecter of persons, robs us of loved ones and eventually of our own breath. Old age creeps up on a man, just at the time when he has reached his prime and has greatly increased his desire to realize many

This is an introductory lesson from one of Dr. Bennion's most widely read and translated manuals, Goals for Living *(1952), which was used for the M Men and Gleaners until 1968.*

of life's riches. Old age can be burdensome and tragic. Millions suffer from incurable diseases such as cancer. Millions are starving or near starving in the world today. Innocent children suffer from the ignorance and weaknesses of their parents. Other millions are victims of hate and lust for power.

No wonder so many poets are pessimistic in their writing.

Men's hearts fail them and they question the worthwhileness of living. All this we see and hear and can understand. Still we say, "Believe in life. Love it despite its tragedy. Be glad every day to be alive." How can we say it?

Reasons to Believe in Life

Question: What things help us to believe and rejoice in life?

Life is rich, full of goodness. We have acknowledged the sorrow and tragedy. Let us look at the other side. What is there to enjoy?

There are people. Not all of them enhance one's faith in life, but many human relationships do. To know a father's or mother's love and confidence, to have a life's companion stand at your side through joy and sorrow, to feel a lad's arms around your neck or to look into his trusting eyes, or to hold the hand of a friend—any one of these experiences can compensate for a good deal of trouble. Yet these experiences are all available to many of us every day.

The other day we were talking with a former student whose life's plans have been thwarted by prolonged military service. We asked him how things were, and he answered: "Wherever I go there are people. And they never cease to fascinate me. I have never met a person who was not interesting to me. I can always wonder what makes him tick as he does."

Will Rogers, the great American comedian of this century, said, "I never met a man I didn't like." Maybe that is why people liked him so much. He believed in man, in every man. He thought as much of the man on the street as he did of the President of the United States, and used the same language when he talked to either of them.

It is great to be alive just to know people—to love them, to converse with them, to work shoulder to shoulder with them, to seek their happiness, to suffer with them, and to laugh and make merry together.

There is nature. Just now she is arrayed in rich autumn hues that change under one's eyes in the setting sun. There is rain—fresh, clean, life-giving rain. There are stars—bright, shining and steadfast in the sky; lakes, rivers, and brooks; meadows, hills, and mountains; and lofty pines and quaking aspen, graceful weeping willows, leafy birch trees, and sturdy oaks. Nature is beautiful and usually bountiful and good to man.

There is art. Music, literature, drama, painting, architecture, sculpture, creative dancing—these things are available to us in number and extent far beyond our capacity to receive. Music or literature alone can give any sensitive soul cause to rejoice in life eternally.

There are everyday common things—work, play, sleep, a glass of water, bread and milk, a fresh peach, a bunch of grapes, a spring salad, ice cream with fresh strawberries, tired muscles, a refreshing shower, birds singing, children laughing—what more does it take than these things to give us faith in life if we have ears to hear and eyes to see?

"One sees what one carries in one's heart," said Goethe. True, life is full of the bitter and the sweet, but man has it within his creative power often to choose the sweet and even to turn the bitter into sweetness. Man need not be simply passive, taking a constant beating from life. He can be active, shaping life after the image he carries in his own heart. Life does not present itself as a finished product. We are all the time working and reworking it for us and even for others after the model of our own despair or hope.

There was a lady in Idaho, a widow, who lost her only two sons in the war. She had been dealt hard blows. She stood alone. It seemed more than she could bear, and she was becoming ill in body and mind. Finally her doctor said to her, "Look here, Mrs. 'Blank,' if you continue as you are now thinking, you will end up a burden to this community. Why don't you forget yourself by helping folks in this town who need you?" She decided to take his advice. She became "Granny" to the whole community. Soon she was beloved by all for her kindness, service, and good cheer. She found a joy as great as any she had ever known in life, perhaps greater.

It lies within our power to create, to give, to plant, to build, to learn, to think, to find new meaning. All these things should lend wings to mind and heart.

Even sorrow and tragedy can become the means of rich living. Jesus suffered with the poor, the sick, the sinner, but he also rejoiced with them and brought them hope, health, and forgiveness. One can learn to rejoice in sorrow. Nearly every cloud has a silver lining for the eye of faith.

Albert Schweitzer, the great French musician, thinker, and medical missionary, concluded early in life that life was tragic and replete with suffering. For this reason, and out of gratitude for his own buoyant health, he dedicated his life to the relief of suffering. He chose to do it in the heart of Africa among illiterate natives. A great man has made peace with the tragedy of life by his love for humanity.

We like the lines from "Renascence," by Edna St. Vincent Millay:

> The world stands out on either side
> No wider than the heart is wide;
> Above the world is stretched the sky,—
> No higher than the soul is high.
> The heart can push the sea and the land
> Farther away on either hand;
> The soul can split the sky in two,
> And let the face of God shine through.
> But East and West will pinch the heart
> That can not keep them pushed apart;
> And he whose soul is flat—the sky
> Will cave in on him by and by.

Even if life were bitter and pointless, how much more pointless it is not to accept it, since we must. To complain or despair of life is to be twice beaten—once by circumstance and once by oneself. Yes, we have at times cause to complain even to high heaven. And we would recommend it, if it would do any good. But it doesn't; it makes us feel worse. It saps our vitality and power. It diverts our attention from the problem to be overcome.

Not to believe in life is to contradict our very nature. Deeply imbedded in nature, including human nature, is the will to live. Man was born to function, to be active, to express himself. When we have hope, live by faith, and take a positive view of life, we are more in harmony with our needs; we fulfill our natures. To be alive and yet in attitude to deny life seems a contradiction that spells nothing but misery and defeat.

Faith in God lends support to faith in life. Even without faith in a personal God, people can believe life worthwhile and more good than bad. We know professed atheists and agnostics who rejoice in living and do everything within their power to cause others to live in good cheer.

A classic illustration of the cheerful acceptance of life by a person without faith in God, Christ, or immortality is found in the writing of the great Roman poet Lucretius, called *The Nature of Things*.The religion of his day was repulsive to him so he proceeded to build a faith in life without religion. He found life itself rewarding and tried his best to teach man to accept it and live it without fear.

The author of Ecclesiastes, though acknowledging his faith in God, was extremely realistic and pessimistic about many things in life and death. He is the author of the famous phrase "All is vanity, all is vanity." Still he could say:

> Go thy way, eat thy bread with joy, and drink thy wine with a merry heart; for God now accepteth thy works. . . .
>
> Live life joyfully with the wife whom thou lovest all the days of the life of thy vanity, which he hath given thee under the sun, all the days of thy vanity: for that is thy portion in this life, and in thy labour which thou takest under the sun.
>
> Whatsoever thy hand findeth to do, do it with thy might; for there is no work, nor device, nor knowledge, nor wisdom, in the grave, whither thou goest. (Ecclesiastes 9:7-10.)

We who believe in Jesus Christ and in a personal Heavenly Father have every cause which the atheist has, and more, to believe in life. Without Deity, man can struggle alone or with other men for values and goals he cherishes. He can be moral and heroic. He can hardly know, however, the gladness of the believer. The unbeliever has no assurance that "the things of the spirit"—such as truth, beauty, love, integrity, friendship—exist apart from mortal men. If there were no God, our goals would be human goals and would be destroyed, should man's life end. (This thought is developed by W. P. Montague, in *Belief Unbound*.) If God lives, the greatest things in human experience remain in him and in our immortal selves, no matter what might happen to men on the earth.

Faith in God means faith in justice, wisdom, and mercy. These things are at the heart of the universe and will prevail. Nothing we can do to help his cause will be in vain. We like the scriptures which follow:

> The Lord by wisdom hath founded the earth; by understanding hath he established by the heavens. By his knowledge the depths are broken up, and the clouds drop down the dew.
>
> My son, let not them depart from thine eyes: keep sound wisdom and discretion: So shall they be life unto thy soul, and grace to thy neck. Then shalt thou walk in thy way safely, and thy foot shall not stumble.
>
> When thou liest down, thou shall not be afraid; yea, thou shalt lie down, and thy sleep shall be sweet.
>
> Be not afraid of sudden fear, neither of the desolation of the wicked, when it cometh. For the Lord shall be thy confidence, and shall keep thy foot from being taken. (Proverbs 3:19-26.)

> Wherefore, brethren, seek not to counsel the Lord, but to take counsel from his hand. For behold, ye yourselves know that he counseleth in wisdom, and in justice, and in great mercy, over all his works. (Jacob 4:10.)

Admittedly, life is difficult and always a bit uncertain and dangerous. We like the courage of the poet-philosopher who penned these lines at the moment it looked quite certain the plane in which he was riding would crash.

> If in some midnight quietness,
> Some roseate burst of dawn
> Or noonday foggy frightfulness—
> These wings would haply fall to earth,
> And the friendly feverishness of life
> Surrender its quick charms
> To the final friendliness of death,
> Enfolding, nescient arms,
> Say this, and only this you say,
> On that not too unwelcomed day:
> "He loved his life but recked it not,
> And gladly died while the blood was hot."
> Then scatter these ashes from a safer place
> While the motors drone this last refrain:
> "He loved life, loved it all;
> Loved this too, this last quick fall!"

Let us have courage to die, but even more, the courage and wisdom to live with faith in life's potential goodness. Let us accept life with good cheer and with fortitude even in its darkest hour. In the Doctrine and Covenants, men are encouraged by our Father in heaven to "be anxiously engaged in a good cause, and do many things of their own free will, and bring to pass much righteousness; for the power is in them, wherein they are agents unto themselves." (D&C 58:27-28.)

The best cause of all is life itself. Let us be "anxiously engaged" in it.

16

"In the Sweat of Thy Face"

Eleven years ago, our grand old neighbor, Bryant S. Hinckley, then eighty-two years of age, walked through his orchard one day to behold an unusual sight in the back of our lot. My brother-in-law, another neighbor, my three sons, aged eight, eleven, and fourteen, and I were pouring footings for a new barn. The old red barn had crashed to earth in a strong wind, and the boys and I decided to build a new one. This was to be rugged, rustic, of our own design, and to be built with our own hands. So off to Weber Canyon we had gone, sixty-five miles away, and hauled down load after load of poles and slabs in a big truck.

What Brother Hinckley saw that summer morning pleased him. He patted the boys on the shoulder and said, "That's the way to do. No boy ever becomes a man until he learns to love to work."

Many young folks look upon work as a duty, a necessary evil, or even a curse. They associate fun with eating, playing, entertainment, or a car ride. If it were not for the necessity of getting money, some might never lift a hand to work.

Work can be fun and can satisfy a person's desires as few things can. When I was fourteen years of age and my brother sixteen, we went to work on a ranch 180 miles from home, driving all day in a chain-driven truck to get there.

Uncle Teddy was our employer, a man who had as much courage in adversity as any man I have ever known. He had a way with boys. Seldom did he give detailed instructions; he simply told us what to do and expected us to do it. The first time we harnessed a team of horses, the collars went on upside down. One day we were told to clear off ten acres of sagebrush. We had never done anything like this before and were making slow progress. So I went to find Uncle Teddy

---

In August 1960 the "Era of Youth" section of the Improvement Era, *edited by Elaine Cannon and Elder Marion D. Hanks, published this personal account of Dr. Bennion's appreciation for the Church's emphasis on work.*

to get him to tell us how to do it. His answer was simply that a neighbor boy, whom we had thought quite stupid, had grubbed out ten acres the previous spring and done a fine job. Nothing more needed to be said; we cleared the field of brush.

Before the summer was over, we had changed the course of a mountain creek, dug a new canal, put in miles of fencing, and helped put up a stack or two of hay every day for weeks. But best of all, we had come to feel strength in our shoulders, backs, arms, and legs. More thrilling than our physical strength, however, was the self-confidence we had gained. No longer were we afraid of tackling any new job.

After working for Uncle Teddy for two summers, I was afraid of no man. I suppose if the Lord had asked me to run the universe, I would have answered,"Yes sir, when shall I begin," so great was the strength, courage, self-confidence, and independence of spirit that I had gained.

In my observations of college students for some twenty-five years, my own earlier experience has been verified again and again. Boys and girls who like to work, who have learned to use their hands, who have stayed with the job in the face of great difficulty, are the happiest and most successful in study and in marriage.

Some twenty years ago two quiet, unassuming freshman boys came to us from their farms in Fielding, Utah. They were not unusually brilliant boys, but were very steady and conscientious. I suppose they had thinned beets day after day until every muscle in their bodies ached. They applied their work habits to their studies, and today they both have Ph.D.'s in science and are teaching at two major universities in the United States.

One spring our fraternity at the institute of religion decided to have a new kind of party. The committee in charge searched out widows, the aged, the afflicted in the vicinity of the university. Then they divided the boys and girls into groups of six, with a captain over each group. Homes and yards were cleaned with enthusiasm, and in fellowship and the vigor of youth.

After the day's work, the groups came together in the recreation hall, where hot sandwiches, salad, ginger ale, and pie à la mode were served.

Then the fellows and girls "kicked up their heels" in a Virginia reel and many other old-fashioned dances. The governor's son remarked, "I've never had so much real fun in one day in my whole life."

Another work experience was equally rewarding. One Sunday morning the leader of the institute priesthood group said, "Brethren, we've talked about priesthood here all winter. Don't you think it's time we did something in the name of our priesthood?"

"All right. What do you suggest?" asked a member.

"Well, let's clean up yards for some widows next Saturday," the leader replied.

In arranging for places to work, a woman was called on the telephone to see if she needed some help. Her reply was, "How much will this cost me?" The answer was, "Nothing. Some college boys want to help you just for fun and fellowship."

This good sister broke down and wept, and said something as follows: "I have been a widow for eight years. I live alone. This is the first time anyone has ever offered to help me in a physical, tangible way."

Think of it! No neighbor, no Boy Scout troop, no Aaronic or Melchizedek Priesthood quorum, no MIA group of girls—all belonging to the true Church of Jesus Christ—had ever thought to put their shoulders to the wheel to gladden the heart of a precious child of God.

A wise Father in heaven knew man's need when he sent Adam and Eve forth from the life of ease in the lush Garden of Eden to eat their bread "in the sweat of their face" with the remark, "Cursed is the ground *for thy sake;* . . . thorns also and thistles shall it bring forth to thee." (Genesis 3:17-18.) These words in Ecclesiastes were meant for us too: "Whatsoever thy hand findeth to do [that is, thy labor under the sun], do it with thy might." (Ecclesiastes 9:10.)

17

From the "Golden Days" of My Youth

When I was a boy of fourteen, I went to work on a ranch in isolated country 180 miles from my home in Salt Lake City. In those days, this was a long way away. In the valley where the ranch was located there were only three families and a few hired men and boys.

One day my boss sent me into the mountains with a hired man to change the course of a mountain creek. Much of the water which came to us through the old channel sank into the sand before it reached the ranch. A new canal had been made. Our job was to connect the mountain stream with the new canal. It was an exciting job and took nearly a week to accomplish.

My pardner, in charge of our two-man crew, was a fine fellow and a skillful, steady worker. He had one bad habit. He was a chain smoker. He didn't offer me any cigarettes, but I must confess his smoking was mighty interesting as we sat around the fire in the early darkness. On the third day at camp, my pardner ran out of tobacco. His Prince Albert can was empty. I watched this good man become nervous, restless, and irritable. He searched the ground around the camp, picking up cigarette butts out of the dirt where men and horses had walked. The nearest store was miles away, and we had only a wagon and team for transportation.

Watching my good friend's misery and helplessness, I vowed then and there that I would never be a slave to a "weed" or drug.

A few years later I was serving a mission in Bielefeld, Germany. Near Bielefeld was an institution for the mentally ill and retarded, called Bethel. Over five thousand mentally handicapped people in all stages of their limitation resided there. In addition, there were won-

---

In a rare mood of nostalgic personal reflectiveness, for a collection called Turning Points *(©1981 Bookcraft Inc., used by permission), Brother Bennion shares some intimate details of his life and his simple gratitude for practical gospel teachings.*

derfully devoted ministers, doctors, nurses, and others who cared for them. Bethel was a little city all by itself.

One day we missionaries toured the little city and found out that it had been established by religious people who had compassion for the ill. We asked about the cause of their illness. The guide said that it was believed that heavy drinking of alcoholic beverages was one important cause.

There are many causes of mental illness and mental retardation; and heavy use of alcohol, we have learned in recent years, is one of them but only one.

A few days after the visit to Bethel, my companion and I were tracting in a nearby village. We knocked on a farmhouse door and were invited in by a rough, growl-like greeting. In the corner of the room was a half-drunken father. Hearing our message, he ordered us to get out of the house "with our ______ Mormonism." As we left, two forlorn-looking sons our age waved goodbye to us.

This was the second time in my life when I was deeply moved to thank God for my Mormon upbringing and for my father and mother who had given me a healthy mind and body.

My wife and I studied at the University of Vienna following my mission. This was during the Depression in 1931-1932. We lived on sixty dollars a month of borrowed money. We had no telephone, no car; we bought no clothes, and we walked or rode the streetcar everywhere we went. Saturday evenings we went to the grand opera house and sat in the top gallery for twenty-five cents each. Sometimes I stood up for fifteen cents.

The end of the month found us often very low on cash. We usually went to the market—which was held in a nearby street—to buy vegetables, fruit, and meat from farmers. Our object was to make a soup to last us until our monthly check would arrive.

One day after we had spent our last pennies on food at the market, as we were leaving I stooped down and picked up some outer cabbage leaves one of the farmers had thrown away. This embarrassed my good wife and she chided me good-naturedly. I told her that a new flavor in the soup the third day might taste pretty good. As we got near to the street where we lived, we heard a young man about my age singing a heart-rending song in the street:

> My mother loves me not,
> My father I do not know,
> I do not wish to die,
> I am so young.

A few people would open their windows and toss small coins to him in the street. I noticed that he not only picked up the coins but also gleaned cigarette stubs and cigar butts from between the cobblestones where men and horses walked. I turned to Sister Bennion and said, "In our poverty I may have to pick up cabbage leaves to feed my hunger, but thanks to Mormonism, I don't have to pick up cigarettes and cigars from the dirty street."

In the years which have followed these experiences of my youth, I have learned that there are things in life and religion that are far more important than not smoking and not drinking. Humility, honesty, chastity, faith, love of God, and love of neighbor are the great fundamentals of religion and of life.

I have also learned that many fine people have developed smoking and drinking habits. I do not judge or condemn them. (Many would quit if they believed they could.) But I shall be eternally grateful to my religion for giving me the incentive to leave tobacco, liquor, and other harmful drugs alone. (I have enough faults without them.) I have also come to appreciate the words of Alma to his son Shiblon: "See that ye bridle all your passions, that ye may be filled with love." (Alma 38:12.)

V
TEACHING AND LEADING

In his office as Associate Dean of Students at the University of Utah, about 1970

18

Teaching Religion by Word of Mouth

Religious fervor is not inherited. One acquires it only to the degree that he associates religion with that which is most real and meaningful in his life—the decisions he makes, the convictions he lives by, his satisfactions, hopes and aspirations, and significant happenings.

How can the teacher help the student identify religion with life? He will, of course, avail himself of progressive educational processes, by which the student experiences subtly his religion in life projects and situations. The teacher will recollect also the influence of example—the warmth of personality and integrity of character of certain of his own teachers. In conjunction with these and others not mentioned, there remains a third method of teaching, one that is much used, abused, and misused. Discredited by some, apologized for by others, and traditionally applied by many, it merits consideration, if for no other reason than because of its wide use. We refer to the spoken word, the explanation of the gospel in the classroom, before the fireplace, over the pulpit, and in the office.

The spoken word, like the written word, need not be so far removed from life. Though I recognize with due consideration all remarks to the contrary, the student does not always learn of life best by contacting it directly. The happenings and impressions of the student's life do not weave themselves voluntarily into a single meaningful wholeness. They flow into a constantly changing maze of feeling and thought. The student depends on the interpretations of others for direction, and words are still some of man's most effective symbols with which to convey meanings.

The literary genius is not untrue to life. Even his "fiction" is drawn

---

In December 1939, shortly after returning from founding the Tucson institute to be director of the Salt Lake Institute of Religion for a second time, Dr. Bennion published the following essay in Week-Day Religious Education, *a periodical for seminary and institute teachers.*

from life itself, where one finds more hate and love, despair and hope, tragedy and joy than have ever been printed in books. Yet the skillful writer with eyes to see and ears to hear and the talent to express his keener insight and deeper understanding singles out tragedy, builds a plot around it, holds our attention to it until we feel it more intensely than in life itself. This is not because he exaggerates or falsifies, nor because tragedy is artificial or foreign to real life. It results from his ability to isolate some feeling or thought, cast the spotlight of understanding on its shadows, and clarify its place on the horizon, whereas previously it had been obscured in a labyrinth of subjective experience.

In this manner Jesus, the artist in parable, interpreted life for his listeners. So real are his illustrations in the Good Samaritan that tourists today trustfully listen to the story while the guide points out the inn between Jericho and Jerusalem to which the Samaritan took the man "who fell among thieves." By the power of the spoken word, Jesus gave to the world a deeper understanding of the word "neighbor" than most men could discover for themselves living among neighbors a lifetime without that interpretation.

Some methods of teaching the gospel, it would seem, are quite foreign to life and the subject itself, carrying within them the seeds of disillusionment. Others appear to be more satisfactory and more consistent with the nature of religion. What follows is an attempt to evaluate certain procedures, and is offered for consideration and evaluation rather than acceptance.

First, the teaching of religion should be student-centered. It should help the student solve his own problems, both those of which he is now aware and others which he will meet in the future. The course of study should be built around such questions. This does not mean, however, that the gospel should be taught as a series of disconnected, isolated, and miscellaneous questions, or even as a series of related questions, as though religion consisted of a collection of questions. There are more effective ways of dealing with such questions as Does God exist? Where are the ten tribes? Is the biblical story of creation true? than treating them directly as the heart of the course. Several reasons seem to support this assertion.

Many questions of the kind mentioned cannot be answered satisfactorily. We do not know where the ten tribes are. All the talk in the world has not proved nor disproved the existence of God. The history of philosophy is witness of this fact. If questions are singled out as the heart of a course, the young student will demand answers

for his satisfaction. In using another method, which will b
later, it is not important that all questions be answered.

Even though we could answer adequately all questions, re
would be at best a miscellaneous collection of answers in the mi
of the student. The gospel of Christ is more than that. It has body
and soul. The student needs a feeling for it as a whole.

To reply to any question effectively, the teacher must build a broad foundation and set up criteria, and clear ground in common with the student. One cannot say merely yes or no. Why not, therefore, do this at the outset, thereby automatically eliminating many problems, anticipating others, and helping the student establish a basis on which to answer questions which will arise when he is beyond the reach of an understanding teacher?

Suppose, for instance, a teacher facing a class of high school or college students studying science treats the question: Is the biblical story of creation true? as an isolated question in a series of other religious questions. How shall it be answered? If the promise of the course is an answer to questions, these eager young minds may demand a yes or no reply. The teacher may be persuaded, by the students' eagerness, to take a stand for the cause of the scriptures and marshal all evidence to show that the Bible story is true and all notions not contained therein are false. Some students will not be convinced and will, as they proceed in science, lose faith in religion. Others, accepting the evidences for the Bible story, will close their minds to scientific findings. Using another approach, practically the entire problem-complex can be eliminated from the discussion, and we do not mean avoided nor hedged, as we shall shortly try to illustrate.

Second, the gospel should not be taught as a complete, final, finished product to be understood with the same detailed finality with which one can understand a chemistry formula. A student should not come out of a class in religion with all the prophecies dated, the celestial kingdom landscaped, the past and future of the Creator understood, and himself ready to step into a place in the council of Deity.

All has not yet been revealed, and we believe . . . that God "will yet reveal many great and important things pertaining to the Kingdom of God." (Article of Faith 9.) Looking backward, this is a dispensation of the fullness of time. Looking forward, "Eye hath not seen, nor ear heard, . . . the things which God hath prepared for them that love him." (1 Corinthians 2:9.) Eternal progress is the watchword. To teach

d of finality—that which tries to explain

even of the rich treasures of truth which
acher, young or old, understands a single
llness and in its far-reaching potentialities.
sence of faith, of love, of priesthood, the
mission of Christ? Why then should boys
ad women be led to believe that they do or
ne gospel in every detail and in its fullness?
Is not the . . . ctice of religion as large and enduring and
promising as that of physics, chemistry, or economics? Who would
dare assume full and final knowledge in one of these fields?

II

The most effective manner of teaching the gospel, we believe, is to lead the student to an understanding of fundamental principles sufficiently broad in meaning, profound in implication, and flexible in application as to be true and effective in the lives of men for all time, if we may judge by human experience to date. The ability to stress foundation principles is one explanation of Jesus' greatness as a teacher. When asked to single out the greatest commandment in the law, He gave two commandments (Matthew 22:37-40) which embraced the entire Law of Moses and more—commandments that can be fulfilled in a scientific as well or better than in a prescientific age, commandments equally applicable in family, civic, educational, and religious life.

When confronted with Jewish masters of the Sabbath—men who had pulverized the commandment, "Remember the sabbath day to keep it holy," so finely that they could no longer find the germ—Jesus recovered it. With one statement, "Is it lawful . . . to do good, or to do evil? to save life, or to lose it?" (Luke 6:9), he gave us a fundamental guide to Sabbath day living that will never be outdated and never wholly fulfilled. Contrast that with the "perfectionism" of the scribes who "understood" the law.

Yes, the teacher should teach the existence of God with all the conviction of his soul. But how? Not by discussing it as a problem, and not by giving the student a final and complete description of the nature of God and his works adapted to the adolescent mind, a description that may leave the student with a conception of the Creator as being not only human but adolescent as well. The student should be taught the basic principles of religion related to the concept of God, that he is personal and a God of love, mercy, justice, goodness, and intelligence; that man can commune with his eternal Father; that the attributes of Deity will not fail one; and that God seeks our cooperation to bring to pass his work. These are safe guides and lasting challenges and stimuli to religious living. Such principles promise satisfaction.

The principles of religion organize themselves quite naturally into a whole view in the mind of the student. Faith, humility, repentance, doing good, forgiveness, mercy, self-control, and love all belong to the same family. Questions or rules for Sabbath-day living lack that same intimate relationship. One could discuss them all year without acquiring a feeling for the gospel as a whole.

Is the biblical story of creation true? (We promised to return to this question.) That question, at least in its present form, ceases to be a crucial problem when the student understands certain basic principles:

1. The purpose of scripture is primarily religious and moral. "For the fulness of mine intent," says Nephi, in writing the Book of Mormon, "is that I may persuade men to come unto the God of Abraham, and the God of Isaac, and the God of Jacob, and be saved."(1 Nephi 6:4.) The first sentence in the Bible also indicates this emphasis: "In the beginning God created the heaven and the earth." (Genesis 1:1.) After one and one-half pages in which the manner of creation is described, the Bible record continues another nine hundred pages describing man's relationship to God and his obligations to fellowmen. Again and again God is affirmed as the Creator of heaven and earth. "The Lord by wisdom hath founded the earth; by understanding hath he established the heavens." (Proverbs 3:19.) Hardly a reference, however, do you find describing the exact process, the "how" of creation. Think of Jesus' emphasis, the greatest religious teacher of all!

2. The revelations of God are given to men "in their weakness, after the manner of their language, that they might come to understanding." (D&C 1:24.) The writers of the Bible were not scientists. Their language did not include scientific concepts as do the textbooks of today. One cannot expect the Bible to be a scientifically written account when its purpose is religious and its language antedates many centuries the age of experimental science.

3. Scientific accounts of creation have as their purpose to describe the process, the "how" of things. Ultimate origins and the purpose or "why" of creation are beyond the scope of science. No matter what the description, science leaves the question open as to whether it was done by God or otherwise.

If the student has an understanding of the religious purpose of scripture; if he comprehends God's wisdom and economy in revealing himself in man's language and in the light of his circumstances; and if he knows the descriptive and developmental nature of scientific findings, he will be able to answer the question as to whether or not the Bible story is true and many more of a similar nature. He will recognize that it is not false but incomplete, fragmentary, and in part symbolical in its scientific or descriptive aspects. He will also rest assured that it is true and wholly true in its main emphasis, that "God created the heaven and the earth" in wisdom and understanding.

If the student has an understanding of the larger relationships involved in the religious and scientific approach to the creation, he will suspend judgment on some aspects of the problem. In fact, he will feel that that is the intelligent thing to do. And he will have acquired sufficient satisfaction to enable him to do so happily, pending further revelation, new findings, and his own increase in learning and wisdom.

19

Good Teaching and Leadership

Everywhere one looks in life, purpose is the great motivating idea which makes people's activities significant. The doctor aims to relieve pain and save life. The coach aims to win the game and, happily, quite often to build strength of character in boys and men. The army trains to protect its country from surprise attack. The carpenter aims to build the house.

It is no different in the Church. The first thing a teacher or leader in MIA must know is where he is going. He must ask himself: "What do I wish to accomplish through this activity or in this class?" The Lord's work does not take care of itself. If it did, he would not need us to work in it. Each teacher must define his purpose to himself—whether he is teaching M Men and Gleaners, conducting a Boy Scout meeting, or planning a Young Marrieds' fireside. If he fails to do this, he is working blindly, like a hunter shooting without a target, or a football player running out of bounds.

Choosing Objectives

A worker in the Church needs to establish for himself three kinds of objectives, or purposes:

1. The general objective of all Church work.
2. The overall objective for his class during the year.
3. A single, specific, objective for each activity, function, or lesson.

He will keep "1" and "2" in mind throughout the year in everything he plans and does. And then, as he prepares each lesson or activity, he aims at a limited and very specific target in harmony with his larger and long-range objectives.

Thinking of People

In choosing objectives, remember that there is nothing on this earth so important as people—men, women, boys and girls, Brother

---

In 1962 the general boards of the Mutual Improvement Associations published Lowell Bennion's compendium, Six Fundamentals of Good Teaching and Leadership. *Reprinted here are parts of the first two sections.*

Jones, Sister Smith, Tom, Dick, and Harry, Mary and Janet—whoever the individuals are who belong to your class or group in MIA.

God himself said that his work and glory in his endless creations was "to bring to pass the immortality and eternal life of man." (Moses 1:39.) In his service, our purpose must be the same as his, or we shall find ourselves working against him.

We should never hold a meeting, teach a class, or plan an activity without asking ourselves: How is this going to affect the people who will participate? Because, ultimately, the only measure of our labors is this: what happened to the people because they came to our class or function in MIA. A class is no better than what happens to the people who attend. Meetings, classes, subject matter, activities are a means to the end; the people are the end.

I. *The general, overall objective*

Our overall objective, then, is to help people gain exaltation in the kingdom of God. Since this is achieved by accepting Christ and living in harmony with his will, workers in the Church might best conceive of their work as: helping people to become real Christians, genuine Latter-day Saints; helping them to understand, love, and live the principles Christ taught, that they might come to know the increasing joy that comes to men when they are growing in the realization of their full potential as children of God.

II. *The basic objectives in each course for the year*

As he plans the MIA year, each leader or teacher should try to write down several objectives for his particular group which he will pursue during the entire year. These should be more specific and adapted to the immediate needs and interests of those in one's class. They may already be stated in the manual or course of study. Whether they are or not, the teacher must find them and be able to state them in his own words. Let us illustrate what these long-range objectives might be for different groups.

A. *The Young Marrieds*

1. To help each member individually live a more rewarding life, consistent with the ideals of the gospel and with his or her role as husband or wife.

2. To help each couple increase in their understanding of and love for each other. This will include helping them to discover and build a community of intellectual, cultural, and spiritual interest which is so important to a growing friendship.

3. To help couples succeed better as parents in establishing happy, successful Latter-day Saint family life.

B. *Boy Scouts*

Suppose you were a Scoutmaster: what would your objectives be in the coming year with thirty boys, ages twelve to fourteen? Would it be to get them all enrolled, in uniform, and taking the *Boy's Life?* No! These are simply a means to an end. Your objectives would have to be stated in terms of something that is happening to each boy's personality and character.

You might proceed as follows: Ask yourself, "What do boys of twelve to fourteen need the most in a long-range program of building Christian character? What would I, as a parent, want the MIA to accomplish most for my boy right now?" You might come up with some objectives like these:

1. To help every boy know of the joy of achievement, know how to do some things very well.

2. To help every boy learn that he is accepted and respected by other boys and men.

3. To help every boy learn that the greatest adventure and fun in life can be had by living in harmony with gospel ideals.

III. *The single objective for each lesson and activity*

As you plan each lesson, fireside, or activity, you must find a very limited and specific objective. In teaching, it is always best to have just one aim in mind. It has been said, "A good talk is one idea organized and illustrated." This is also true of a good lesson—just one idea, organized and illustrated, and of vital importance to members of the class. Do not misunderstand. Several ideas can be introduced in every lesson, but they should, to be most effective, always be related to a single major objective. All concepts should hang together and point to one big one.

It is not enough to have a single subject, such as faith. This is too big and too broad a theme for a single lesson. One could write a book on the subject of faith. Some teachers conscientiously feel that they should teach everything that is to be known about faith—what it is, how we gain it and lose it, wherein it differs from belief and knowledge, in what sense it is a gift of God, its relationship to grace and works, and the life's story of all the great men of faith, such as the brother of Jared, Abraham, Peter, Alma, Joseph Smith, and Wilford Woodruff—all in one lesson. Obviously, one would get lost covering so much subject matter in one lesson even though everything was related to the general subject of faith.

One should find a more limited and specific aim within faith, which is needed by the students, and seek to achieve this in one evening. Then, next week, another should be chosen. The following are some objectives under the topic of faith, each suitable for a single lesson:

1. To help students understand just what faith is—distinguishing it clearly from belief and knowledge.

2. To help students realize how essential and constructive faith is in one's life.

3. To lead students to see how they can increase their faith in the gospel of Jesus Christ.

4. To help students distinguish between a blind faith and a faith that is not blind.

Any one of these objectives—and there are many more available—is large and important enough for a single lesson. To have several objectives is to weaken all of them. The mind can really grasp only one idea at a time effectively.

Another example of having a single objective for one lesson may be illustrated in the lessons for the Laurels in the area of courtship.

One lesson deals with chastity. The single and only purpose of this lesson is to inspire girls to want to keep their chastity. Every idea and illustration in the lesson should lead to this objective.

Another lesson deals with dating. Obviously, this subject has many facets, and a teacher could be led in many directions by it. Hence, the teacher, with a knowledge of her girls and their needs, should decide on the most important idea or attitude needed by her girls which she can put over in relation to dating. It might be one of the following:

1. Dating should be a means of building real friendship.

2. Going steady, except after a good friendship has been established and prospects for marriage are good, is a foolish trap to get caught in.

3. Affection should never become an end in itself, or destroy things more important than itself.

Revealing the Objective

The question is often asked: Should the teacher write his objective on the chalkboard at the beginning or even at the end of the lesson?

This, we believe, depends on the kind of lesson that is being taught. If one is dealing with factual, objective material and is seeking—primarily—to convey information, then it might be very helpful to declare one's objective in the beginning. For example, a new Boy Scout leader announced the first evening he met his troop of eight boys, "Next week I am going to teach you how to shoot a gun." Twenty-five boys showed up the following Tuesday. Or, if one were to teach a lesson on the topography of Palestine, the teacher might state his purpose and carry it out.

However, when one's purpose is to affect people's lives—to bring about changes in attitudes, feelings, and otherwise influence human behavior—we believe it is much wiser for the teacher to keep his purpose to himself. For example, suppose his purpose were to inspire greater honesty in the lives of his class members, and he wrote on the board, "Today, I am going to inspire you all to be honest." What would be the result? Would not some students, jealous of their right to choose, say to themselves, "Like fun you will. I'll show you that you can't!"

Teaching a lesson has much in common with telling a joke or a story, which should carry its own point or message. It is a sad day when one tells a joke and then has to reveal the point of it. On the other hand, how effective is a well-told story that carries its own message, such as the parable of the Prodigal Son.

A teacher who would influence human behavior keeps his purpose clearly in mind in planning and teaching a lesson. However, he does not rob his students of the free, creative thrill of arriving at their own conclusions and resolutions. Many a lesson has been ruined by moralizing and by endless repetition. If the lesson is well-given, sensible, and inspiring in character, the student can be trusted to draw a good conclusion.

Understanding Human Nature

As a lad of fourteen I went to work on a ranch. One day the boss sent me up into the mountains with a man twice my age to change the course of a mountain creek. We were losing the water as it came down the old channel in the valley, so we decided to bring it to the ranch in a newly constructed canal.

With the enthusiasm and folly of youth, I jumped into the creek and proceeded to dig a channel that would lead to the newly made canal. I began to shovel out gravel and dirt from the bottom of the creek with vigor. My older and wiser co-worker tapped me on the shoulder and said, "Son, just pick up the larger rocks and let the water do the rest of the work. It will wash the dirt and fine gravel with it."

This was my first lesson in working with nature. I learned that life is much easier this way. One's strength can be used to accomplish much more if one works with, rather than against, the laws of nature and of life.

My second lesson came during World War II when I was trying to get by on a limited rationing of gasoline and also attempting to keep an old car running. I learned to gauge my speed so that I would seldom have to stop at a red light. This conserved gas, brakes, and general wear and tear. Other drivers frequently sped by me, only to slam on their brakes at the next semaphore light. Then they sat tensely waiting for a green light, only to gun their motors, waste gas, and speed up for a stop at the next light.

If we are to teach and lead people in the Church, we need to understand more about human nature. For if we understand people, we can get through to them and will have a better chance of seeing gospel teachings take effect in their lives.

Students resist the teacher and his ideas if he is working at cross-purposes with their thinking and feeling. They build up resistance and reject the teaching if it is not presented in a way that is congenial to human nature.

Each individual is unique. He lives in a different world from everyone else. He interprets the thinking of the teacher, not in light of the teacher's thinking, but in the context of his own experience. When we teach a group of individuals, each living in his own world, how can we possibly work in harmony with the human nature of each individual?

This would be quite a hopeless task were it not for another fact about human nature, namely, that people also have much in common. Each has a unique heredity and environment, even children of the same family, but they also have things in common. The wise teacher respects individual differences, but he also learns to work in harmony with those aspects of human nature shared by all men. And, we may ask, what are these facets of human nature shared by all?

Men have basic needs in common. All men hunger for food, thirst for liquids, seek air to breathe, and have other physiological needs such as rest and relaxation. Even more important for the teacher to remember is the fact that people share social, psychological, and spiritual needs. All wish to be acceptable to other human beings, to express themselves creatively and adventurously, to feel their own worth, to find a purpose and meaning in life.

Consciously and subconsciously people strive to satisfy these needs. Much of life's motivation to act is in anticipation of their fulfillment. The effective teacher is aware of these needs and strives in his personal relations with students, in his manner of teaching, and even in the things he teaches, to help students satisfy their spiritual and psychological hunger. The gospel lends itself both in spirit and in idea to the gratification of man's basic spiritual desires, as we shall see later on in this lesson. But first, let us spell out these basic human needs more explicitly. What do students of human behavior generally agree are man's most basic human needs above and beyond the physiological ones?

1. A feeling of belonging, of acceptance by other human beings. This idea was expressed simply, and never more truly than in the early pages of the Bible, wherein the Creator declared: "It is not good that man should be alone." This applies equally to young and old, male and female. Men are social by nature. "No man is an island." Each must feel that he is wanted and needed by others. Each must love and be loved to fulfill his nature.

2. Creative self-expression of adventure, new experience. Man was born to function. Watch a newborn child. It begins life struggling for breath, crying, twisting, and squirming. Endless activity, insatiable curiosity, and love of adventure characterize the growing child.

Inactivity is a sign of death. In a living person it may be pathological. The quiet, shy member of your class may be greatly lacking in deep emotional satisfaction. In his silence he may be conjuring up more troubles for himself than the happy, outgoing youngster who is more disturbing to your class.

The young people in your class hate routine and are bored with dull generalities. They want to be challenged with new ideas. They want to use their hands, imagination, and minds. They would like to think that the gospel is as exciting—in its own way—as a new car.

3. Self-approval or self-esteem. Every human being is struggling continuously to feel his own worth. Each person in your group needs to feel his own importance, to be successful in his own eyes, to have a great deal of self-respect.

In our experience, too few people are genuinely self-accepting. Even those who appear to be most proud—the bully, the conceited, the snobbish, the rude, the loud, the "show-off" type, and the domineering, authoritarian individual—are likely unaware of it themselves and are just trying to cover up for a deep-seated sense of inadequacy and inferiority. There are no real egotists, but those who act that way in search of ego fulfillment and status.

4. A sense of actualization, a feeling that one's total life has meaning and purpose. As people move toward adulthood and live out their days on the earth, they need to feel that their total living has meaning, that they somehow fit into the total scheme of things. That is, people need values, ideals, purposes, and faith—the kind of things which a testimony of the gospel of Christ can give them.

Satisfying These Needs

The teacher and leader in the Church should try to work in harmony with these needs and help rather than frustrate his students in their efforts toward fulfillment. He is not simply a teacher of subject matter, nor is he simply a teacher of students. His aim should be to teach ideas to students and provide activity for them in a way that will help them satisfy their basic needs. (We will now make a few suggestions under each need as to how this can be done. The teacher will think of many more out of his own experience.)

1. *Belonging, acceptance, love.* How can a teacher give this feeling to each member in his class? How can he help each student to feel accepted—not for what he can do, but just because he is who he is and what he is? Jesus, it is well to remember, loved even the sinners and publicans. They felt his love, because "then drew near unto him all the publicans and sinners for to hear him." (Luke 15:1.) There are a number of things a teacher can do to help each member of his class feel part of the group.

a. The arrangement of the room itself can do much. Make it a clean, pleasant, warm, friendly, and comfortable place in which to meet. Arrange the chairs in a circle or, if need be, in two rows in a semi-circle.

b. Include everyone in discussion. This is done easily and fruitfully in a class under twenty or twenty-five by having each one in the circle, starting at teacher's left or right, give his views on an issue. In a larger class that must be seated in rows, the teacher can start at one end of a row and have each one react to a question or issue. The teacher can also point simpler questions to the more timid or less well-informed and more difficult ones to those who are better informed.

c. Some teachers are not good listeners or learners. They are so eager to tell the class all they know that even their questions are a farce. They prefer to answer their own questions; students are only allowed to nibble at them, and they invariably give the wrong answer. A teacher must have respect for the thinking of his students. He need not and should not agree with them always, but he should protect the dignity of the person. This is an art.

d. Immediately before and after class, a teacher should have the opportunity to show interest in those who need his interest most. There is a tendency for teachers to visit with students whom they enjoy or who are most responsive. They should not neglect the quiet, lonely, or even belligerent youngsters. Casual conversation, the calling of a person by name, a pat on the shoulder, a shake of the hand, a personal inquiry, a deserved compliment—these things may be quite as effective as the lesson itself. They require no extra time or exhausting effort, but just thoughtfulness.

e. An occasional social project or field trip planned for real fellowship can also help. Some students do not excel in the classroom, but they might do very well repairing toys for a Christmas service project. Others excel in eating. The feeling of acceptance is gained through pleasant group experiences. It takes a good variety of them to give all students this feeling of belonging.

The above methods, and others a teacher can think of, will be of no value unless he has a genuine interest in and liking for people. Paul's words are so true: "And though I bestow all my goods to feed the poor, and though I give my body to be burned, and have not charity [the pure love of Christ], it profiteth me nothing." (1 Corinthians 13:3.) Every teacher should examine his own conscience to see how he feels toward each of his class members. If there are those whom he does not accept, these are the ones he had better serve the most in order that he might learn to love them.

2. *New experience, adventure, creative self-expression.* How can a teacher, especially one dealing with youth, help them to satisfy their great urge for self-expression and do it in a manner consistent with the ideals of the Church?

a. The teacher can be enthusiastic, genuinely interested in, and excited about the lesson or activity. This attitude is contagious, enabling students to experience the teacher's love for the thing at hand. If a teacher would only remember how much is at stake each time he faces a class, he would not have great difficulty in meeting his class with eagerness and readiness.

b. The teacher should make sure in his planning that the students are going to have a learning experience. Not only should a teacher have a single aim, but it must be either entirely new to his students or be a substantial enrichment of what they already know. Our students have minds. They desperately need adventure in the realm of the mind. This is more rewarding and far less dangerous than youth's search for excitement on the highway, in drink, or in crime and sin. Teacher, what new idea of significance is your class going to learn the next time you teach them?

c. Friendship is always a source of adventure. Many of the methods of achieving acceptance indicated above are also extremely adventurous. Prayer, worship, service, kindness—these may be rich in spiritual adventure, especially when they are shared by the group. Too often we think of adventure only on the pleasure level.

d. Self-expression means participation. A Boy Scout must learn skills, do a good turn, take part in raising the flag, swim, hike, and play with his associates. Mia Maids, Explorers, Laurels, M Men, and Gleaners must be involved in the planning of their activities. They need responsibility. Teachers and leaders should do fewer things for them and use their imagination to let the young people do more for themselves, for each other, for the Church, and for the community. It is what a person does, what he accomplishes, his satisfying experiences, which fulfill his basic needs and build his character.

3. *Self-approval or self-esteem.* This is a most difficult need to fulfill, especially for those who for some reason, often unknown to themselves, are greatly lacking in this resource. What can the teacher do?

a. Achievement is a real source of self-esteem. Young people, and older ones as well, have a great need to be successful. Too often we try to make people happy and keep them close to the Church by giving them a lot of attention, awards, rewards, and even bribes. These things do not satisfy the inner man. Many a spoiled child turns with hate and disrespect on his parents who have done everything for him except let him prove his own worth by real accomplishments. More imagination should be used by parents, teachers, and leaders to have youths give of themselves, carry responsibility, and serve them and the Church. A mother loves her child so deeply because she has given and sacrificed so much for it. The same psychology applies to youth. Young people will love the cause if they give richly and meaningfully to it.

Achievement is quite a specific thing. A leader must plan carefully and persevere greatly to enable each youth in his care to learn skills in such areas as discussion, reading aloud, leading, speaking, presiding as a class officer, playing games, dancing well, participating in music and drama. It is important that we measure our labors, not in terms of activities and group statistics, but in what is happening to each person in our class. What is he learning? What is he achieving? Wherein does he feel and know his own strength?

b. Self-approval is also won by the genuine approval of others. The teacher or leader should see that each student is approved quite frequently by at least one person, namely, the teacher himself. Sometimes a leader will have students of such maturity and fine spirit that he can encourage one or more of them to give moral support to a person in need. This must be done with the utmost caution and tact.

c. Self-esteem comes from integrity. Integrity means wholeness and oneness. To have integrity, one must have purposes, values, and ideals, and then pursue them. Any assistance the teacher can give to youth to inspire them and to help them succeed in the pursuit of these things will build self-esteem.

4. *A philosophy of life—faith, testimony, purpose in one's total living.*

a. To help a student find a genuine and growing faith in the gospel of Jesus Christ is the sum and substance of all of our teaching and leadership. This will be greatly facilitated if the other needs, already discussed before, are on the way to fulfillment in the lives of our students. A student, for example, who is loved by others can usually find it easier to believe in a loving Father or to appreciate Christ's life of love. A boy who is having high adventure in gospel living will have no need to kick over the traces. A girl who has self-esteem can more readily exercise the faith in herself and others which the gospel so clearly teaches.

b. Acquiring faith and testimony is a gradual process. Even sudden and miraculous conversions are usually followed by ebb and flow, like the tide. Students should not be told that they either have a testimony or they have none. Rather, let them know that it grows like a tree and bears fruit. Find ways of strengthening their faith through teaching and through other experiences, such as in worship, service, and achievement. Testimonies, like friendships, are built of many single experiences. Testimony is inseparably linked with one's total life-experience. It must be a growing tree with many roots to nourish it.

Summary

. . . We should work with human nature rather than against it. This is perhaps best achieved by thinking of people as persons who have needs or desires which somehow must be gratified. These desires seem to be—on the psychological and spiritual level—(1) belonging or being accepted, (2) creating self-expression or new experience, (3) self-approval or esteem, and (4) a philosophy of life based on the gospel of Jesus Christ. . . .

Finally, it may be said that the gospel is perfectly designed to satisfy man's spiritual needs. Love, the very heart of Christ's teaching, satisfies man's need to belong. Faith, freedom, and creation satisfy man's urge for adventure and creative self-expression. The dignity and worth of every human soul harmonize beautifully with man's need for self-approval. Our task is to take the gospel out of the books and plant it deeply in the lives of men, for, truly, human nature will thereby find and fulfill itself.

20

The Joy of Teaching

One afternoon a junior student at the University of Utah who was majoring in elementary education came to my office and said she had a problem with her Sunday School class. She was teaching twelve-year-old boys and girls. They were out of hand. And I asked her, after her description, "What do you have in mind when you prepare your lesson during the week?" Her very honest and interesting reply was, "How to keep the children quiet while I give the lesson."

If giving a lesson were the end of all teaching, the most effective way might be to gag the children, hog-tie them, and play a phonograph record. Brother Robert Thomas [Professor of English at BYU and the previous speaker] has beautifully told us that teaching is more than giving lessons; it is giving them with understanding, with knowledge, and with love. If the Lord will bless me, I would like to suggest that there is one more step in teaching, if we would know the joy of giving as teachers.

I learned this from one of my students who was in a class on marriage and family life. I had been very much occupied in telling these unmarried students all that I knew about marriage. After class I noticed an older student lingering; and, when they linger, they usually wish to talk. He came up to me and said, "I'm a sophomore medical student. I do very well in my present work. I can memorize and learn and pass examinations. But," he said, "next year I go to the hospital and make tours with doctors, and they will interrogate me about patients. I am frightened to death whenever I speak to anybody. Can you help me?" That was in the middle of the quarter. I said, "Yes," but I did not know how at the moment.

The next time we met in class I wrote on the board the word "Children." It was a small class seated in a circle, and this medical

---

This address was given at a conference of the Deseret Sunday School Union on Sunday, October 7, 1962, and was printed in the April 1963 Instructor, *under the title, "The Joy of Giving."*

student was about in the center of the circle. I said to the class, "We'll start on my right and each one of you say anything you want about children. Raise a question, state your wishes, do as you will, but say something."

When it came his turn, he had to speak. There was no pressure there; it was his turn. The rest of the quarter we handled the course in this fashion. Not only that, but we put him on the spot and fired questions at him and talked with him again and again. He came up at the end of the quarter very, very grateful for the degree of confidence that he had gained to face his professor the next year.

This experience gave me another idea. If you have ever taught a class on reasons for faith in God, you perhaps will have experienced (especially if you have taught college students this subject) that those who were convinced were of the same opinion still; and those who were doubting were perhaps still doubting after your rational explanations.

So this time I went into the class, having been taught the value of individual participation by the medical student, and I told one or two experiences in my own life which had given me faith in God. One time was when I had done something foolish and wrong, and had been humbled to my knees and felt the Spirit of God answering my plea for forgiveness. Another time was when I had felt deeply grateful for the life of a child. Those were moments when I had felt God near me and when prayer was real and answered.

After I had mentioned these experiences, I said to the class, "What experiences have any of you had which have made you realize the reality of God's existence?" A boy spoke up—very much to my surprise because he was a playful sort of chap, a bit loud, and not the spiritual type at all on the surface. He said, "A week ago Friday evening, I went to the Roof Gardens at the Hotel Utah with students from the LDS Institute—about 150 couples. It was a beautiful moonlight night as we stood there looking over at the lighted temple and the Angel Moroni. As I looked at those young people, my friends, for the first time in my life I really knew that God lives."

Other students spoke up in class and bore witness to their faith in our Father in heaven, each out of his own unique experience. It is thrilling for a teacher not to lecture to the class, but to initiate something which brings thought and feeling from the group.

One Easter Sunday morning I returned to my Sunday School class of university students and said, "Faith in Christ doesn't mean anything in the abstract. Faith in Christ means whatever we have faith in because of our faith in him. I'd like each one of you on the back row to stand up in turn and declare, 'I have faith in this or that because of my faith in Christ.' "

The first three or four students gave the answers one would expect. And then a tall Indian boy stood up—a Hindu, twenty-five years of age—and said "Because of my faith in Christ, I am not afraid to die."

I said, "Did you used to be afraid to die?"

"Yes," he answered.

"When did you lose this fear?" I further asked.

"When I became converted to the restored gospel of Jesus Christ."

How thrilling in a class to hear a young man of twenty-five say and mean it, "I am not afraid to die."

As we went down the row, a girl about twenty-five years of age stood up and said, "Because of my faith in Christ I am not afraid to live."

I said, "What do you mean? Did you used to be afraid to live?"

"I did. I was worried about myself, my future; I'm unmarried"—and she continued to speak frankly of her concerns. But, she said, "I found faith in Christ. I found a trust in my Father in heaven. I have found things to live for, things to do. I'm not afraid anymore."

(You will pardon all these personal stories, but I was told to speak this way about the joy of teaching.) I had an experience last winter in a Book of Mormon class. We were coming to Alma, chapter 36, in which Alma the younger confesses his wrongdoing and tells his son about the wonderful joy of his conversion. As I prepared this lesson, I thought of a young man in my class who had recently been divorced, who had been in to talk with me, and whose life, at the moment, seemed empty; he felt he had ruined it.

I knew how much he needed to make a fresh beginning, to know that repentance means a clean slate if it is complete. So I tried to convey to the class the feelings which Alma relates in chapter 36. The young man spoke up and said, "Brother Bennion, I believe in repentance; but how do you get the assurance of forgiveness, and how do you get the strength to have a new mind and become another person after you have made serious mistakes in life?"

This question gave me an opportunity to talk about how fellowship with Jesus Christ and service to him could give one a new spirit and a sense of forgiveness and renewal.

Another member in this class told about how he had overcome a great weakness by relating his shortcoming to the partaking of the sacrament. He let the sacrament go by for several Sundays. While it went by and during each week, he prayed to God in the name of Christ that he might overcome his particular weakness. After a few weeks he overcame his difficulty and told us how he sat with tears in his eyes as he finally partook of the sacrament with gratitude to the Savior for the strength which he had received through faith in him. Never had the sacrament meant so much to him.

A few weeks later a girl in this same class handed me a note. It read something like this: "Ever since I was in elementary school, I have had two weaknesses which have plagued me. I was not able to overcome them until that lesson in which we learned about turning to Christ for strength to overcome our sins." She said, "Now I believe I have conquered them in the same way in which that boy overcame his wrongdoing."

Brothers and sisters, the people we teach are afraid. They have feelings of failure and guilt. And they need to believe in themselves, trust their own thinking, and lose themselves in loving their fellowmen.

I believe that the greatest moments of teaching consist mainly of knowing, understanding, and loving our students; but, in addition, we have in some way to open the door for them to give back to us—give of themselves, if you will—to find their faith and their courage, to find themselves.

There are many ways by which we can help them to do this. I only mention one or two. I think if we were to look into our own lives to know our own fears, hopes, and aspirations, we would understand their needs. I believe too that if we would study the life of the Savior and see his wonderful ways of drawing sinners to him, of rebuking people and having them still accept him and follow him, we would get many insights into the best ways by which we could let students give of themselves and find themselves. May we do this with all diligence, humility, and love, I pray, in the name of Jesus Christ. Amen.

VI
LEARNING HOW TO KNOW

At the ranch, about 1967

21

What Ought I to Do with Life?

What is life and what ought I to do with it? One of the most fascinating aspects of history is the struggle of mankind to understand life, this thing which is so interesting and dear to us and yet so difficult to comprehend. Great thinkers of past civilizations have left us their conclusions. Some have called life a blessing; others, like Buddha, have taught that life and the desire to live are the source of all our troubles and that we must escape from life.

All the explanations of the sages of the past have failed to satisfy the man of today. In earlier civilizations man was much more concerned about the world in which he lived than he was about man. Moreover, life was more simple, with fewer explanations. It was, no doubt, easier to choose between them.

In recent centuries mankind has increased rapidly on the earth. Man has produced many goods. He lives and thinks in terms of these products of his hands and mind. Not only his material life but also his intellectual life is far richer and more complex today than ever before. And yet all the accumulated knowledge and the numerous theories of men leave us with the fundamental question: What ought I to do with life?

The problems of life have not changed so much as have our living conditions. We still begin life in the same manner. We entertain and worry our parents in much the same way. In modern times schoolteachers in increasing numbers have been added to the list of those whom we vex and cause to wonder. As we approach young manhood and young womanhood, our schoolwork or the task of earning a livelihood tends to make us reflective. Or some new experience in

---

Not long after he received his doctorate and returned home from Europe (December 1933), Lowell Bennion wrote What About Religion?, *a lesson manual for M Men and Gleaners (sixteen-to-eighteen-year-olds) of the Church's Mutual Improvement Association. This is the first chapter of that manual.*

life, such as the blunt questions of someone younger, the conversations of an old man, the loss of someone close to our lives, or the responsibilities of parenthood, awakens us to the realities and problems of life.

There is only one thing we should do about any problem—try to solve it. Most people make an effort, either feeble or great, to find the solution. Many of them conclude that there is no solution to be found, and just keep "livin'." They adjust themselves to their lack of success and go on sailing. Some drift through life like a ship without a sail. Others find a rudder which guides them to one port after another, although they must always decide which way to turn the rudder.

Here we shall not concern ourselves so much with that which other people do. Each individual must meet life's problem himself. It is a personal matter which we shall discuss together. The burning question is: Who can tell me what I ought to do? Where can I look for an answer or for help?

Science

Science has been slow in coming into its own. The Medieval church jealously tried to monopolize all avenues to truth by denying that reason, as expressed in experimental science, was a path leading to knowledge. Its error deprived mankind of the blessings of science and eventually destroyed much of man's faith in that which he had thought to be true religion. The fact that the source of religious truth—revelation from God—was, as is very evident, lacking in the church of the Middle Ages, coupled with the fact that the principles of Christ were at low ebb in practice, added one misfortune to another.

In our day the situation has been quite reversed. We have learned to acknowledge and encourage scientific research and to benefit from scientific discoveries. We are interested and active in scientific pursuits. Today men look to science for enlightenment where they once turned to religion for guidance. Therefore I may well ask: What does science offer me in the solution of the problem? What ought I to do?

Science teaches us how to do things—what can be done. It has given us the tools and means of reaching certain goals or attaining certain ends. When the pioneers left Nauvoo, they had one of three choices as to how to get to the Rocky Mountains—in wagons, on horseback, or on foot. Today we have the same possibilities and, in addition, the automobile, the bus, train, or airplane. Science has increased our means and ways of doing things.

Why did the pioneers go west? Did they base their decision on science? The fact that they could go in a wagon did not determine their decision. The problem for each one was, "What ought I to do? Stay here in a prosperous section of the country where land is cheap, fertile, and available or keep my faith and go to the unknown, ill-reputed West?" It was a question of values. Science could tell them what the possibilities were and how to attain each possibility, but not which one should be chosen.

Today science offers the young man called to go on a mission the possible routes and means of transportation to his field. It tells him how to get there. That question does not worry us anymore. The thing the young man wants to know is, "Ought I to go?" Science will further tell him what his possibilities are: going to school, going to work, or going on a mission. But again it does not make the choice. The choice depends on one's philosophy of life.

Science produces the airplane which may carry mail or passengers. It may be used to rush aid to a sick child or assistance to a lost party. Or it may be used to bomb and destroy civilizations. Science puts in our hands the means to maintain or to destroy life. It leaves man to decide what he will do with that means. That will depend on his reverence or lack of reverence for life—a problem which is not controlled by science.

The accomplished physician of today understands, in many cases and to a certain extent, how to preserve and prolong life. The accomplishments of medical science are marvelous and have been of great benefit to mankind. Compared with the craft of the primitive medicine man, its results are astounding. The conscientious physician works on the assumption that life is worth saving. And yet he knows no more about the meaning of life perhaps than did the medicine man. His science has taught him how to save life but not that life is worth saving.

If I can learn from some source or other what I ought to do, science will render me great service in helping me to understand how to do it.

Everyday Experience

Experience is a good teacher. Science is but one form of experience pursued methodically with definite aims in view. What are the sources of experience? We have (1) the experience of past ages recorded as history, (2) the experience of associates, if we care to consider it, and (3) our own experience.

The chief disadvantage of experience is that it is limited. We know too little of history. Our associates and elders are only human, as are we; hence their experience is limited to a few years. It is highly instructive but not absolute. Men have different experiences and interpret them differently. Men whom we respect and honor for various reasons have had different experiences, cherish different ideals, and give different advice. Whom should I follow? My own experience, although invaluable to me and very personal, is greatly limited. It alone has not told me what I ought to do. On the contrary, it has just led me to ask the question and ponder over it.

Finally, the old adage, "Experience is a dear teacher," is only too true. The man who lost his fortune in the stock-market crash may vow never to speculate again—sweet consolation to him if he is old and in dire need of the necessities of life. The man who loses his good name or his own self-respect ordinarily would not do it a second time—if he had it to lose.

We do not wish to minimize the value of experience. Life is an experience. Experience is, however, experimental. It seldom leads us to absolute truths. As in the case of science, its chief value lies in telling us what can be done based on what has been done. It points out the various paths men have chosen in the past. It is particularly uncertain as to the future, since new situations are always opening up in the lives of nations and individuals.

Human experience, vast and interesting as it is, has not as yet solved the problem of life. Men are asking more and more: What ought we to do?

Religion

The very fact that science and experience, including philosophy, have not as yet given us absolute truths nor answered the question "What ought I to do?" is sufficient reason to give religion a chance. What does religion claim to have that these other fields of thought and life do not give us? It claims as its own an original source of knowledge and power not recognized in the method of science. (Although many scientists may believe in religion, it is not a part of the science itself.) That source of knowledge and power is God.

Consider the two possibilities: (1) a life in which man is left entirely on his own resources to solve the mysteries and problems of life, and (2) a life in which another Being, far superior in intelligence and far richer in experience, points the way and offers a guiding hand. One may argue that both possibilities are challenging. That is true. The difficulty with the first is that it involves a tremendous amount of waste and often disaster and failure. The individual life seems often to be wrecked before one discovers what one ought to do.

The second possibility, in which God plays the directing role, is by no means without a challenge or devoid of the chance of being both ingenious and courageous. No one in his right mind has ever insisted that we know too much or that God has done everything for us. Life is still teeming with problems and questions. Man is still engaged in a struggle with nature, with man, and with himself. The difference in these two proposed possibilities lies in the fact that under the direction of God, we are all sure of our goal and the journey of life can be enjoyable and profitable.

The very purpose of religion is to tell us what we ought to do. It does so by giving us new light on the meaning and purpose of human life. It even goes a long way in teaching us how to live. For example, the Word of Wisdom is a guide in matters of mental and physical health, and the Great Commandment, "Love thy neighbour as thyself," is a key to happy human relations.

Religion inspires idealism and courage, which express themselves in action. Glance back through the pages of history and see how religion has changed the world—not always for good, because it has been misunderstood, misinterpreted, and even falsified. In your mind try to erase the lives of the great religious leaders and their movements from history. How does the picture look? Whatever your verdict may be, you will admit that religion has played a tremendous role in the past. That alone should stimulate us to consider it.

How has religion affected the lives of individuals? What did it do to the life of the first member of your family who accepted Mormonism, whether he was one of the early pioneers or a recent convert from the old country? How has it changed your life directly, or indirectly through the lives of your parents and grandparents?

Yes, you will say, religion offers an answer, promises to be a real help—even indispensable—if it is true and if God lives. You want to be sure that religion is something more than another name for a certain part of philosophy. You wish to know that it comes from God and is not just man's wondering and thinking about God.

Mormonism claims to be a revealed, and not a man-made, religion. We have seen the need for such knowledge that God could give to man. If that need is felt, then let us consider together in ensuing discussions what the message of religion is and finally on what grounds such a message and answer to our problem rests.

22

Faith: Values and Limitations

Faith permeates the religious life as sap runs through every branch of a living tree. Faith is as vital to religion as the circulation of the blood is to the body. Faith nourishes and motivates the religious life as the root system feeds a plant. Without faith, religion loses its most distinctive element. Our most basic beliefs about God, Christ, and man rest in good part on faith. Our most fundamental ways of living religion, such as repentance, service, love, and forgiveness, are expressions of faith. It is logical, therefore, that the first principle of religion is generally considered to be faith.

The very fact that so much of religion rests on faith is disturbing to some earnest college students. In their philosophical studies they are encouraged to question, to doubt, and to be critical. In their scientific studies they are taught to think factually and objectively—to weigh, measure, observe, and describe with the faculties of the mind and the senses wide awake. To ask a student thus engaged in critical thought and careful experimentation to accept things on faith sometimes seems to him to be asking too much. Religion appears sometimes to rest on mere credulity, something for which trained minds have little respect.

It is the purpose of this chapter to examine the nature of faith, to consider what it is, its values and limitations. Its relationship to knowledge and belief also needs to be considered. In short, an effort will be made to ascertain whether faith has a legitimate and helpful role to play in the life of the student.

Faith, like so many important intangibles of life, such as truth, beauty, and goodness, is not easy to define. And yet it must be given

---

In 1959 Lowell Bennion published Religion and the Pursuit of Truth, *his most thorough study of the different ways of knowing the truth and of the contributions the various disciplines and components of life can make to religious seeking. Reprinted here are parts of the section on how the adventurous, creative quality of faith is crucial to the pursuit of religious truth.*

some definition, or one's contemplation of this principle will be confusing and meaningless. The scriptures exhort us to live by faith. They illustrate its nature on many pages, but define the term only two or three times and then only briefly. In Hebrews we read: "Now faith is the substance of things hoped for, the evidence of things not seen." (Hebrews 11:1.)

And in Alma we read: "And now as I said concerning faith—faith is not to have a perfect knowledge of things; therefore if ye have faith ye hope for things which are not seen, which are true." (Alma 32:21.)

A number of definitions from writers and thinkers will be given here, and then what seem to be the essential elements of faith will be extracted.

> Faith is that power within us which impels us to act without our knowing the result of that act. (F. B. Hammond.)

> Faith is the personal resolve to take risks, to adventure forth on a hazardous quest (living is always a hazardous quest; we stand in jeopardy every hour). . . . Faith, then, is loyal and courageous affirmation of the highest values man envisages. It is a bold and risky confidence in the response of reality to our deepest needs and highest interests. (From Joseph A. Leighton, *The Field of Philosophy* [New York: D. Appleton and Co., 1930].)

> Faith is a hypothesis, held in all humility in the absence of ultimate proof and in the hope of an increasing clarification. (Jonathan Swift.)

> Religion deals on the side of faith with the uncharted region of human experience. (Gilbert Murray.)

> The faith-state is the sense of the exceedingness of the possible over the real. (William James.)

> The fact of accepting or the disposition to accept as real, true, or the like that which is not supported by sensible evidence or rational proofs. (*Webster's Unabridged Dictionary*.)

> Faith is at once an affirmation of truth and surrendering to the truth affirmed. Apart from the first it would be blind; apart from the second, without practical significance. (Morgan, in *Encyclopedia of Religion and Ethics,* 5:589.)

> Faith is reason grown courageous. (Sir Wilfred Grenfell.)

> Faith is to act with confidence in realities not factually and not rationally known nor proven. (Anonymous.)

> Faith is the sphere of the possible. (Anonymous.)

Goethe said: "Human life divided by reason leaves a remainder." Faith deals with that remainder.

Considering the above statements about faith, what, may we conclude, are its basic characteristics?

The Essential Elements of Faith

I

While one of the most essential ingredients of faith is feeling, it cannot be confined to feeling alone. Faith also includes and presupposes rational factors such as belief, the power of imagination, and the ability to construct hypotheses. However, unlike knowledge, which is abstract and symbolic of reality, faith is concrete experience. Faith is felt. Belief and hypothesis are swallowed up, as it were, by feeling, which becomes the dominant emphasis in the experience of faith.

To say that faith is essentially feeling does not discredit it. Life itself is experienced more in feeling than in thought. Motivation to work, play, love, and create is born largely of feeling, and all of life's satisfactions are felt.

A freshman student became considerably upset one day because her psychology teacher had said in class that if feeling were taken out of religion, there would be nothing left. The student, of course, had interpreted the statement as a criticism of religion. But whether or not it was a criticism, it needed amplification and qualification. In the first place, religion is more than feeling. The great religions of mankind contain ideas which relate concretely to human behavior. Anyone who has read Deuteronomy, Amos, Isaiah, or Luke would know this. But—and this is equally important—if religion did nothing more than help man feel right and feel deeply about life, it would be justified, because feeling is a large part of living. Humility, faith, and love are essentially feelings, or attitudes; and they make their rich contributions to life. No apology need be made for faith because it is, in good part, a state of feeling.

Because faith is linked with feeling, it need not be evanescent and whimsical, without substance and, like a soap bubble, easy to burst, even though the faith of some people is of this kind—blind, inconstant, and without foundation. A strong, solid, and enduring faith is grounded in knowledge and experience. And, like aesthetic feeling, Christian love, and other emotional states, faith may not only abide, but may increase in strength and richness. Later in this chapter the relationship of faith to knowledge will be discussed. Then it will be seen how a solid faith is grounded in knowledge and experience.

II

Faith varies in strength and character from person to person, and even from time to time in the same person's life. This is to be expected of something so personal and subjective as faith. Faith then is not cut and dried, is not fixed and static, but is something as dynamic as life itself. It may lie anywhere between mere hope and certitude, which is a feeling of complete assurance. Between these two extremes, faith of various degrees is experienced by almost everyone. In some things, a person's faith is as strong and sturdy as an oak tree; in other things, it may bend with the wind like a weeping willow tree. Faith is a product of one's total life-experience. As this experience increases, one's faith in certain people and in things and ideas is bound to increase or to decrease.

III

Faith relates to the unknown, to things unseen or not yet realized. This is evident in many definitions quoted above, including the two from Hebrews and Alma. Here again faith is different from knowledge, for knowledge relates to the past. Knowledge is awareness of reality through repeated and verifiable experiences. If one knows a thing, he no longer needs to have faith in it, as Alma declared: "Yea, there are many who do say: If thou wilt show unto us a sign from heaven, then we shall know of a surety; then we shall believe. Now I ask, is this faith? Behold, I say unto you, Nay; for if a man knoweth a thing he hath no cause to believe, for he knoweth it." (Alma 32:17-18.)

Faith is the sphere of the possible. It is an hypothesis, suggested by the existence of some facts, but projecting beyond these to the realm of what might be or could be. This characteristic of faith is readily illustrated in a couple's feelings about marriage. The typical couple approaching marriage will say that they know they will be happy. This they cannot possibly know from experience or logic. Having never been married to each other and being aware of the unhappiness and the divorce statistics for married people today, a couple can only believe and feel that they will succeed. Marriage is consummated in faith, and this should be recognized by the participants. The success of each marriage is only a possibility envisioned by faith.

IV

Faith is adventurous and creative. It not only is the sphere of the possible, but is also the power which often makes the possible come into being. Faith is that remarkable quality of the human spirit which first envisages the possibilities of life, then lives as though these possibilities were realities, and by this action often makes them real. In the realm of knowledge, one conforms to what is; in the realm of faith, one creates life after the image carried in his heart. Faith adds another dimension to life. Recognizing the borders of knowledge, it transcends them.

Jesus recognized this wonderfully creative, dynamic power of faith. He likened it unto a mustard seed and said that he who had faith even as a grain of mustard seed could move mountains; that nothing would be impossible to him. Faith is like a seed because of its great potential to multiply itself, to increase reality. Faith is like yeast in its capacity to expand and enlarge whatever it becomes a part of. Faith is like a tree that takes root, grows, buds, blossoms, and bears fruit. . . .

V

Faith impels action. In the language of James, "Faith without works is dead." One might also say that faith without works is not faith, but mere belief. Then belief is not feeling, or assurance, but is a thing of the mind. A person says he believes something is so when he thinks it is, but is not sure. Belief might be called uncertain knowledge, or one's best guess about something. Many beliefs do not compel action; they are merely opinions concerning things. For example, even though he attends the University of Iowa, a student may believe that Ohio State University will win the conference football championship. This is purely an intellectual conclusion; no action is taken to support the belief. Such a person may even cheer against the team he believes will win. Faith, in contrast to belief, is a conviction which leads to action. And actions mirror quite accurately the character and strength of one's faith.

Faith That Is Blind

In our discussion of faith thus far, its positive qualities have been stressed. Indeed, if men could always exercise faith in things not seen and not yet realized which are good and true, living by faith would always prove rewarding.

The truth is, however, that people experience much the same feeling of hope and assurance in things that are not good. One can also place his trust and faith in that which is not true. This experience turns out to be blind faith—not the kind that is based on knowledge and experience or quickened by the spirit of Deity. And yet it is commonly called faith and has feelings in common with it.

Two illustrations may help: A couple marries with little understanding of each other's personalities and with even less knowledge of the nature of marriage. But their minds and hearts are full of hope, adventure, confidence—attitudes which accompany the feeling of faith. Their blind faith often leads them not to bliss, but to the divorce court. Or, to cite another example, two men form a business partnership. Visions of mutual benefit and profit gladden their hearts and blur their vision of reality. They too visualize unmade profits as already won. But their naive trust in each other may also be shattered on the hard anvil of reality.

Men can also be disillusioned in religion. Through the ages, in the name of religion, men have frequently and continuously been exercised by a faith in things which appeared to be real, and in things which could not fulfill their hopes. They have worshipped gods of wood and stone made by their own hands. Divine favor has been sought through sacrifice of the firstborn. Revelry, prostitution, infanticide, suicide, flattery, deception, bribery, and lip service have been used to ingratiate the gods, and even God, but to no avail. Religious feeling can be as blind as any other expression of faith. And when it is blind, it takes a person out of touch with reality just as does any other ill-founded faith.

Faith and Knowledge

Faith should not be considered a substitute for knowledge. Whenever knowledge is available, it should be used. For it is generally better to live by knowledge in particular things than by faith, if knowledge is available. A man would rather know that he has money in the bank when he writes a check than to write it in the faith that the money is there. It is better for a man to know that his bride-to-be has a good character than to marry her without knowledge of this fact. It would be better to know the cause of cancer than merely to have faith that by refraining from eating certain foods one would not become a victim. An appreciation for the great role of faith in life should never deter us in our search for knowledge. *It is knowing the truth that makes men free.*

Faith is a means of reaching out to gain more knowledge, like a searchlight casting its beam ahead into the "uncharted region of our existence." Man lives in a law-abiding universe. This is the faith of both the scientist and the religionist. Man satisfies his needs and attains his goals by learning and by lending obedience to both the laws of nature and the moral laws of God. Faith was never intended to be a blind substitute for knowledge, but rather an impelling motivation to seek and to know reality. The Savior seems to indicate this in the following statement: "Then Jesus said to those Jews *which believed on him, If ye will continue in my word,* then are ye my disciples indeed, and *ye shall know the truth, and the truth shall make you free.*" (John 8:21-22; emphasis added.)

In Alma's inspiring discourse on faith (Alma 32:27-43), the object of the experiment with faith which he recommends is that it will lead us to knowledge. Men of faith need not be indifferent to knowledge nor in any sense minimize its worth in order to glorify faith. There is ample need of and room for both a sound faith and all the knowledge we can gain. The gospel plan teaches the wisdom of walking by faith in this life. It also teaches us to seek knowledge and to obey the laws of life. No matter how much knowledge a person gains, he is increasingly aware of how much of his life is lived by faith.

A sound faith needs roots. It should, as has already been mentioned, be grounded in knowledge, experience, and revelation. Like a house, its walls should be laid on good foundations lest in time they crack and crumble. Faith should not be considered an enemy to knowledge, nor a competitor. The student should not feel compelled to choose between faith and knowledge. Let him gain and use knowledge where it is available. Let him walk by faith where knowledge is not available. Let his faith include, but transcend his knowledge.

The relationship of faith and knowledge is not like this:

Faith *or* Knowledge

It may be more truly represented in this way:

Faith ⇨ Knowledge ⇨ Faith ⇨ Knowledge

There is no genuine faith without some knowledge. However, knowledge, by its very nature, is limited. Any quest for it is a venture in faith. Any acquirement of it only makes one aware of his need for more faith.

Faith as "reason grown courageous" will ever be an essential need of life. The simple faith of a child is a beautiful and touching thing to observe. Sometimes, however, under the storm and stress of life, it proves to be as fragile as a piece of pottery. It is difficult, if not impossible, for a person to retain his childhood faith as he grows to maturity. Why should he not strengthen and mature his faith until it is the full expression of his whole mind and heart? The late Guy C. Wilson frequently quoted the following statement to illustrate the relationship of faith and reason:

> Faith is a conviction born in the mind that has looked at all the facts available and found in them a meaning with which the soul can rest in peace. It does not abhor an invitation to think—for it is the result of the thinking of a mind that is candid and unafraid. (Author unknown; from notes taken at a lecture by Guy C. Wilson.)

Religious Faith

Faith, as it has been discussed and illustrated thus far, is not limited to religion. In every walk of life, as one lives in the present and looks to the future, one necessarily exercises faith—lives in anticipation of accomplishments and realities not yet known. The attitude of faith is necessary in all human relationships: in marriage, business, sports, politics, war, and peace.

Even science and philosophy, which place so much value on the use of reason, are based on certain assumptions of faith. The scientist, for example, trusts his senses, believing that they report the world quite accurately. He believes also in a world of law and order, of cause and effect. He believes he can think and that thinking is worthwhile. These assumptions, he feels, have been verified through science. Still they remain assumptions. Although the doctor assumes that life is worth living, he cannot prove it with all his science. Faith underlies all of his work in the highly honored practice of medicine.

Religion has no monopoly on faith, nor is the experience of faith in religion wholly different from the experience of faith in everyday life. In both instances one faces the future and the unknown with a limited knowledge and with a feeling of hope and assurance. Religious faith is characterized largely by a difference in its objective.

Characteristics of Religious Faith

1. Religion gives man faith that his life has meaning and purpose. In daily life and in the specialized sciences, faith is usually expressed in some particular thing or process. In contrast, religion is primarily concerned with the meaning of man's whole existence. Is the universe indifferent to man's fate, or is there an intelligent Being who is re-

alizing his benevolent purposes in human life? Most religions are based on the faith that life is not a matter of chance, not the result of the operation of impersonal forces, but is the result of divine wisdom and planning. . . .

"Wherefore, brethren, seek not to counsel the Lord, but to take counsel from his hand. For behold, ye yourselves know that he counseleth in wisdom, and in justice, and in great mercy, over all his works." (Jacob 4:10.)

The man of religious faith believes that life is meaningful and potentially good because it is the creation of God who "counseleth in wisdom, and in justice, and in great mercy, over all his works."

According to our Christian faith, man's life on earth is purposeful, part of a divine and eternal plan. And though we don't have all the answers about many particulars, our religion sustains us in the positive feeling of faith toward the whole of life.

2. A second characteristic of religious faith, closely allied to the first, may be called a total commitment. Just as religion is an attitude of faith in the overall meaning and purpose of life, it is also a total and complete commitment on the part of the true believer. In daily life we commit ourselves again and again to some task or obligation. We sign contracts, make loans, register for courses of study, promise to love, honor, and cherish one another in marriage, and swear an oath of allegiance to the constitution of our country. These are individual and specific commitments, some of which are only of short duration. None of them embraces our complete feeling about the whole of life.

Religious faith means the dedication of one's whole life "in search, reverence, and service" to the object of one's faith, to the great purpose of life. Religion means a commitment of the whole self to that which is supreme, highest, and best in life and in the universe. Religious faith is no partial, limited, or temporary loyalty. It is a devotion to the whole of life in its highest spiritual meaning now and forever as long as religious faith is real. This complete commitment is often indicated and encouraged in scripture. . . .

> O, remember, my son, and learn wisdom in thy youth; yea, learn in thy youth to keep the commandments of God. Yea, and cry unto God for all thy support; yea, let all thy doings be unto the Lord, and whithersoever thou goest let it be in the Lord; yea, let thy thoughts be directed unto the Lord; yea, let the affections of thy heart be placed upon the Lord forever. Counsel with the Lord in all thy doings, and he will direct thee for good; yea, when thou liest

> down at night lie down unto the Lord, that he may watch over you in your sleep; and when thou risest in the morning let thy heart be full of thanks unto God; and if ye do these things, ye shall be lifted up at the last day. (Alma 37:35-37.)

Jesus' words to Nicodemus, who came to him by night wishing to know how to enter into the kingdom of God, illustrate the wholeness of religious conviction. Jesus said to him, "Verily, verily, I say unto thee, Except a man be born again, he cannot see the kingdom of God." (John 3:3.) Nicodemus was confused, thinking Jesus meant he had to be born again of his mother in the flesh. But Jesus had reference to finding a new faith, becoming a new person in one's religious and moral outlook, living a new spiritual life. Baptism by water and the gift of the Holy Ghost were means of helping man to bear witness of his spiritual rebirth.

3. Religious faith is idealistic and aspirational. All the great religions of mankind are striving to help men to be better persons, to live on a higher moral plane, to forsake hate, greed, and selfishness; and to be just, kind, and merciful toward their fellowmen. Isaiah's plea, in the name of Deity, is typical of this characteristic of religious faith:

"Wash you, make you clean; put away the evil of your doings from before mine eyes; cease to do evil; learn to do well; seek judgment, relieve the oppressed, judge the fatherless, plead for the widow." (Isaiah 1:16-17.)

The entire Sermon on the Mount, given in Matthew 5–7, is a call to idealistic and nobler living, challenging man to be like God in his impartiality and love—"Be ye therefore perfect, even as your Father which is in heaven is perfect." (Matthew 5:48. Note verses 43-48.)

Faith in the improvement of human nature, in man's perfectability, slow, long, and discouraging though it be, is implicit in the Hebrew, early Christian, and Latter-day Saint faiths. This is true not only of individuals, but is also the goal of society. Prophets of God have been concerned continuously with the establishment of a righteous people of Zion, a social condition among men where justice, mercy, peace, and good will may prevail. . . .

4. Another characteristic of religious faith is this: It involves the will; it calls for moral and spiritual action. Religious faith inspires moral effort. In contrast, often when one, in faith, projects a hypothesis in science to explain the facts, the imagination is simply being exercised and the scientist acts upon intellectual hunches and curi-

osity. When a man acts on faith in business, he does so for economic gain and perhaps in the spirit of adventure. But neither in business nor in science is man often required to exercise his full moral or spiritual capacities, whereas religious faith calls for self-discipline, self-control, humility, repentance, meekness, and other attributes of character.

5. Finally, in religion as in any other field of life, we will ever walk by faith in this life. It is not true that the whole of religion is simply a matter of faith, as some people are heard to say. The brotherhood that men share in the name of the gospel of Jesus Christ is real, and its joyous fruits can be known by direct and repeated acquaintance. Likewise, the worth of the moral and religious teachings of the Sermon on the Mount can be verified in everyday living. The good fruits of repentance, humility, and love can be tasted, as can be the bitter fruits of arrogance, pride, and hate. However, it appears that man will never outgrow his need of faith in the overall meaning and purpose of his life. And, no matter how strong one's testimony of God, Christ, and personal immortality may be, it contains elements of faith as well as the witness of the Spirit. We would not wish it to be otherwise. Religion too should be dynamic, creative, and great adventure if it is to satisfy man's moral and spiritual aspiration.

Granted that religious faith has many desirable features, that it would enhance life by giving it increased significance and motivation, the question still arises, how does one gain this faith? Is it a gift from God? Or may it be won, even as knowledge, by one's own effort? The answer is neither simple nor single.

Avenues to Faith

1. The scriptures bear witness that there is a light emanating from Deity which inclines men to believe in God and to have faith in that which is good:

> For behold, my brethren, it is given unto you to judge, that ye may know good from evil; and the way to judge is as plain, that ye may know with a perfect knowledge, as the daylight is from the dark night.
>
> For behold, the Spirit of Christ is given to every man, that he may know good from evil; wherefore, I show unto you the way to judge; for everything which inviteth to do good, and to persuade to believe in Christ, is sent forth by the power and gift of Christ; wherefore ye may know with a perfect knowledge it is of God. . . .
>
> Wherefore I beseech of you, brethren, that ye should search

> diligently in the light of Christ that ye may know good from evil; and if ye will lay hold upon every good thing, and condemn it not, ye certainly will be a child of Christ. (Moroni 7:15-16, 19.)

In this sense, faith is a gift of God. But it lies within the power of man to receive or to reject the influence of the Spirit of God. The gift of faith, like a muscle, becomes strong with use and weak with neglect.

2. A second avenue to faith is study. The scriptures contain beautiful stories, reflections on life, wise counsel, evidence of God's dealings with his prophets, and propositions to which our minds and hearts respond with faith. This they cannot do, however, unless we are, through diligent inquiry, acquainted with the content of religion, unless we expose ourselves to the word and make ourselves receptive to its influence. Jesus said, "Ask, and it shall be given you; seek, and ye shall find; knock, and it shall be opened unto you."(Matthew 7:7.)

3. A sure way to build faith is to live by faith. Even as we know flavor by tasting, so we can also come to feel and know in our hearts the truth and worth of religion by partaking of it. Jesus said, "to those Jews which believed on him, If ye continue in my word, then are ye my disciples indeed; and ye shall know the truth, and the truth shall make you free." (John 8:31-32.) On another occasion, he also answered the question of how we can know the truth in this way:

> Now about the midst of the feast Jesus went up into the temple, and taught. And the Jews marvelled, saying, How knoweth this man letters, having never learned? Jesus answered them, and said, My doctrine is not mine, but his that sent me. If any man will do his will, he shall know of the doctrine, whether it be of God, or whether I speak of myself. He that speaketh of himself seeketh his own glory: but he that seeketh his glory that sent him, the same is true, and no unrighteousness is in him. (John 7:14-18.)

One learns the value of work by working, of play by playing, of food by eating; and one learns the value of faith by exercising faith, of love by trying to love fellowmen. Even so, if one would have faith in God, he must at least say to himself, "It could be that he lives. I shall give the idea a fair trial. I shall do his will. I shall read the scriptures, especially the life of Jesus, and I shall try to live as God would have me live. I shall at least give religion a fair chance in my life."

However faith may come to one, it does not come fully mature. Like flowers, trees, and children, it must grow and increase. This need for gradual growth in faith is explained in Alma's great discourse (Alma 32:14-43) in the Book of Mormon. The writer is fair and suggests that we exercise only enough belief to make an experiment with faith. His words deserve a careful reading.

A Postscript

In this discussion of faith we have been dealing with it in a broad and general way—in a sense which might fit any religious group. Each religious movement also has its own particular objects of faith. The Moslems declare faith, for example, in Allah and in Muhammad as his prophet. The Jews declare, "Hear, O Israel: the Lord our God is one Lord."

Latter-day Saints declare their faith in many things. The most comprehensive, though by no means complete, statement of our faith is given in the thirteen Articles of Faith. At the heart of these lies the most central principle of all—*faith in the Lord Jesus Christ.* To Latter-day Saints, Christ is central. Through him we can overcome death, ignorance, and sin. Through him we can come to know God and attain unto eternal life.

23

"Seek Ye Wisdom"

My dear brethren and friends: President [David O.] McKay has asked me to talk to the youth of the Church about education. I am not particularly grateful for this task, but I am thankful for his trust and faith in me. I am also grateful for the example which he has set for us in the field of education. President McKay loves the Lord with all his mind, as well as with his heart and soul. I know this from personal experience.

On several occasions when I have dared to impose upon him with problems that were very critical to me, I have always come away satisfied in my mind as well as in my heart. One thing he taught me when I first began to teach in the Church has been extremely helpful. He said, "Brother Bennion, remember, words do not convey meanings; they call them forth." I speak out of the context of my experience, and you listen out the context of yours, and that is why communication is difficult. I don't expect to be fully understood tonight nor that you will agree with everything that is said, and I certainly invite President [Hugh B.] Brown to qualify and correct anything that he feels he should.

It is also inspiring to me that President McKay in his ninety-fifth year should be thinking of the future and putting himself in the place of youth as he planned the theme of this meeting.

If we take a look at Church history, we find that education has played an important, proud role. The process of education began even before the Church was organized. We usually think of the beginning of the Latter-day Saint movement as having taken place in the Sacred Grove in that glorious First Vision of the Father and the Son. To me this is not entirely accurate. The initial beginning of our faith took place, I believe, in the mind of a youth. The boy Joseph in his fifteenth

---

This address was given at the priesthood session of general conference, April 6, 1968, and was published in the June 1968 Improvement Era *and in the official Conference Report.*

year had questions; he was searching; he was eager to know. You should read again the familiar story, his own story, in the Pearl of Great Price. I was struck this week to notice what an emphasis he placed on learning, on asking. At a time of considerable controversy and great emotional excitement, he said in retrospect, "My mind was called up to serious reflection." And the biblical passage which stirred him the most was that famous verse from James, "If any of you lack wisdom, let him ask of God. . . . " (James 1:5.) "Never," he wrote, "did any passage of scripture come with more power to the heart of man than this did at this time to mine. . . . I reflected on it again and again, knowing that if any person needed wisdom from God, I did." (Joseph Smith–History 1:12.)

Unknowingly, and unconsciously perhaps, the boy Joseph carried out the admonition of the Savior, "Ask, and it shall be given you; seek, and ye shall find; knock, and it shall be opened unto you." (Matthew 7:7.)

There is no finer symbol or characterization of the Mormon movement to me than to think of the boy Joseph going to the woods, in his own words, "on the morning of a beautiful, clear day, early in the spring," kneeling, offering a prayer, asking questions of the God in heaven. Joseph's search did not end there. The gospel and Church of Christ were not revealed from heaven in their entirety like the blueprints of an architect's building plans. Rather, Joseph continued to ask questions. He had searching questions that he was asking to find solutions to his problems, and he received "line upon line, precept upon precept; here a little, and there a little." (D&C 128:21.) Only in response to hungry minds, to earnest questions of the boy prophet and of his associates, did the Father, Son, and Holy Ghost, it seems to me, reveal their mind.

Very soon after the First Vision, Joseph not only prayed, but he also studied, as has already been indicated in President McKay's remarks.

The first temple built by the Latter-day Saints in Kirtland, Ohio, the most sacred of all buildings in the Church, was also used for the School of the Prophets. There they studied not only scripture and theology, but also Hebrew and German; and they were taught to learn by study and also by faith, and to seek wisdom out of the best books.

It is remarkable to me too, brethren, that when the Saints came to the West, struggling to conquer the desert under the leadership of that very practical leader, Brigham Young, that he, a man without formal education, talked about education a great deal. He was always encouraging the Saints to study science and all things. In fact, he said that Mormonism embraces all truth; even if the infidel has it, it belongs to us.

We have a proud history of education in the Church that includes the development of auxiliary organizations, academies, colleges, Brigham Young University, institutes and seminaries. Generations of Latter-day Saints have been inspired by this philosophy and by the beginnings of our faith to go on in higher education. Our fathers, grandfathers, and great-grandfathers have gone east and west in this country, with faith that any knowledge they could gain was consistent and in harmony with the gospel of Jesus Christ.

What about our education today in the Church? Are you and I as hungry to know? Are we aware of our lack of wisdom? Are our minds burning and hungering and thirsting for knowledge, as I think Joseph's was, and Brigham Young's, and my father's, and others? We inherit land and money and debts and other things, but education is not inherited any more than character is. The German poet Goethe said, "What from your father's heritage is lent, earn it anew to really possess it." We inherit only the opportunity, the tradition, and I hope the motivation to seek learning and wisdom and education.

I think there are several reasons why you young people should be earnestly engaged in all kinds of education, including secular training. The first reason I would give is that we live in a technological age. Unskilled labor is fast diminishing, going by the boards. Unskilled jobs are decreasing. They are poorly paid. One is expendable if one's only talent is common, untrained physical work. On the other hand, there has never been such a demand for trained people, both technical and professional. Back in depression years engineers came out of the universities and were glad to take a job at a filling station or any other kind of work. Today, anybody who is trained as a teacher, social worker, nurse, doctor, lawyer, dentist—name what you will—is in great demand, is well paid, and I think, generally speaking, his work is more interesting than that of common labor, though not always.

The frontiers which Mormons have known in the past—the desert, the plains, the prairies, rugged mountain passes, "hole in the rock"—are no longer there. Today's frontiers are human and social, spiritual and moral. They were mentioned in this morning's meeting by several of our speakers—air pollution, water pollution, crime, delinquency, family disorganization, war, racial strife. The resolution of these problems calls for training, as well as for character and faith.

Secondly, I believe that we should seek education for education's sake. I would not spend my time encouraging young people to get more education simply to make more money, or to live a life of ease, or to gain status in this world. My chief reason for encouraging education is that I believe that the essence of man is his brain, his mind, his spirit; and I think a person who does not cultivate his mind will not fulfill his life. His life will end in frustration and disappointment.

Let me illustrate concretely, if I can. Last summer I was in the mountains with some young boys, and one day they found a nest of robins, just ready to leave their mother's nest. The boys wanted to take these robins and put them in a cage. I suggested that the robins would die if they did but let them do it; and sure enough, the boys put these little robins in a cage, gave them water, grain, and grass, and in two or three days they were dead. The reason they died is that birds do not belong in cages. Birds were made by the Creator to scratch in the earth and to soar in the sky. Birds have wings to fly. Put a bird in a cage and you destroy his nature.

Now you and I also find ourselves sometimes in cages, cages of our own making, and though we don't always die in these cages, we sometimes die a moral and spiritual death; and we find life shallow and meaningless. I haven't the time tonight to do any more than mention the kinds of things that get us in these cages, but in my experience alcohol does (I should have said "in my *observation*"). In my observation, these mind-expanding drugs do also. I have talked with a number of students and young people who have been caught up in this latest effort to find the meaning of life by running away from it, and what I observe is nothing but tragedy.

You and I don't indulge in alcohol, LSD, or marijuana, but we find ourselves in other cages. One of them is sitting as a spectator of life watching TV day and night. It is wonderful to watch a show occasionally, to refresh oneself and get away from the cares of the day, but to spend hour upon hour watching the trivia that comes across our movie house screens and TV screens sometimes is, I believe, a great disservice to one's life. Another tragic aspect of the life of contemporary man, in my judgment, is our hunger and thirst and lust for material things. We want new clothes, cars, homes, furniture, and drapes, and we spend most of our time, many of us, trying to achieve these material things with which we can identify. I think people who spend most of their life trying to make money and accumulate material goods will wake up with a taste of ashes in their mouths by and by.

Jesus said, " . . . for a man's life consisteth not in the abundance of the things which he possesseth." (Luke 12:15.) And he also said, "Be not anxious about the morrow, what ye shall eat and what ye shall drink, and wherewithal ye shall be clothed, but seek ye first the kingdom of God." (Matthew 6:34.) And I think he meant by that, seek ye first humility and repentance, meekness and integrity, mercy and peaceableness, purity of heart and sacrifice for fellowmen, and love—things of the spirit.

Buddha said, "In eating, fearing and sleeping, men and beasts are alike. Man excelleth the beast by engaging in religious practices; so why should a man, if he be without religion, not be equal to the beast?"

When I first read this, it struck home. In eating, fearing, and sleeping, men and beasts are alike. Man excelleth the beast by being human, by engaging in things of the spirit, of the mind, of the heart.

Brethren, how often do you contemplate the wonderful qualities and aspects of your mind? Imagination is one of the qualities of a human mind that I cherish deeply; it is the ability to take single images and to put them into a new image that has never existed before. Only a human being can reorganize life around him after his own image. Only the human mind, so far as we know, enjoys memory and can transcend time and space. Only human beings can keep the entire past with them. You and I can live with Jesus, Beethoven, Socrates, and our grandfathers. Animals only live in the present, driven by instinct. Only human beings have language, the power to symbolize feelings and ideas and to communicate. Imagination, memory, language—these are wonderful gifts of the human spirit.

Until a year or two ago I kept a pig. My pig never got his eyes above the trough, except when I came to feed him; and, brethren, when I went out to feed my pig, I thrilled at the color on Mount Olympus, and I pondered its geology, and worshipped at the foot of the mountain. I sang "O Ye Mountains High" to myself alone, and "For the Strength of the Hills." I like animals, but believe me, I am grateful for those qualities which are distinctly human and which are divine.

You and I were not only created in the physical image of our Father in heaven; we were also created in his spiritual image. And if the glory of God is intelligence, then the glory of man is also intelligence. If God is Creator, man must be creative to satisfy his soul. If God is love, man must be loving. If God is a person of integrity, then we must also be honest, to be true to our own nature, which we have inherited in part from him.

Another reason why I believe in education is that it is not enough to believe the gospel; it must also be understood, if we wish to live it. Ancient Israel lived their religion after a fashion, but were rejected by God for lack of knowledge. Hear the words of the prophet Hosea:

> Hear the word of the Lord, ye children of Israel: for the Lord hath a controversy with the inhabitants of the land, because there is not truth, nor mercy, nor knowledge of God in the land. . . .
>
> My people are destroyed for lack of knowledge: because thou hast rejected knowledge, I will also reject thee, . . . seeing thou hast forgotten the law of thy God. . . .
>
> For I desired mercy, and not sacrifice; and the knowledge of God more than burnt offerings. (Hosea 4:1, 6; 6:6.)

Brethren, the gospel is to be understood, as well as believed. The gospel has a beautiful structure about it. It has form. It is something like a beautiful Greek edifice, if you will. The Ten Commandments are related to each other; they hang together beautifully. They strengthen each other. The Beatitudes form, in the words of a scholar, a map of life, each one building on the preceding one. The wonderful attributes of God reinforce one another and give us a marvelous basis for a relationship with him. It seems to me that we need to reflect deeply upon the gospel of Jesus Christ in terms of its great fundamentals, and then we need to relate these fundamentals to the issues of the day.

How many of us apply the Golden Rule in business, in race relations in our country today, in relations between nations? Do we always remember free agency, as we deal with our co-workers, with our children, with our wives?

Just one more thought, brethren. By encouraging its youth to gain an education, to study at universities, the Church is encouraging our young people to think, and to think critically. Parents, church leaders, and even some of our students are afraid that in the process of learning, and of learning to think critically, some of our students will lose their faith. I must confess that some Latter-day Saints, college youth, do lose their religious faith as they encounter secular learning. However, I believe that this is not due primarily to their thinking. Some of our youth who do not go to college also lose their faith.

There are a hundred and one reasons why young people lose faith. Some who do go to college leave their religion behind at a very shallow level while they proceed to work on their Ph.Ds. Some discard religion before they have ever known it, before it has taken root in their lives. Others lose faith because they cease to practice religion and study it and live it. Still others lose faith because we their parents and teachers and leaders have not listened to their questions, have been too quick to condemn, have not respected their free agency and their honest thinking. Some lose faith because they do not distinguish between gospel principles and the actions of men. I recall a girl who lost her faith because a returned missionary asked that his engagement ring be returned. People live lives as a whole, and many factors influence their faith.

I dislike very much to see a wedge driven between faith and reason, between secular learning and religious living. It has been my great privilege to have known thousands of college youth who are bright, eager students in every field—in philosophy, in the social sciences, and in every other science. Thousands have kept the faith and are truly committed to both God and learning. But these people walk with humility, both in religion and in secular thought.

Last Sunday I was privileged to attend a priesthood meeting and Sunday School in Madison, Wisconsin. In these meetings graduate students, professors, businessmen, and intelligent wives were enriching each other's thinking immeasurably. This is a beautiful thing to behold, and it is happening in many areas of the Church. In the life of every Latter-day Saint, faith and morality, born of religion, should be wedded to all the knowledge and learning we can get from every source. It is not an easy marriage—faith and reason—and one will have to treat the other partner with great respect. Like marriages between men and women, there will be ongoing adjustments; mistakes will be made; forgiveness will be required; and some divorces will occur. But much of the conflict between faith and reason lies in the person, just as failures in marriage are usually due to limitations in husband or wife, or both, and not in the institution of marriage.

I repeat, let us not drive a wedge between faith and knowledge. We need both. I love my bishop, who is a businessman, and I have sought his counsel in spiritual and family affairs, but should the need arise, I shall not ask him to remove my appendix. The great problems facing us in the world today are far more intricate than an appendectomy. We need to unite all the faith and idealism the gospel can provide and to combine it with all the wisdom of human experience, no matter who has it.

Not all education is found in textbooks or in university halls. I have time to mention only one illustration in closing. I know a little lady listening in tonight who is nearly ninety-four years of age. When she was approximately ninety, she began to practice the organ. Last year the power went off in her home, in her apartment where she lives alone, and her daughter phoned and said, "Mother, is the power off?"

"Yes."

"I will come and bring you home to dinner."

And her mother said, "No, thank you."

"What will you do if the power doesn't come on?"

She answered, "I will light a candle and play my guitar."

I had a wonderful father who was an educator, but I have learned, I think, as much from this little woman who is my mother as I have from my father.

My message to you in closing is this: Light a candle. Light the candle that is within you, the candle that is your own eternal intelligence, which has also received the imprint of divinity in the spiritual creation of our Father in heaven.

I pray that we Latter-day Saints living today may learn to love the Lord our God with all our mind, as well as with our hearts and with our souls; I pray that we may hunger and thirst after righteousness, and after truth, and I ask it humbly, in the name of Jesus Christ. Amen.

24

Scriptures: Values and Limitations

Inspired of God but in Man's Language

Elder John A. Widtsoe had an interesting point of view on scripture: "The message of the scripture is divine; the words in which it is clothed are human. Failure to make this distinction has led to much misunderstanding. Intelligent readers will separate the message of the scripture from its form of presentation." (*The Articles of Faith in Everyday Life* [YMMIA and YWMIA of The Church of Jesus Christ of Latter-day Saints, 1949], p. 60.)

This same idea is stated in scripture itself: "For my soul delighteth in plainness; for after this manner doth the Lord God work among the children of men. For the Lord God giveth light unto the understanding; for he speaketh unto men according to *their* language, unto *their* understanding." (2 Nephi 31:3. Italics added.)

As one reads scripture, one must think not only of God and his purposes, but also of men, of the writer, and of his audience, and not expect perfection. Brigham Young implies this in his forthright style:

> I am so far from believing that any government upon this earth has constitutions and laws that are perfect, that I do not even believe there is a single revelation, among the many God has given to the Church, that is perfect in its fullness. The revelations of God contain correct doctrines and principle, as far as they go; but it is impossible for the poor, weak, low, grovelling, sinful inhabitants of the earth to receive a revelation from the Almighty in all its perfections. He has to speak to us in a manner to meet the extent of our capacities. (*Journal of Discourses* 2:314.)

Man plays a most significant role in both translating and creating scripture. The Lord's instruction to Oliver Cowdery explaining why

---

This selection includes parts of three chapters of Understanding the Scriptures *(Deseret Book, 1981).*

he failed in his attempt to translate the Book of Mormon applies also to the receiving and writing of revelation.

> Behold, you have not understood; you have supposed that I would give it unto you, when you took no thought save it was to ask me.
>
> But, behold, I say unto you, that you must study it out in your mind; then you must ask me if it be right, and if it is right I will cause that your bosom shall burn within you; therefore, you shall feel that it is right.
>
> But if it be not right you shall have no such feelings, but you shall have a stupor of thought that shall cause you to forget the thing which is wrong; therefore, you cannot write that which is sacred save it be given you from me.
>
> Now, if you had known this you could have translated; nevertheless, it is not expedient that you should translate now. (D&C 9:7-10.)

My favorite passage in all of scripture on the nature of revelation is found in the Doctrine and Covenants. It applies equally to scripture because much scripture is a record of revelation.

> Behold, I am God and have spoken it; these commandments are of me, and were given unto my servants in their weakness, after the manner of their language, that they might come to understanding. And inasmuch as they erred it might be made known; and inasmuch as they sought wisdom they might be instructed; and inasmuch as they sinned they might be chastened, that they might repent; and inasmuch as they were humble they might be made strong, and blessed from on high, and receive knowledge from time to time. (D&C 1:24-28.)

Revelation is of God and is authoritative for the believer, but it is given in man's language and weakness, in his own thinking and understanding. Much of it is correction of sin and error or affirmation of correct thinking—but always in words man understands. Men do violence to scripture if they ascribe every word of it to God.

Various books of scripture reflect the character and style of their respective authors: Paul's eloquent descriptions of the saving grace of Jesus Christ, John's great emphasis on love, and James's down-to-earth practical religion are all inspired, but each is unique in language and content. In studying the scriptures we should appreciate the contributions of both Deity and human writers.

There is much in scripture that is so beautiful, powerful, and rich in meaning that one can believe it is wholly of God. Examples are the

Ten Commandments, the Beatitudes, Paul's eulogy on love (1 Corinthians 13), the twenty-third psalm, Doctrine and Covenants 121, and Micah 6:6-8. The authors certainly rise above their own capability under inspiration of Deity in these and many other passages. But they use the words of men and they reflect their own feeling as well as divine inspiration. . . .

Other passages of scripture reflect the author's viewpoint or are conditioned markedly by the circumstances and comprehension of his audience. This is true particularly of some of the narrative and historical portions of the Old Testament, which are not always on the same high plane that characterizes the writings of the prophets. For example, 2 Kings 2:23-24 tells the story of Elisha as he was mocked by little children who said to him, "Go up, thou bald head." It says that when he cursed them in the name of the Lord, two "she bears" came out of the woods and attacked forty-two children, supposedly killing them. This implies divine retribution for their lack of respect for a prophet. I, however, am unable to imagine Jehovah, Jesus Christ in the meridian of time, the same Jesus Christ who loved little children, turning bears upon them in their innocent folly. In my judgment the author meant to show respect for the prophet Elisha, but lacked understanding of the character of God in ascribing such action to him.

The commandments in the law of Moses are, for the most part, just and humane and superior to the ethical standards of surrounding tribes and nations. Much of the law is on as high a plane as the teachings of Jesus. That is illustrated in the holiness code found in Leviticus, chapters 19–26. The Israelites were told not to reap the corners of their fields nor to glean their vineyards and grain fields, but to leave them for the poor and the stranger. (Leviticus 19:9-10.) This is also illustrated in the beautiful story of Ruth. Israelites were taught to be no respecters of persons but to respect the poor as much as the mighty and to love the stranger as one born among them. On the other hand, there are practices in the law of Moses that are related to the times and that we would consider unethical today. Hebrews as well as Gentiles were sold into slavery in ancient Israel, but within this practice, slave owners were admonished to release slaves after a given period of time and to send them away with a stock of goods from their master's storehouse.

Under the law of Moses there was no tolerance of the dissenter from Israel's faith. Anyone professing other gods and encouraging others to do so was to be stoned without pity. This is a far cry from our eleventh Article of Faith, which allows all men to worship what they will. It is understandable only if we remember that Israelites lived among peoples steeped in idolatry and that Israelites were sorely tempted to imitate their neighbors. (See Deuteronomy 13.)

According to the law of Moses, a rebellious son who refused to change his ways was to be brought before the elders and stoned to death. (Deuteronomy 21:18-21.) In this way serious problems in family life would be done away within Israel. Despite all the problems faced between parents and children today, I am glad that we are no longer commanded to kill sons who are beyond control.

The law of Moses is a complex, fascinating combination of just, considerate, and humane laws sprinkled here and there with laws that seem unduly harsh and even unjust. The only explanation I know for the limitations of this great effort to establish a righteous society in Israel is to ascribe them to men. In some instances, God may have accepted and condoned a lower law to meet human need, as he did in letting Israel have a king. In other instances, I believe writers of Israel's history gave credit or blame to God for actions and decrees that were unworthy of him under any circumstances.

Reading in Context

Shakespeare's remark in the preface to this book is worth repeating:

> In religion,
> What damned error, but some sober brow
> Will bless it, and approve it with a text
> Hiding the grossness with fair ornament?
> —*Merchant of Venice,* Act 3, scene 2

Over the centuries men in various churches and sects quoted single verses or passages of the Bible to prove their particular beliefs. Sometimes these texts are used correctly; at other times they do violence to the author's meaning. Using a passage of scripture isolated from its large setting is called textproof method. It is often unfair.

A colleague of mine was asked to review a book of which he was extremely and justifiably critical. It lacked historical accuracy, logic, and substance. He did say in one sentence that it was well-written. The publishers then latched on to that one favorable comment. Ignoring his total review; they quoted it as propaganda to promote the sale of the book, a nonscriptural illustration of quoting out of context and dishonesty.

Context means *with the text.* There are three kinds of context: (1)

the immediate setting of a passage, (2) its place in the book of which the passage is part, such as Amos, Job, or Galatians, and (3) its relationship to the gospel as a whole, especially the fundamentals.

In the Context of the Passage

It is perfectly proper to quote a single verse or two of scripture, but in doing so one should have read what precedes it and what follows it. Otherwise he may misrepresent the author's idea. The following story illustrates this.

One evening in a city in Switzerland a Mormon missionary gave a talk to non-Mormons on the nature of God. He endeavored to demonstrate that the Father was a real person—a Creator, Revelator, and Father in whose image man was made. Suddenly a minister in the back of the hall cried out, "God is a Spirit," quoting from John 4:24. In this verse, Jesus was not trying to describe the whole nature of God; he was emphasizing the role of spirit in God and man as part of a brief discourse on how to worship. He was trying to teach the Samaritan woman to worship "in spirit and in truth."

In that same meeting a few moments later, the minister spoke up again, saying, "God is love," quoting correctly from 1 John 4:8. He was using the verse to prove that God is love and nothing else. If we turn to this verse, however, and read the verses before and after that complete the thought (verses 7–12), we see again that the main interest was to inspire people to love one another. To achieve this, the author stressed God's great attribute of love. The Father's love for us is so great that he is the embodiment of love; this is one of his greatest attributes. But he is also more than love. The next verse says: "In this was manifested the love of God toward us, because that God sent his only begotten Son into the world, that we might live through him." (1 John 4:9.) Love alone cannot send us a savior, cannot create worlds, cannot bring to pass the resurrection. Love is a quality that cannot exist except as a single attribute. It lives through those who exercise it.

In their missionary zeal, Latter-day Saints are sometimes guilty of quoting verses out of context. Isaiah 4:1 speaks of the day when seven women shall take hold of one man and ask to be called by his name. In the past, it was common for missionaries to defend the practice of plural marriage with this verse, which to them was a prophecy of the practice of plural marriage. We might well gather this notion by reading this verse alone. If, however, we begin reading in chapter 3, from verse 16 to the end, we readily see that 4:1 belongs to the same train of thought as Isaiah 3:16-26. Isaiah sees that war is coming to Judah, and that the proud women of Judea, who are more concerned with decorating their faces and bodies than they are with the affliction of the poor in Israel, have made their contribution to the downfall of the nation. Not only have they lived in vain and idle luxury, but they have encouraged their masters to cheat and lie to get gain, living lives offensive to God and destructive of national unity and strength. What happens to women in time of war? Their men fall in battle and they become widows. Marriage meant much to the women of Israel; hence, in the day of calamity (which was near at hand) there might be seven women to one man. Isaiah was depicting the consequences of war brought on by unrighteousness. His prediction applies widely in human experience and is not a prediction of plural marriage.

In the Context of the Book

Each of the standard works is a collection of many writings or books. The Old Testament has thirty-nine, the New Testament twenty-seven, for example. Each passage of scripture is part of a writing or book within one of the standard works. It should be interpreted as part of that writing or book.

Part of one verse in the beautiful twenty-third psalm reads: "Thou anointest my head with oil." In a Sunday School class one day a teacher used this statement to prove that the anointing of the sick was practiced in the Old Testament. It may have been, but this was not the verse to use to prove it. The entire twenty-third psalm is a song of thanksgiving and praise to the Lord. "Thou anointest my head with oil" is a symbolic way of acknowledging the bounteous blessings and goodness of the Lord—as the entire psalm attests. If you wish to prove that the anointing of the sick was used in biblical times, turn to the book of James, a work of forthright admonition and instruction, and there you will find this explicit teaching: "Is any sick among you? let him call for the elders of the church; and let them pray over him, anointing him with oil in the name of the Lord: and the prayer of faith shall save the sick, and the Lord shall raise him up; and if he have committed sins, they shall be forgiven him." (James 5:14-15.)

In Ezekiel 37, a vision of this prophet is recorded wherein he saw a valley full of dry bones and then saw flesh and sinews come upon them; "Breath came into them, and they lived." (Ezekiel 37:10.) Verses 1-14 of this passage have been used to prove the resurrection. It is probably not Ezekiel's purpose in this passage to establish the doctrine of individual resurrection. It is quite obvious, if one reads the entire book of Ezekiel, that the prophet is talking about the restoration of Israel as a nation, as a people, with dry bones as a symbol of their captivity. The resurrection can be established much more clearly and abundantly in the New Testament or Book of Mormon. (Note Alma 40, Luke 24, and 1 Corinthians 15.)

Latter-day Saints should also read the rest of chapter 37 with Ezekiel's purpose in mind. Verses 15-28 tell the oft-repeated account of the prophet being commanded to write upon two sticks, one for Judah and one for Joseph, Judah being interpreted as the Bible and Joseph as the Book of Mormon. If we read the entire passage in the context of the total book of Ezekiel, we find that the prophet is predicting not only the coming forth of two books or records, but also the restoration and reunion of the two nations—Israel and Judah. The Bible and the Book of Mormon are records of Judah and Joseph, respectively, and the coming forth of these two records heralds the eventual reunion of the two nations and should someday even contribute to Israel's unification. The coming forth of the Book of Mormon fits into this large hope and faith of the prophet Ezekiel. Latter-day Saints often ignore Ezekiel's great interest in unifying Israel and Judah.

To see how a great passage of scripture assumes even more meaning when read as part of an entire writing, refer to 1 Corinthians, one of Paul's most interesting epistles. Paul had learned that there were contentions among the Saints (1:10) and all manner of strife, divisions, and sins (3:1-3). Some of their strife was over the gifts of the gospel. Some could speak in tongues, some could not; some could interpret, others could not. In chapter 12 Paul explains the gifts of the gospel and how different gifts are enjoyed by different members but not all by all. In chapter 14 he explains that the gift of tongues is not the most important gift of the gospel nor is it a necessary one. [Between these two chapters], in the most meaningful eulogy of brotherly love ever written in scripture, Paul points out the supremacy of love over all other gifts. Without charity (meaning brotherly love and, in Moroni's words, "the pure love of Christ") we are nothing.

> Though I speak with the tongues of men and of angels, and have not charity, I am becoming as sounding brass, or a tinkling cymbal.
>
> And though I have the gift of prophecy, and understand all mysteries, and all knowledge; and though I have all faith, so that I could remove mountains, and have not charity, I am nothing.

> And though I bestow all my goods to feed the poor, and though I give my body to be burned, and have not charity, it profiteth me nothing. (1 Corinthians 13:1-3.)

Chapter 13 can stand alone, but knowing chapters 12 and 14 adds rich meaning to it.

In the Context of the Gospel

A young architect once gave a group of students and me a choice insight into how to interpret scripture. He was talking about architecture, a highly complex field that embraces art, science, and mathematics. He said architects use three basic guides when planning a garage, house, or a cathedral: Is it sound? Is it functional? Is it beautiful or aesthetically pleasing? These wonderful guidelines are equally useful to the client who is building or buying a home.

Religion too is a vast, complex field. The scriptures, our best record of religion, are tremendously composite, varied in style and origin, written by scores of authors living over centuries. To interpret scripture fairly, intelligently, and meaningfully, we need some guidelines comparable to those of the architect. There is a logical, meaningful, conceptual structure to the gospel just as there is to architecture or any other discipline. Gospel principles belong together; they support and enrich one another. The gospel may be likened to a mosaic. It has a design, a set of ideas that are consistent with each other and that together give meaning to life. The person who would understand religion should not pulverize the gospel and think of it as an array of separate facts and ideas. Like architecture, the gospel has its fundamental concepts and principles. These need to be kept in mind as we read single verses or contemplate individual ideas in scripture. To illustrate, I suggest that there are some fundamental concepts regarding God and man that should always be remembered as we read the scriptures.

Our conception of God the Father:

1. He is the Father of all men.
2. He has certain moral attributes, such as justice, impartiality, integrity, love, mercy, forgiveness.
3. He is law-abiding.
4. He is more intelligent than all other persons.

Our conception of man:

1. All men are children of God.
2. All men are brothers.
3. Men are that they might have joy.

4. Men have the capacity through obedience to the principles of the gospel to progress eternally.

5. Men have free agency.

6. Men were created in the image of God.

These concepts concerning God and man represent only a partial listing to illustrate the value of interpreting scripture in the light of fundamentals.

A Case Study

In Alma 34, which is a profound and rich chapter, we read:

> And now, as I said unto you before, as ye have had so many witnesses, therefore, I beseech of you, that you do not procrastinate the day of your repentance until the end; for after this day of life, which is given us to prepare for eternity, behold, if we do not improve our time while in this life, then cometh the night of darkness wherein there can be no labor performed.
>
> Ye cannot say, when ye are brought to that awful crisis, that I will repent, that I will return to my God. Nay, ye cannot say this, for that same spirit which doth possess your bodies at the time that ye go out of this life, that same spirit will have power to possess your body in that eternal world.
>
> For behold, if ye have procrastinated the day of your repentance, even until death, behold, ye have become subjected to the spirit of the devil, and he doth seal you his; therefore, the Spirit of the Lord hath withdrawn from you, and hath no place in you, and the devil hath all power over you; and this is the final state of the wicked. (Alma 34:33-35.)

How do we interpret this passage? Is there no opportunity whatever for repentance in life beyond the grave? Some people think so, and that may be right with regard to those who are spiritually dead. Taking this passage by itself, with no reference to other gospel fundamentals, we could easily conclude this. But let us remember that God is our Father—a loving, merciful Father—and that his work and glory is to redeem his children. He is not likely to give up easily nor quickly. Judging by the attitude of his Son, the Father would, we believe, never close the door to repentance for his children.

Some, such as the sons of perdition, may sink so low that they lose the power to repent because they "die as to things pertaining unto righteousness." (Alma 12:16.) Perhaps others who have procrastinated their repentance may find the faith and power to repent in the eternal world. This is our faith when we do work for our kindred dead, some of whom, no doubt, were first-rate sinners. We are not discrediting Amulek's plea to repent now. It is the sensible thing to do, for happiness in this life as well as for our eternal welfare. And no one knows who will have the strength to repent hereafter.

The whole gospel cannot be taught in one sermon. However, as we interpret a sermon we can and should do so in the context of the gospel as a whole.

I learned long ago that single verses must be interpreted in the context of the gospel as a whole. A returned missionary said to me that he was in a hurry to get married in the temple because if he were—even though he might commit sin except murder and the shedding of innocent blood—he would still enter into his exaltation. He based his faith on Doctrine and Covenants 132:26, which says:

> Verily, verily, I say unto you, if a man marry a wife according to my word, and they are sealed by the Holy Spirit of promise, according to mine appointment, and he or she shall commit any sin or transgression of the new and everlasting covenant whatever, and all manner of blasphemies, and if they commit no murder wherein they shed innocent blood, yet they shall come forth in the first resurrection, and enter into their exaltation; but they shall be destroyed in the flesh, and shall be delivered unto the buffetings of Satan unto the day of redemption, saith the Lord God.

We might agree with him if we consider this verse in a vacuum. But in the light of the gospel, no unclean thing will enter the presence of God. And no forgiveness is possible without repentance. No verse of scripture intends to give license to sin.

I do not accept any interpretation of scripture that denies the impartiality or love of God or the free agency and brotherhood of man. These concepts are too basic to the gospel to be denied by someone's interpretation of a verse of scripture.

No part of the gospel stands alone, any more than a part of a house does. And just as each part of a house derives its meaning and function in its relationship to the whole house, so it is in the gospel. Single gospel ideas must be viewed as part of a whole plan or perspective. We should try to see the gospel as a whole, not as a series of isolated concepts.

Standards of Evaluation

How do we decide which teachings in scripture are valid for us today? How do we distinguish between that which is universally and eternally valid and that which was meant for a particular time and place and which may not be applicable now? How do we determine that which is of God and that which may have crept into scripture through the errors or misinterpretation of well-meaning writers, scribes, or translators?

To answer these questions, we should employ all the guidelines thus far discussed in this work—the background, authorship, correctness of translation, context, and religious intent. But these are not enough. To avoid error or justifying our own desires, we need additional rational and spiritual helps. What are some of these?

Consistent with Gospel Fundamentals

If we study all scriptures, certain fundamentals emerge clearly. One is the character of God. Over and over again in all four scriptures Jesus and the prophets bear witness that God is our Father—just, impartial, merciful, forgiving, law-abiding, creative, and intelligent. If we believe the scriptures, we can depend on God's integrity and love.

Isolated passages may portray him as wrathful or jealous or capricious, but these attributes do not square with the above-named qualities of character. Therefore, passages that appear to portray him so negatively must be reviewed and interpreted carefully to preserve the integrity and consistency of his character. For example, the word *jealous,* as we use it, usually describes weakness in human character, based on a feeling of inadequacy and insecurity, and often nurturing envy and hate. Surely God is not of such a character. Actually, the word *jealous* in its scriptural usage may mean *one cares*. Webster gives an archaic meaning of jealousy as "earnest concern or solicitude; vigilant watchfulness or care." In the new Latter-day Saint edition of the Bible, the word jealous taken from the Hebrew "qannah" is interpreted as "possessing sensitive and deep feelings." (See Genesis 20:5, footnote b.) This makes sense. Likewise in human experience a person who knows wrath is usually out of his mind, beyond self-control. Our Father must experience righteous indignation as did Jesus when he drove money changers from the temple courtyard. Yet the Savior was always in control of himself.

I do not accept any interpretation of scriptural passages that portrays God as being partial, unforgiving, hateful, or revengeful. It is more important to uphold the character and will of God than it is to support every line of scripture.

Clearly portrayed in the scriptures are certain concepts of the nature of man. Taken as a whole they repeatedly teach or imply free agency, the brotherhood of man, God's concern for man, man's responsibility for his own behavior, and certain basic ethical requirements such as those that we find in the Decalogue. Certain isolated passages, if taken singly, may seem to deny some of these principles. For instance, in Ephesians Paul states, "For by grace are ye saved through faith; and that not of yourself: it is the gift of God: not of works, lest any man should boast." (Ephesians 2:8-9.) This passage seems to imply that salvation is wholly an act of grace. This kind of interpretation and logic may have led John Calvin, the great French Protestant reformer, to teach predestination. Many Protestant groups rely wholly on the grace of Christ. If we study all scriptures, including Ezekiel, James, the Book of Mormon, and Doctrine and Covenants—as well as Paul's writings—we will find that the grace of Christ plays a large role in our lives. But to make it efficacious in relation to our sins, we must also exercise faith unto repentance. To maintain that man has no role in his own salvation besides simple acceptance of Christ is to make free agency, repentance, and personal spiritual growth quite meaningless. I believe the scriptures strike a happy balance between the grace of Deity and the faith and works of the individual, both being essential to life and eternal salvation.

Consistent with Christ's Spirit and Teachings

Since Christ is the Son of God and unexcelled in his own character, mind, and close relationship to the Father, since he inherited all the rich background of the law and the prophets, and since we profess to be his disciples, he should be our ultimate standard as we interpret and use the scriptures in our own lives.

If any concerns, attitudes, and practices of the Israelites, Nephites, Lamanites, or Latter-day Saints contradict the Savior's teachings, we should study them further. First, we must be sure our interpretation is not at fault; then we should not accept and practice principles and policies that are contrary to Christ's spirit and example. Brigham Young stated this thought very well: "We have taken this book, called the Old and the New Testament for our standard. We believe this book and receive it as the word of the Lord. Not but there are many words in this book that are not the words of the Lord, but, that which came from the heavens, and which the Lord has delivered to us, we receive, and especially the sayings of the Savior." (*Journal of Discourses* 12:309.)

Continuous Revelation

Since men are not infallible, and since life is dynamic and characterized by change, continuous revelation is needed to correct errors of the past and to implement the basic, eternal principles of the gospel into the policies and practices of both individuals and the Church today. We need prophets—men called and inspired of God—to interpret the meaning of the gospel for our time.

Needed also in the Church's and our personal interpretation of scripture is the gift of discernment through the Holy Ghost and the light of Christ. The truths of scripture were inspired of the Holy Spirit. Therefore, their interpretation should be guided by the same spirit that produced them.

Common Sense

A fine German brother and former mission president said to me one day as he helped me build a room in our house, "I go to Sunday School and listen to all kinds of gospel interpretations. I have decided not to believe anything that doesn't make good 'horses senses.' "

Faith takes us beyond knowledge, but I don't see how any interpretation of the scripture can be enlightening if we don't understand it. I think too that we should question interpretations that contradict common sense, good judgment, verified experience, and the counsel of wise and good men and women. I believe reason should confirm what we believe to be the inspiration of the Holy Ghost, and I believe we also should check our own thinking by the Holy Spirit.

Oliver Cowdery, in his failure to translate the Book of Mormon, learned the necessity of combining thinking with divine inspiration in the work of the Lord. (See D&C 9:7-10.) I believe the counsel given to him applies to the interpretation of scripture as well as to its translation.

In Christ's great summary of the religious life he said, repeating an ancient law, "Thou shalt love the Lord thy God with all thy *heart,* and with all thy soul, and with all thy *mind.*" (Matthew 22:37. Italics added.)

An interpretation of scripture can be trusted when it (1) is consistent with gospel fundamentals and with the teachings and spirit of Christ, (2) is confirmed by the promptings of the Spirit, (3) appeals to our ethical judgment, and (4) has won agreement among persons of good will. Of such a nature as this is the memorable revelation received by President Spencer W. Kimball on June 8, 1978, in which the priesthood was made available to all worthy male members of the Church regardless of race. This revelation is wholly consistent with the impartiality of God, the love of Christ, and the free agency of man. It appeals to our ethical judgment, has been received by men and women of good will, and has been confirmed by the Holy Spirit in the minds and hearts of Church leaders and members overwhelmingly. It has been accepted by the Church and has become part of our modern scripture, the Doctrine and Covenants.

VII
LEARNING HOW TO LOVE

With Merle in front of the Notre Dame Cathedral in Paris, 1931

25

The A, B, Cs of Dating

Wayne and Sally had been going together quite steadily for months. They were in college and had had a grand time at dances and other socials. Both were active in the Church, and much of their association had been in church meetings and socials. Their friendship had not been narrow, and certainly was not in the rut of affection discussed in our last lesson.

They liked each other so well that he quit going to his own M Men class and joined the M Men in her ward so they could be together more often. The M Men and Gleaners of her ward had classes, firesides, and other activities together. The fellows and girls were one big happy, sociable family.

At Christmas time the combined group decided to sponsor a lovely Christmas dance. The officers knew of the close friendship and also of the capabilities of Wayne and Sally and asked them to be a committee of two to plan and sponsor the dance. This they agreed to do with enthusiasm. The party turned out to be a grand success.

Two weeks later Wayne went for a ride with his M Men leader. In the course of the conversation, he said, "Brother Smith, if you had to choose between two girls, one who was very capable, positive, and efficient and one who was more retiring and whose possibilities were probably great but undeveloped, which would you choose?"

After a moment's reflection, Smith said, "Wayne, if this already-made girl were just what I wanted, I believe I would take her; if not, I'd rather take a chance on helping to develop this other girl into the kind of person she and I wanted her to become."

One year after the Christmas party Wayne married not Sally, but this other girl, this one who was more modest and less positive in her ways. His teacher-friend asked him why. He said, "Because I

This selection is taken from Today and Tomorrow *(1942), a manual for fifteen- and sixteen-year-olds in the Young Women's Mutual Improvment Association that was used throughout the years of World War II.*

worked with Sally on a committee and discovered that she couldn't even take a suggestion from me." Do you see the connection between marriage and committee work? It is easier to learn about the total personality of an individual in one good committee project than it is in a year of going to shows and dances or in superficial talk. Serving on a committee, you find out who is dependable, who can give and take and is flexible enough to see and appreciate points of view other than their own. Initiative and imagination are revealed. "Pride and prejudice" are uncovered. Since learning of this and like experiences, we teach as a maxim: "Do not marry anyone with whom you have not worked on a committee."

Choosing a Roommate

Suppose you were going away to college or to work and you were given the privilege of choosing a roommate for the next four years. Once she was chosen, you two would have to see the thing through. What qualities would you ask for in this roommate? Make a list on the blackboard or on paper. Would you like the person you room with to be honest, dependable, trustworthy, a bit flexible? State and explain your wishes.

You will live with the person you marry, not for four years with periodic vacations in between, but for life and forever. Your association in marriage will be more intimate and more extensive. Surely, you would want the boy you marry to have the same basic qualities you would choose in a roommate, and others as well. How can you discover these qualities, besides serving on a committee? What kinds of things—activities, events, and associations—reveal character, the mind, disposition, ideals, attitudes, and the habits of a fellow? Let us make a list:

Personality-Revealing Associations

I	1. Committee 2. Work 3. Play	III	1. House parties 2. Firesides 3. Home visits
II	1. Study 2. Reading interests 3. Conversation 4. Attendance at and reaction toward sermons, lectures, concerts, shows	IV	1. Canyon outings 2. Hikes 3. Travel

Seeing each other:

V { 1. Under criticism | 3. Facing disappointment, sorrow, loss
2. In embarrassing situations | 4. When unexpected

Attendance at shows and dances does not reveal personality extensively because such activities are prepared occasions in which boys and girls play the role of recipients. The entertainment is arranged for them. These other activities, listed above, call for more activity and varied responses. They are far more revealing. We shall illustrate one activity in each group.

1. Work: A girl who works in an office said recently, "I hope I may have the privilege of working in an office for a few months with the man who proposes to me. You can't be with a person eight hours a day in the drudgery and opportunities of an office without learning to know the character, disposition, and mind of a person to a high degree, if you have eyes to see and ears to hear." How true!

2. Intellectual Interests: A girl who is mentally alert, ambitious, and eager to learn will not be happy with a fellow who is dull and dead intellectually. How can she evaluate a boy's mental powers? It is difficult to come right out and say, "Brother, what are your main interests in life? Do you believe in God? Do you appreciate Beethoven's music as well as Schubert's? What magazines do you read? Who are your favorite authors? What is your I.Q.?" A barrage of questions like these shot at a fellow in machine-gun fashion, or even from week to week, would alarm and embarrass most anyone.

There is a better way to get the same insight into a fellow's mind. Go to church with a group and casually develop a conversation afterwards about the things heard in the sermon. Immediately interests and attitudes on basic questions of life will be revealed. Go to a lovely concert or a good lecture and see how your friends respond. Engage in conversation for a few hours sometime and see what interests are present.

3. Social Gatherings: House parties, if well planned, reveal a lot, because one sees friends as they react toward other people. One learns if they are courteous, considerate, interesting, good sports, and unselfish. One night a group of students held a house party. All went well during the enjoyment of a tasty buffet supper. Afterwards games were played. Among them was a guessing game in which one person was "on the spot" and had to think fast of famous persons whose names begin with the letter C. Some of the rest of us had already been in his position and had been embarrassed a bit by our ignorance

and had lost out. Now it was his turn. When he failed to remember a person soon enough, he was not only embarrassed but became quite upset, acted like a four-year-old who will not play because he is not winning.

Present at the party was this fellow's girlfriend! His attitude, expressed while playing one game, opened her eyes as his good dancing, car rides, and handsome appearance had not done in a year's time. To see each other in one's home is to see a person in a situation most nearly like one's own marriage will be.

4. Outings and Travel: Boy Scouts have been playmates for years in the neighborhood without learning as much about one another as they have learned in a week at a Scout camp where living and working together really unveils character and personality. Neighbors have thought themselves to be acquaintances of long standing, until they have taken a trip together. Then they knew they had never really known each other before. The experience of travel invariably makes people closer friends or estranges them from one another. It does not leave them untouched.

Boys and girls cannot travel together before marriage, except after they have become rather serious. Then a short trip, chaperoned by one of the families, is a good thing. Group hikes, outings, and canyon parties make a fine substitute for travel in the early days of friendship and courtship.

A group of college boys and girls went as a class to study the geology of the Southern Utah parks and the Grand Canyon of the Colorado. One of the boys on the trip reported that, through lengthy conversations and a great variety of activity, he had learned more about the character of some girlfriends than he had discovered all year at school in frequent association with them. He learned which were good sports, what their imaginative and intellectual powers were, and where their interests lay. It was a revelation to him to know girls in ways other than on dates of the routine type, such as at shows and dances.

5. In Trying Circumstances: Crises and unusual circumstances often reveal character more quickly and surely than occasions of comfort and tranquillity. If a person can take criticism and be grateful for it, he will be easy to live with. If criticism is resented and excuses are made for one's mistakes all the time, such a person is emotionally immature and not ready for marriage.

A boy, just turned three, was visiting a dairy farm. Led on by the insatiable curiosity of a child, he climbed on a big new tractor. In the process he fell off and struck his head. After a little crying, he turned to the tractor, kicked it, and said, "I don't like you, Mr. Tractor." Some adults show the same kind of infantile behavior. Criticism reveals it. . . .

Most revealing is the manner in which a girl or a fellow reacts to such crises as loss of a loved one, sudden financial reverses in the family, unfair treatment shown toward her by someone, honors received, or any serious disappointment.

Types of Dating

Fellows and girls may be classified in their dating habits into one of four groups:

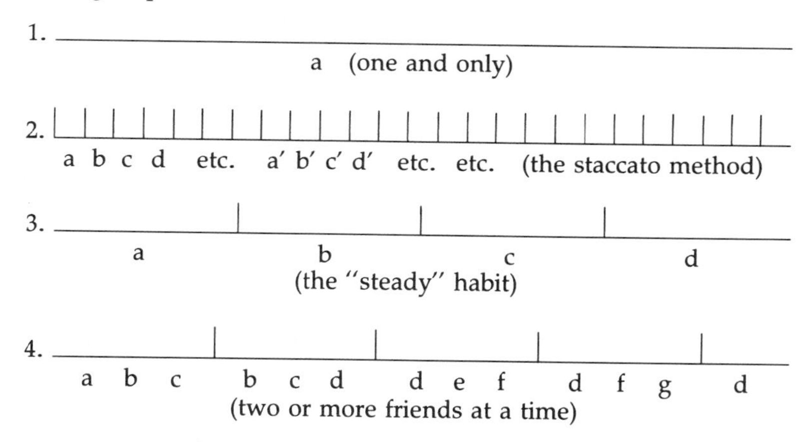

1. The One and Only. A generation or two ago quite a few of our parents and grandparents married the first and only person with whom they had ever dated. This experience is less common among young people today. Evaluate this type of association. What are its values and its limitations?

Childhood sweethearts who go on to a happy marriage must have quite smooth sailing compared with the waves of disappointment some people seem to ride. They certainly may have a long life together, one into which no one else has intruded, not even for a moment.

This "one and only" system also has its serious limitations. It limits one's circle of friends from which to choose a personality ideally matched to one's own. It does not provide for comparison of one friend with another. If a girl falls for a boy in the teens, would it not be better for her to go out with several boys, at least for a time? If she really loves number one, she should be all the more sure and confident after having compared him with the others.

2. The Staccato Method. Sometimes fellows and girls go out with a different girl or boy on every date, never taking the same one out more than once or twice. One boy within our acquaintance kept a notebook in which were listed the 176 girls he had taken out. This was several years before his marriage. He had worked out a code by which he evaluated them. What are the values and limitations of this staccato method?

In the early years of dating, dates are usually infrequent and this method is good experience. Later on, in college or elsewhere, fellows and girls who go out with many different acquaintances, once or twice each, run into some serious limitations, according to their own confessions. A girl can't really get to know fellows by just having a superficial acquaintance with a large number of them. Nor can a boy know girls in this way. They become fickle and shallow in their relations with the opposite sex if they continually skip from one to another in their dating.

3. The "Steady" Habit. The most common relationship for many fellows and girls to fall into is the habit of going steady. No matter whether they are fifteen or twenty, they cannot think of more than one boy or one girl at a time. So a fellow takes out the same girl for a year or two, then another, then another, and finally marries the last steady girlfriend. What are the values and limitations of this method?

It seems natural for a boy to be attracted by one girl at a time. Then too, we are creatures of habit. Having once mustered the courage to ask a girl out or to go with a boy, and having lived through the first date successfully, why not repeat the experience? It becomes convenient to go out with the same person repeatedly. One knows what is expected and what to expect. One can be a little more free and less formal.

On the negative side, this method has serious limitations. To go steady with a boyfriend takes a girl "out of circulation" and robs her of the rich experience of knowing several fellows well and of being known by them. Should the relationship break up, as it often does, it takes a girl a little while to get back into a circle of other friends who wish to step her out. Going steady with one person does not allow for comparison of that person with other boys at the same time and on equal basis. Finally, whenever a couple go together all the time, they naturally become involved; they become more serious.

Often they fall into this state of seriousness quite unaware and unprepared. This bears illustration.

A boy and girl went with each other practically steady the last two years of high school. Their interest in and affection for each other grew gradually and steadily. They really enjoyed one another's company. The girl, with good reason to do so, began thinking seriously of the future. The boy found it out and broke off the association abruptly. Why? Not because anything had given him reason to change his opinion of her, but because he was not prepared to think of marriage. He had four or five years of schooling, a mission, and the possibility of military training ahead of him. He had no money and no assurance of success vocationally as yet. He was simply unprepared for the seriousness of the situation in which he found himself. His girlfriend was deeply hurt—and with good reason, for she was thinking one jump ahead of her boyfriend.

4. Two or More Friends at a Time. This fourth method of dating is called the a, b, c system. In this pattern of behavior a boy goes out with two or three girlfriends over the same period of time. That is, he alternates his dates more or less and becomes well acquainted with several girls at the same time. He may drop a, b, or c and add d and so on. The one thing he does do is go out with at least two girls and date them often enough to know and appreciate them well. What are the values and limitations of the a, b, c method?

The only limitation ever presented by college students is that they don't have time and money to divide their association between two or among three girls. This objection is of doubtful merit and is offset by many favorable factors.

This method combines all the values of the other three methods and avoids their limitations. You have an opportunity to know people well as in (1) and (3). Your acquaintance is broad as in (2). On the other hand your acquaintance is not superficial and shallow as in (2), nor does it limit your choice and comparative values as in (1) and (3). You do not get involved, if you are sincere, so long as you have two or three boyfriends in the same season.

In short, the a, b, c system gives you many good friends whom you can come to know well and compare with one another at the same time. You will not become involved in a serious situation before you wish to and get caught in a trap, as it were. It will be easier for you to keep your association with fellows on a creative basis, to keep out of a rut of affection, if you have two or three good friends. You will gain a knowledge of "boy nature," and become a better judge of character and personality than you could be in the other three systems. You will have had a rich experience and background of friendship, out of which an intelligent and happy courtship can emerge and grow into a happy and successful marriage with the friend of your choice.

"From Friendship to Marriage"

As long ago as 1711, Joseph Addison wrote, "Those marriages generally abound most with love and constancy that are preceded by a long courtship." To which we might add, by a courtship which reveals character and personality most intelligently. There is something exciting, romantic, adventurous, and movie-like about falling in love with a fellow in a dazzling courtship of a few weeks' or months' time. All studies show that there is danger in this approach to marriage, which increases the divorce rate and the unhappiness record of marriages.

The ideal is to go from friendship to marriage, not from marriage to friendship. The difference may be illustrated below. (A) shows how top-heavy a marriage may be if it has no basis in friendship; (B) shows how well grounded and firm, like an Egyptian pyramid, a marriage is that has its basis in friendship—ideally in the a, b, c system.

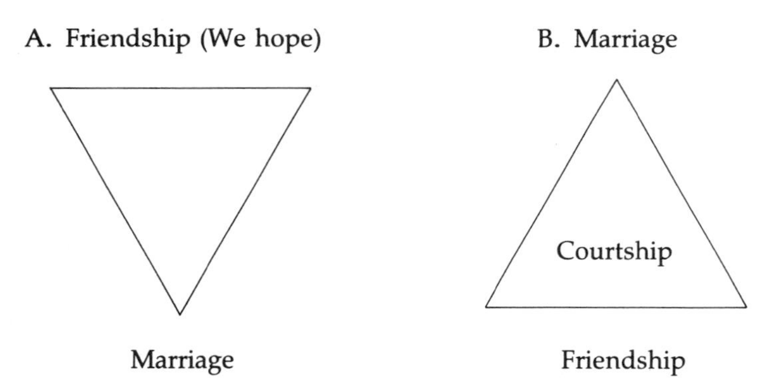

The steps between friendship and marriage should not be too abrupt. Let the line below represent a continuation of the a, b, c system, (4) above.

going steady | private understanding | pin | ring | marriage announcements

A girl has already become well acquainted with a numbe boy friends, a, b, c, d, e, f, g, and h. Out of this rich backgrou has learned to evaluate boys and to know what she wants. Boy emerges as the choice of her mind and heart. She is already we acquainted with him before she goes steady. After going fairly steady, a private understanding is reached. The two become adjusted to the idea of a partnership without complicating it with public opinion. A pin or an engagement ring should not ordinarily be accepted until marriage is in sight a few months away. Announcement of the engagement is usually made four to six weeks before the marriage.

A girl who believes in and seeks the LDS ideal of an eternal marriage cannot go far wrong if she will realize that love is a part of life as a whole, that she must marry a fine fellow of good character and wholesome personality, and that to find such a person she ought to have years of creative and rich friendship with girls and boys through which she can learn to know human nature and "boy nature." Out of this rich, intelligent, and interesting background, she can then select a boy with whom she can realize the highest purposes of marriage.

Pray Over Your Choice

When you find yourself someday thinking and talking seriously about a fellow, and before you make any final promises, go to your Father in heaven in prayer and ask him to help you make a decision. Marriage is the most important step a girl who marries takes in life. Why pray about anything if not about marriage? Pray, and do not marry without a feeling of assurance inspired from on high.

26

…eatest of These . . .”

At the risk of being commonplace, I have chosen to speak with you tonight on an old theme. My justification is twofold: It is among the most important things in life, and it still goes largely unheeded.

Some nineteen hundred years ago Paul established a community of Christian believers in the seaport city of Corinth. After teaching them for about eighteen months, he continued on his way, leaving his Corinthian saints to develop their religious life without his guidance. And what a travesty of religion they made in his absence. Word came to Paul that one of their chief concerns lay in who among them possessed the greatest spiritual gifts. Paul was moved by this circumstance to write about what is important in religion:

"Though I speak with the tongues of men and of angels, and have not [love], I am become as sounding brass, or a tinkling cymbal. And though I have the gift of prophecy, and understand all mysteries, and all knowledge; and though I have all faith, so that I can move mountains, and have not [love], I am nothing. And though I bestow all my goods to feed the poor, and though I give my body to be burned, and have not [love], it profiteth me nothing." (1 Corinthians 13:1-3.)

Paul's meaning is clear. He gave to morality, specifically love, a supreme place in the religious life. Without it everything else—faith, theology, ecstatic gifts, sacraments, authority, offerings, church activities—are as "sounding brass or a tinkling cymbal" and profit nothing.

This point of view did not originate with Paul, though he did give it eloquent expression. Jesus had said that everything in the Jewish canon of scripture—the Law and the Prophets—depends on the love of God and love of neighbor. Centuries before him a group of Hebrew prophets, especially Amos, Hosea, Micah, Isaiah, and Jeremiah, had

---

Dr. Bennion delivered this address at the baccalaureate services of the University of Utah, June 3, 1956.

utterly rejected the formal "religious" worship of ancient Israel because the people, in daily life, practiced neither justice nor mercy.

The words of Amos must have felt like the sting of a bee as he cried, in the name of Jehovah, "I hate, I despise your feast days, and I will not smell in your solemn assemblies. Though ye offer me burnt offerings and your meat offerings, I will not accept them. . . . Take thou away from me the noise of thy songs; for I will not hear the melody of thy viols. But let judgment [justice] run down as waters, and righteousness as a mighty stream." (Amos 5:21-24.)

Even more impressive is Micah's characterization of the relative importance of things in religion: "Wherewith shall I come before the Lord, and bow myself before the high God? Shall I come before him with burnt offerings, with calves of a year old? Will the Lord be pleased with thousands of rams, or with ten thousands of rivers of oil? Shall I give my firstborn for my transgression, the fruit of my body for the sin of my soul? He hath shewed thee, O man, what is good; and what doth the Lord require of thee, *but to do justly, and to love mercy, and to walk humbly with thy God?*" (Micah 6:6-8; emphasis added.)

In our Judeo-Christian tradition, a religion without love is a vain and futile thing. Before we seek to appraise the thinking of Paul, Amos, or Micah, let us reflect a moment on the meaning of love. As a word, written in a sacred book, it is only a symbol of reality. All words are but symbols of feelings, ideas, and things, as you well know. Let us try to suggest the reality which the word *love* symbolizes.

The Meaning of Love

Some of you graduates are being married this week. Paul was not talking about the romantic feeling which you have for one another. As a matter of fact, he seems to have had mixed feelings on the subject of love in marriage. Brotherly love is not the kind of emotion one feels for his girlfriend on a moonlight night. If he does have brotherly love for her on such an occasion, it is not inspired by the moon. Romantic feeling, taken by itself, is far too selfish and possessive, and at times fickle, to be identical with brotherly love. Nor is love of neighbor synonymous with friendship, though it usually is a rich ingredient thereof. The unique essence of friendship lies in its mutuality, in the sheer delight two people have in each other because of the richness of their common interests and values. Friendship also includes admiration, which need play no role in brotherly love.

Brotherly love has some essential and distinctive features. (1) It is utterly selfless, consisting of a warm, outgoing, unselfish desire for the welfare and happiness of another person. In Paul's language, love "envieth not, vaunteth not itself, is not puffed up, doth not behave itself unseemly, seeketh not her own." Hence, in love of neighbor there is no thought of reciprocation, no calculating for a reward either here or in heaven, but simply the spontaneous, whole-souled interest in the other person's good. (2) It follows that brotherly love is not something that has to be earned or merited on good behavior by the recipient. I heard a man say once, "I will not forgive that man his wrong until he gets down on his knees and pays me double for all my losses because of him." If forgiveness must be earned or doubly earned, the word *give* should be removed from the center of it. Forgiveness is an expression of love, and love is a gift. If it were earned, it would have to be called justice, reciprocity, or recompense. (3) Since love is both unselfish and unmerited, it is impartial. A real test of Christian love lies in its impartiality. This Jesus well knew when he told his disciples to love their enemies that they might be children of their Father in heaven: "for he maketh his sun to shine on the evil and on the good, and sendeth rain on the just and on the unjust." (Matthew 5:45.)

Brotherly love impels us, with equal desire, to seek the good of sinner and saint, of the stranger as well as of our own kin, of Jew and Gentile, of white and colored, of the common man and those in places of honor. Therefore, love knows no geographical boundaries, no racial barriers, no cultural prejudices, for it recognizes the intrinsic worth of every human being.

Several reasons should inspire in us this impartial feeling of good will toward men. Many of us believe in the Fatherhood of God and that he "hath made of one blood all nations of men for to dwell on all the face of the earth." (Acts 17:26.) Others may agree with Bertrand Russell, the distinguished British philosopher, who bids us "not weigh in grudging scales [people's] merits and de-merits, but let us think only of their need," because we face a common doom and need one another's faith and courage.

I believe there is an even better reason than either of these to love people impartially. It is this: Love needs no motivation, no justification, no reason. By its very nature, love fills one with good will toward all men. As Shakespeare said of mercy, one of love's offspring, "The quality of mercy is not strain'd; / It droppeth as the gentle rain from heaven upon the place beneath." (*The Merchant of Venice*, Act IV, scene 1.)

There is one more characteristic of love which I wish to mention this evening. Love impels one to action. It is doing, giving, helping, serving. And love is fruitful, "like a tree with blossoms in the spring," in the words of Romain Rolland. "Love aims to satisfy human needs. It looks beyond differences of race, class, capacity, talent and appearance, and sees men in their likeness one with another; for they are all subject to pain, suffering and death; and all hunger for food, water, shelter, companionship, freedom, creative self-expression, and self-esteem."

Knowledge Without Love

Paul said that without this kind of love, which we have tried to characterize briefly, other things profit nothing. Not only is the religious life without love a "tinkling cymbal," but this is true also of the educated life. I would go further and maintain that education, unaccompanied by love of men, is worse than nothing. My reason for making such an assertion is this: Among other things on earth, people are supreme. (You will readily recognize my bias here, since I am one. Since you are also, I hope you will agree.) And I believe that one human is as precious as another. I believe that we should strive above everything else to help people realize their basic and common needs.

Knowledge is a power which can be used for good or ill. A psychologist may employ his skill to help a person come back to reality and to find happiness in it; or he may use his skill to sell people something they can't afford to buy and don't need, or to hate the Jews, or to love war. The educated man without love is a constant threat to his fellowmen. He is brother to dictators, authoritarians, and the unscrupulous. Those who live for selfish interests, without concern for human values, are aptly described by an ancient Taoist writer: "Those who make wealth their all in all cannot bear loss of money. Those who make distinction their all in all cannot bear loss of fame. Those who affect power will not place authority in the hands of others. Anxious while holding, distressed if losing, yet never taking warning from the past and seeing the folly of their pursuit—such men are the accursed of God." (Ballou, *Bible of the World,* p. 532.)

And, may I add, a curse to people.

An educated life without love is not only a curse to others, but is deficient in itself. Through the mind alone, to quote Paul, "we know in part," and "see through a glass darkly." Rationally we cannot know life fully or intimately. Our intellectual view is partial, restricted, complex, and leaves us quite dissatisfied. One who is guided by reason alone is likely to come to cynicism and despair. The way of reason needs to be supplemented by a rich life of feeling. For it is in affective states, such as aesthetic experience, worship, and love, that we enjoy moments of complete self-fulfillment, moments which are wholly meaningful in and of themselves.

Love Without Knowledge

If knowledge without love is inadequate and even harmful, the opposite is also true. Love without knowledge and wisdom may bring futile and injurious results. We have no desire to disparage either reason or love. Together they give promise of a perfect marriage. Either alone is like a marriage without a mate. I would like to suggest a few reasons why love needs the guidance of knowledge.

Life is more than subjective, more than feeling. We live in a world of objective reality wherein we must cope with the forces of nature and of human nature. The history of mankind has taught us that a satisfactory relationship to much of this world of reality is best established through the scientific method—by methodical, rational, controlled experimentation and observation. The germ theory of disease, wonder drugs, the principle of gravitation, a knowledge of the essential elements of soil fertility have come to us not through prophet or poet, but through science.

Suppose I had a loving heart. Even so, none of you who know me would come to me to have your appendix removed, your teeth filled, your house built or decorated, or your auto repaired. If you should, even love would diminish in the world.

Not only do surgical operations deal with reality, but every human problem is equally grounded in tangible reality. Without knowledge we can blunder in economic, social, political, and other human problems even as I would in surgery.

Love and Knowledge

Love, allied with knowledge, is our need. When these two work together, "all is well, all is well." This is illustrated in the life of that loving genius of our time, Albert Schweitzer. While but a youth, he recognized the tragedy of life. Instead of succumbing to despair, he assumed an obligation to give back to life its precious gifts to him. Reverence for life became his all-consuming passion. To heal men's souls, he first became an organist, an interpreter of Bach. This was not enough, so he became a minister, serving the poor of Paris. Still sensing his lack to fulfill men's needs, he returned to his alma mater, the University of Strasbourg, and studied medicine. Upon graduation, he took with him his wife—a nurse trained in the treatment of tropical illnesses—and went to the heart of Africa to serve "the least of Christ's brethren." The brilliant mind, loving heart, and skilled hands of Albert Schweitzer have been healing men's bodies and souls for over forty years. We are not Albert Schweitzers, but we have knowledge and two hands, and we can increase in love. And each of us in his own way can be inspired of love and guided by knowledge.

May I conclude these reflections by suggesting to you a few areas and situations which are crying to us for the application of both love and knowledge.

Opportunities for "Intelligent" Love

A generation or two ago marriages were held together in good measure by social forces such as the economic dependency of women, the interdependency of husband and wife, and the disgrace of divorce. Today these social forces exert diminished control. Marriages succeed in America if they satisfy the personal desires for happiness of husband and wife. . . .

If marriage is to be the source of such completely satisfying personal values, then certainly those who enter therein must bring to it the fine qualities of friendship and brotherly love, as well as romance.

The modern family has been robbed of many of its former functions—economic, recreational, cultural, educational, and religious. What is left to the family? The most important function of all: the satisfaction of the basic emotional and spiritual needs of its members. Only in the home can children be assured of love and self-respect born of self-discipline. And only parents with genuine love can satisfy these needs. Knowledge helps, and so does patience.

Our modern urban life has estranged man from man. Too often we know each other only as functions—as someone who delivers the paper, sells us the meat, or as kids who run across the flowerbeds. We need to take the time to visit with our neighbors, to guide our neighbors' children into rich experiences of friendship and learning, play and creativity. These things are of greater worth than the accumulation of goods "where moth and rust doth corrupt, and where thieves break through and steal." (Matthew 6:19.) Love dictates that we know each other as persons, not simply as names and functions.

Our community and social problems become increasingly complex. They cannot be resolved by love alone, nor by knowledge alone, nor by men individually. There is a need for men and women, inspired by a loving concern for human values, to meet together and pool their wisdom and experience for the common good. To be sure, every man should take care of his own family and work in his own church. Let everyone retain his individual taste in clothing, literature, music, matrimony, and theology, and let him take pride in his own genealogy and heritage; but let him also be a citizen of the community and of the world.

It is a deeply rewarding and spiritual experience to meet around the table with associates from other disciplines and with men and women of Catholic, Protestant, Jewish, and a humanist faith, there to plan and work for some need common to all men. "No man is an island." (Donne.)

> Nothing in the world is single;
> All things by a law divine
> In one another's being mingle:—
> Why not I with thine?
> —*Percy Bysshe Shelley*

The world is our stage.

All the problems of mankind are, in the last analysis, human problems, caused by human beings who are frustrated and confused in their search for self-fulfillment. They will not be solved by military strength, economic aid, or legislative statutes alone, though these are necessary along the way. Peace and happiness will come to the world when we learn to love our fellowmen and learn how to express that love in a manner that will be acceptable to them, consistent with their need for freedom, creativity, and self-respect. Ignorance and selfishness are our chief enemies; love allied with knowledge and wisdom, our chief hope.

The Ideal and the Real

When I was graduated from this university in 1928, we had a way of separating the ideal and the real. Earning a living was the real world, and love of men the ideal. We have come to believe differently. *The ideal is the real.* Love is not in the clouds, but is the deepest of human needs. As Dostoevski has one of his characters say, "Fathers and teachers, I ponder What is Hell? I maintain that it is the suffering of a being unable to love."

The individual's fate on earth has always been uncertain, as Job so beautifully attests: "Man that is born of woman is of few days, and full of trouble. He cometh forth like a flower, and is cut down: he fleeth also as a shadow, and continueth not." (Job 14:1-2.)

But whether life be long or short, kind or unkind to us, we will not have spent it in vain nor without meaning and joy if we learn to love our neighbor as ourselves.

As you well know, the fate of the nation and of humanity has become quite as uncertain as the life of the individual. Here, too, our hope lies in love that is allied with knowledge.

We began with Paul; let us end with him: "And now abideth faith, hope, and [love], but the greatest of these is [love]."

God bless each of us to believe and practice love, I pray in the name of One who did, even Jesus Christ. Amen.

27

Toward a Happier Marriage

Since early childhood, in the Mormon church two ideals have been constantly placed before us: a good marriage and chastity. We have tonight heard beautiful, inspiring talks by President David O. McKay and President Joseph Fielding Smith on this same subject.

There is nothing that I would wish for young men, there is nothing I would ask for my own sons, more than that each of them might find happiness in a good marriage—the kind of happiness which their father has found with their mother—and for them to know the joy of having sons as fine as they are.

My young brethren, there is nothing on earth that can satisfy the whole man and make the struggle and the adventure of living so worthwhile as a good marriage. And chastity is so important because it is the foundation of personal happiness, of making a girl happy, and of a happy marriage.

We have the feeling, my brethren, that we are not succeeding too well in the Church today in regard to marriage and chastity. I do not mean to imply that we are not doing pretty well and that we do not have wonderful marriages and virtuous, clean young people in the Church. But I am told that the divorce rate in Utah a year or two ago was higher than the national average.

I know from personal consultation the tragedy that comes into the lives of boys and girls when they break down their moral standards before marriage. I have the deepest sympathy for people who fail in marriage and who fail to live up to this great ideal of chastity. I believe in repentance and forgiveness, but I would like to try to say in a practical way something on the positive side to bring about happier marriages and finer moral living.

What is causing so much divorce and the breaking down of our

In April 1958, Lowell Bennion gave this address at the priesthood session of the LDS general conference. It was subsequently printed in The Instructor *(June 1958) as well as in the official Conference Report.*

moral standards? This is a complex subject; let me suggest only one possible explanation of it.

One day a girl came into my office—a fine Latter-day Saint girl—with tear-filled eyes.

I said, "What's the trouble?"

She replied, "I want to get married."

I said, "That's a worthy goal."

"But," she continued, "my father doesn't want me to marry the boy I'm in love with."

"Why not?"

"Father says he is spineless. My mother doesn't want me to marry him either."

"Why not?"

"She says that after the marriage, he will not be as polite and courteous as he is now."

I said, "What do you think of this boy? Is he spineless? Will he be courteous to you after marriage?"

"I don't know," she replied. "But I love him, and isn't that all that matters?"

I said to her, "It's all that matters, if you have the right kind of love; but the kind of love that people know in a typical courtship in our society is not big enough for marriage."

It is so common for very young boys and girls to become interested in each other; to date repeatedly, steadily, and frequently; to exchange affection increasingly; and then, after a period of what I would like to call "romanticized recreation," they get married and expect happiness.

Let me tell the unmarried that marriage is more than romanticized recreation. Marriage is more than dates and affection. True, romantic love is part of marriage, a very beautiful part. But in addition, marriage is a business and financial partnership. Moreover, marriage is especially a human relationship—an everyday and all-day and continuous companionship between husband and wife. This is one of the beautiful aspects of it. It is also the realistic part.

The big thing in marriage is to know how to live together, to understand each other, to be congenial and cooperative. Then, after the children come, the very difficult and interesting task is to have a congenial relationship between parent and child, and in the family as a whole.

Recreation and romance alone are not the right kinds of relationships to prepare people for a business partnership and for the human relationships which we find in marriage and family life. I was told that of boys and girls who were married while in one high school in this valley, within one year 50 percent of them were divorced. I cannot say that this is true for sure, but I can believe that it might be.

I would like to suggest to you unmarried young men, who, in this land of America, have all the freedom in the world, who have all the leisure, the money, automobiles, and opportunities to help you choose your companions for life, how to prepare for marriage.

In this wonderful period from about the age of twelve to whenever you are married—twenty-one, twenty-three, or twenty-five, or what age it might be—instead of plunging right into a courtship relationship in your young high school years and being so terribly concerned about the romantic aspect of life, why not think ahead and take a long view? Think in terms of preparing yourself for marriage.

I have three suggestions to make in this connection:

First of all, use these years to prepare yourself to be a good husband and father. Learn how to work, because after you are married, you must work to be happy. Learn a vocation which will satisfy your mind, your soul, and your creative urges. Learn how to live with other people; first in your own home and in your neighborhood. Learn to love to work in the Church—something you can do all the days of your life. Learn to read good books, to listen to beautiful music, to serve your neighbor. Build within yourself resources that will make of you a mature, manly adult by the time of your marriage.

And secondly, in your relations with girls during these wonderful years—these promising years—do not settle down to a steady relationship in your early teens, when you have had little experience in understanding yourself and girls. Rather, build friendships—many friendships. Do not take yourself quite so seriously in courtship in the early years. Make friends with several girls. Take out two or three over the same period of time. There you will have comparative value. You will get to understand girls and to know them as friends. You will understand your relationship to them and learn how to communicate with them. You will lay the foundations of fine human relations with the opposite sex. Associate on a group basis a great deal.

And third, brethren: After you have proved yourself to be a man, after you are ready to earn a living for your family in good measure, after you have much to offer to your prospective wife, then I suggest that you look around to find a girl who has much to offer to you and to your great purpose in building a good family life. Choose from among all the fine girls that you have known, or find another girl with whom you may build an enduring friendship. And go slowly with this girl, building a broad, deep friendship with her.

After you are friends; when you know that you can be business partners; when you know that you can enjoy each other's companionship; when you know you have common ideals, purposes, and desires for life, and that you can help each other to fulfill your very beings, then let romantic interest develop gradually, may I say, and find its fulfillment after marriage. I know that if a young man will build his marriage on the foundation of friendships first, culminating in a single friendship with a wonderful girl, and will let romance come last, his marriage will be as solid as a pyramid. People who become romantic first and then get married will have to wait until after the wedding to see if they can be friends. Some of them find they cannot be friends.

Every year, except when we have a bad frost, I go out to my little peach orchard around the first of September, and there I pick beautiful tree-ripened peaches—peaches with that golden color which drop into your hand with a slight turn of the peach. The youngest boy in our family cannot wait until the first of September. He dashes out into the orchard the end of July, when the first red comes on the peach. Eagerly he picks the peach and bites into it. Finding it hard and bitter, he throws it, and often a peck of other green peaches, on the ground. What is the difference between his approach and mine? In February I prune the trees. In May I start to thin the peaches, to cultivate the soil, and to irrigate once a week in the night. With great love and affection, I watch the peaches grow and I wait, with self-control, until the peach is ripe. My little boy cannot wait.

So it is with love, my young friends. Those who will build friendship, who will build Latter-day Saint ideals of character into their own lives and prepare themselves for marriage, and who will wait and practice self-control until they are mature and until they earn the right to a deep love, will know what real love is—the kind of love that is part of life—the fruit of a good life together. Those who are interested only in the taste and the flavor, and who rush into a romantic relationship, often taste a bitter fruit.

Now, my dear brethren—you who are fathers, teachers, leaders, and bishops—our young people live in an age of great temptation. They need help and guidance. I would like to make five specific, concrete suggestions on how we can help them to court and prepare for marriage more wisely.

The first one is this: I think we should discourage and not promote too early dating between the sexes. The other night a mother came to me and said that her eleven-year-old daughter, who is in the sixth grade, insists upon using rouge and cosmetics and wants a date every week with a boy in the same class.

The other Saturday I came home and found our twelve-year-old son preparing to go on a date with an eleven-year-old neighbor girl to a private dancing party two blocks away, at a home in which we were not acquainted. I took the liberty of breaking up the date with as much grace as I could.

Brethren, if our young men must wait until they are twenty, twenty-three, twenty-five, or even twenty-nine, until they are married, why should we rush this boy-girl dating relationship? Why should we encourage it too much through the schools and through our Church groups? I would say let us be careful.

Secondly: You cannot just dam off human nature, any more than you dam off water. If you dam off water, it will break out in another place. If you dam off human nature, it too will break out in some unwholesome way. So, while we are discouraging early dating, I think we must substitute something in its place. My second thought, then, is this: Make life meaningful and rich for the boy as a boy, and for the girl as a girl, during these early teen years; in fact, all through adolescence.

If a boy can find himself through work, through gaining skill, through learning, through fulfilling responsibility, and can get basic satisfactions within himself during these years, he will not be overly dependent upon his relationships with girls. He will not hunger for a steady relationship nor for a deep affectional relationship with a girl to prove his own worth or to find security within himself or self-esteem.

Can we make priesthood work so interesting in itself for our young men that it will satisfy their souls? Boys must have satisfaction!

Can we train a girl to develop her talent, her music, her household skills, even to have experiences in service, in worship, in responsibilities, so that she is not looking at a boy all the time—maybe only half of the time?

Just think of all the stimulation which comes to them to be romantic and to have romantic interests, from movies, advertising, and from their own biological natures. Let us make activities for boys meaningful to boys and activities for girls meaningful and rewarding to girls. Let their social activity be just part of their lives during these adolescent years.

The third suggestion I have to make is this: You bishops, teachers, and leaders do not know how much fathers need you. An adolescent boy is seeking to become an adult and to be independent, and he is seeking the companionship of those his own age. Many a wonderful boy, unconsciously, has to almost rebel against his father during these middle teens in order to feel himself a man and to be independent. But this boy still needs friendship and companionship of men, of adults. He does not have the same feelings of rebellion toward you men that he would feel, perhaps unconsciously, toward his father. Let me illustrate.

The other night, at a wedding reception, a lovely girl of fine parents in our community was the bride, married in the temple. As her Mutual Improvement Association teacher came through the line, the bride threw her arms around her teacher and said, "Oh, thank you for helping me to have this experience today. You did so much for me." Here is a girl with a wonderful mother, but she needed also the help of this extra person to keep her ideals and goals high; to give her strength during these critical years.

I plead with you, brethren, and with myself, that we not think of our young men in terms of numbers or statistics, that we do not think of our work in terms of activities or even in terms of groups; but that we think of these young men individually and think only of the nearness that we have to them, of our understanding and our love for them. If we can stay close to them, then we can talk to them about these personal things.

My fourth suggestion concerns itself with this problem of dancing all evening with the same girl and of going steady so young. Sometimes we can use young people to help us help other young people. Let me give an illustration.

Down at the institute of religion in Tucson, Arizona, twenty years ago, we had forty boys and forty-five girls who came to Mutual. The boys were prone to dance after Mutual with the same girls each night. Four or five girls sat on the sidelines.

One day I said to a returned missionary, who was professing his great faith in the gospel of Jesus Christ, "Do you love your fellowmen?"

He said, "I do."

"Does that include your fellow sisters too?"

He said, "Of course."

I said, "I doubt that. Every Tuesday night you find a little girl here and dance with her for a half hour. You are not concerned with what other girls are doing. Why don't you find another returned missionary and you two see to it that every girl here has at least two dances every Tuesday night?"

He said, "I will. I had never thought of applying the gospel to my social life before."

Well, these two young men soon had those girls happy and everybody dancing. It worked beautifully.

I believe you should speak to a group of the finest, most popular young leaders of your wards, of your MIA groups, about this problem of dancing all night with the same girl. They do not like to do it. They do it because it is the socially acceptable thing to do. They are afraid, as individuals, to break down the custom. If you put the problem to them, brethren, and suggest that a few of them trade partners and then remind them of it once a month and watch it, I believe it would work.

I think we need to use our imaginations and have meaningful associations between our young men and young women other than dancing. Try a "work party" sometime where you have M Men and Gleaners, broken into committees, helping the widows of the ward—serving with their hands and then coming together afterward for an old-fashioned supper, for singing, for prayer. It gives young people a chance to know each other in a marriage-like way and tends to break up narrow romantic relationships among them.

My last thought is this: Try an indirect approach. A man does not overcome the habit of drinking by talking about drinking or thinking about drinking. A person does not avoid unchastity by fighting himself. There is only one way to rise above our selfish, narrow interests. That is the way that has been pointed out to us repeatedly by the General Authorities.

I heard Elder Harold B. Lee say, ten years ago and again at our seminary convention two months ago, "I don't care much what you teachers do, if you will only create a love for God in the hearts of these young people you teach." I believe that this is very sound advice. If we could teach a boy to love God, really love God with all his heart, other things would fall into their places. If we could teach a boy to be a true disciple of the Lord Jesus Christ, other things would fall in their proper places. If we could just teach a boy to have respect for every other human being, these courtship problems would fall into their proper places. If we could teach a boy to have self-respect, his behavior would be good and ideal.

A Presbyterian boy, a medical student, said to me in a personal conversation, "Some of the Mormon boys at the dorm smoke and drink. They are good fellows, too." Then he said, "I don't smoke and drink."

I said, "Why not?'

He said, "I used to be tempted, but now I have found a kind of spiritual feeling for life that is based on my faith in God. And smoking and drinking just don't seem to fit into that feeling which I have."

Can we, fellow workers, do as well by our young people?

My young brethren, I pray with all my heart that you will use wisdom in your youth and lay the foundations for happiness in marriage by building friendships, by being chaste.

We older men—we teachers and leaders—God help us to help them to this end, I pray in the name of Jesus Christ. Amen.

28

"Thou Shalt Love . . . Thyself"

Ten young people were called up before their stake M Men-Gleaner class, and each was asked to name one thing in his or her character or personality which needed to be eliminated or improved. With little hesitation they began to report their habits of procrastination, degree of envy, lack of patience, withdrawal in social situations, lack of self-confidence, quickness of temper, or sharpness of tongue.

The same group was then asked to name one thing in their personality of which they were proud, one quality in which they rejoiced. They immediately became quite flustered and rather apologetic. It took time and prodding to get them to think of their good qualities.

This experiment has been repeated with a number of groups and with much the same reaction. People are conscious of their limitations. They live with their failures and sins but seldom consider their strengths and their virtues. Recently in another MIA meeting several boys and girls were asked: "Each of you give one reason why you are glad to be a human being." One replied: "The idea has never occurred to me."

Again it took something equivalent to a block and tackle to draw from these young people the reasons they had for rejoicing over their capacities for life; their capacities of mind, heart, hands, senses, and soul—of a human being.

Anyone who counsels with young people knows how many there are who reject themselves, who feel they are little better than the dust of the earth, who hang their heads low. Self-rejection seems to be at the core of so many people's troubles, either as the cause or the concomitant.

Even the loud, boisterous, and rude braggart or show-off, who appears to be an egotist of the first order, is often found, on closer acquaintance, to be a person who feels quite as inferior as the shy person who withdraws into his corner. This phenomenon is so com-

---

This essay was published in the April 1962 issue of the Instructor.

mon that it leads one to believe there are no egotists in this world, but only people who appear to be.

Students of human nature believe self-acceptance or a feeling of one's own worth to be one of the most basic psychological or spiritual needs of every human being. The other need, which has priority, is the need to belong to others, to be wanted and loved. These two needs seem to be inseparably linked in the life of each individual. Man, conscious of himself and others, must feel accepted by them and by himself to enjoy life. One is quite as important as the other.

There is no escape from oneself. One can ignore God and refrain from speaking to fellowmen; but who can escape himself except the mentally ill person who withdraws from reality and lives in a world of unreality—the schizophrenic. One can and does, of course, greatly distort one's self-image, but live with this self-image, whatever it be, he must.

Jesus, with his profound insight into human nature, indicates that he understood the worth of every human being in the sight of God and also the need for men to feel one another's worth and their own as well. He had a wonderful way of drawing both publicans and sinners to him. They were searching for their own worth and redemption from guilt and rejection, and Christ knew how to help them recover their self-respect. Many heard him say, and doubtless believed his words, "Go thy way and sin no more," or "Thy sins be forgiven thee; thy faith hath made thee whole."

Self-acceptance is not only a joy in itself and a prerequisite to the spiritual health of the individual, but it is also a prerequisite to living other gospel principles of great worth. A person, for example, who hates himself is not free to love his neighbor. He is afraid to give of himself and will likely use his neighbor and his faults to build up his own ego. And since he feels that he cannot elevate himself, he is likely to seek to bring his neighbor down to his own level through criticism and gossip. Starved egos are inclined to feed on others as parasites, or cling to them as leeches. This they do quite innocently and unconsciously.

If one cannot accept himself, he is self-involved. This precludes the maturity of meekness and the open, inquisitive, teachable attitude of humility. A person so concerned with himself has great difficulty in being objective, in concentrating on his studies, in pursuing a knowledge of the reality about him.

Similarly and tragically, the person without self-love often feels estranged from God. How can he be beloved of God, he reasons, when he hates himself? And even though it can be explained to him that God's love is constant, impartial, and unmerited, this he cannot feel.

In the Savior's memorable summary of the Law, he spoke of two commandments, the one like unto the other—love of God and love of neighbor. He also recognized a third person to love when he repeated the Mosaic admonition, "love thy neighbour as *thyself*." Just what his thinking was toward love of self, he did not, to our knowledge, elucidate. However, he obviously either took it for granted or affirmed it when he told us to love one another as ourselves.

With the need and desire for self-acceptance so great, it is tragic indeed that so many people depreciate themselves. One may well ask, why? Human nature is extremely complex and little understood, and the suggestions which follow are tentative, even though written with conviction.

Man is moral by nature. He not only acts but also continually evaluates his behavior in terms of good and bad. Man is a dreamer, an idealist, and sometimes is discontent with what he has and is. He is inclined to measure himself by that which he would like to be. As an idealist, he always falls short of the ideal. Failure, sin, and accompanying guilt haunt his introspective path as a tiger stalks its prey. Heavy is the burden of guilt which such men carry.

A second reason for self-rejection may be the inability of many people in our complex age to find adequate and meaningful ways to express themselves. Life is meaningful to the extent that it is purposeful. If people cannot define and pursue goals which satisfy their human needs and aspirations, their lives remain unfulfilled. They may feel useless to themselves and, to that degree, worthless.

Third, some people confuse humility with self-depreciation. They apologize, feel themselves unworthy, incapable, and "meek" in order to give evidence to themselves that they are religious. The Savior's remarks that the last in his kingdom shall be first and the least shall be greatest are interpreted by some to mean that one must reject himself to be acceptable to God. This point of view certainly is a distortion of the meaning of meekness and humility. Meekness means self-control at its highest, a freedom from feelings of self-pity, self-concern, and futility. Humility includes self-acceptance so that one is free to learn and to relate oneself to fellowmen and Deity. True humility and meekness are not incompatible with a feeling of one's own worth but are, in part, the fruits of such a feeling.

So great is the need to feel one's worth that we grasp, often unconsciously, at every possible means of attaining it. One common way is the acquisition of material possessions far beyond physical needs. Women fill their closets with "changeable suits of apparel." Why? Not primarily to keep warm or comfortable but to give their egos a lift through the eyes of others. Men buy new and big cars. Why? Not for safety and comfort alone, but also to "be seen of men." Men and women together build homes far beyond the necessities of shelter and comfort. Why? May it not be because it is so easy to identify themselves with that which is tangible and visible? May it not also be that our very lust for luxuries bears witness of our inner poverty of soul?

A quick, momentary, and illusory way of lifting one's self-image is to depreciate others, especially those whom we envy and in whom we recognize some superior quality or position. Much gossip and criticism of other persons has its root in our desire to pull people down to our level. It is easier to pull down another person than to build up oneself, and so, in our desperate need to feel our own worth, we are prone to do this. Likewise, a person who cannot see or face his own limitations is quick to shift the cause of his deficiency from himself to those with whom he associates. The failing student may blame his failure on his teachers, "none of whom are competent." The lost son blames his mother.

Authoritarianism, this habit of exercising "unrighteous dominion," so beautifully described in D&C 121:34-46, has part of its foundation in the conscious feeling of insufficiency on the part of the possessor of a little authority. It is a characteristic of small persons who do not feel comfortable nor secure in their positions. To convince themselves of their worth, they must strut, give orders, and harass their fellowmen. By contrast, a person who feels creative within himself, who loves his fellowmen, who is genuinely humble, has no need to hurt others or to ride rough-shod over his subordinates or colleagues.

Thus far we have observed how common it is for people to reject themselves, and yet how great is the need to feel their own worth as human beings. We noted that man, as a child of God and disciple of Christ, has every reason to accept himself, but this he seldom does. Burdened with failure, sin, and their accompanying despair and guilt, he rejects himself. But, finding it impossible to live in complete self-rejection, he grasps at every straw to build up his self-image. He accumulates goods to "be seen of men"; he gossips and debunks others; he imitates Hitler and Napoleon—all to little or no permanent avail.

How then, may we ask, can a person build his feeling of worth on solid foundations? And how can we, as Church workers, teachers, and leaders, help youth to find their own worth so that they will not destroy themselves in such vain attempts to act important? Drinking, smoking, carousing, reckless driving, and stealing are essentially futile efforts on the part of youth to make themselves feel important.

Man is more than animal. His self is not fully realized merely through these procedures. He must be engaged in distinctly human endeavors. He has a mind which craves use and satisfaction. His capacity for emotional life is great. He needs to love and be loved. Man is an idealist; his eyes look to the stars. He is a dreamer; he beholds the moon. He has a memory, imagination, and the power of reason.

He who would know his own worth must live a distinctly human life—he must think, serve, imagine, belong, create, laugh, and weep. What does this mean to the leader of youth who would help them find themselves? Let us suggest some needs of youth which must be fulfilled if they are to know their own worth.

1. Youth need love. Each needs to be accepted just as he is—not for what he can become or for what he ought to be, but for what he is now. Somehow, he must feel his own goodness and strength before he can become good and strong. Young people need friends, wholesome friends. They need to belong to a group of peers who like them for what they are. They need to be active participants in such a group, feeling and doing things together. It is not enough to be simply in the same seminary, Explorer, or Sunday School class with others. They must have rich and meaningful social, spiritual, play, and work experiences in common, regularly and repeatedly.

2. Youth needs creative adventure. Opportunities are innumerable. Just plain, good fun is worth having in days of storm and stress, but their adventure should go beyond pleasure. Their minds hunger for adventure; they need to learn new ideas—specific, concrete, and exciting concepts in school, in church, and in the home. Every time a teacher prepares to face a class he should ask himself: "What new idea or deeper comprehension of an old idea will my students take out of class today?"

3. Youth need success born of their own achievement. Every lad needs desperately to excel in something. Praise, compliments, and flattery are as soap bubbles unless he experiences his own growth

and increase. Boys and girls need to do, successfully and repeatedly, specific and concrete things, such as playing games, making things with their hands, expressing their own thinking, playing musical instruments, tying knots, building things, repairing cars, sewing clothes, painting pictures, singing in groups, helping those in need. They need to have responsibilities to carry out under supervision and with appreciation. They need to do difficult things which test their strength, their courage, their endurance, and their ingenuity.

Youth need not to be pampered and coddled and protected from the struggles of life as much as they need hardship and big tasks to accomplish. A boy is eagerly and quite naturally trying to be an adult. He has qualities of body, mind, and soul which need fulfillment. They make up the self he is seeking to find.

4. Youth needs to repent. Nothing, perhaps, destroys a person's feelings of worth so much as a sense of guilt born of sin. Young folk do not grow up without doing things that are wrong and that they recognize as being evil. Awareness of this gap between their behavior and their ideals destroys self-respect and estranges them from themselves.

Repentance is not easily achieved. Much thought should be given to ways of helping youth to repent. The following suggestions may help:

We should not try to minimize the evil of their sin and attempt to make it unimportant. On the other hand, we should distinguish between the sinner and the sin, letting the youth know that we respect and accept him even if he has done wrong. This we cannot do unless we truly love him. Young people usually measure up to our expectations of them, so we should put faith and trust in them. When we preach repentance, we should also speak of forgiveness and let people know that these two principles go hand-in-hand. And finally, we must help a boy who is dejected in spirit by leading him to life's genuine satisfactions—opportunities to be creative, to serve, to succeed, and to find fellowship with his peers.

5. Youth needs to recognize the divinity that is in him. A child of God, he has partaken of his Father's nature. His is a great capacity for divine attributes. His glory is also knowledge, wisdom, and intelligence. Like the Father, he too would create "worlds without number." Like the Father, he too must be honest, free, loving, and giving to satisfy his own soul. He too has a feeling for the beautiful and is aesthetically responsive to nature and human nature.

Somehow, leaders of youth must restore individuality to life, helping each young person rejoice in his own uniqueness. Each young person needs to learn to think his own thoughts, to create with his own hands, and to sense his own sonship of God. Leaders must help a youth to help himself, to know himself, to rejoice in himself.

A boy who respects his body will not destroy it with alcohol, tobacco, and lust. A boy who respects his mind will not dissipate it in idleness or ugliness. A boy who respects his Father in heaven will not profane His holy name.

Somehow, we must help every youth find his own worth as a human being and a beloved child of God. When he finds it, he will find it much easier to do that which becomes a human being and a child of God.

29

Overcoming Prejudice

A dark-skinned girl from India enrolled in a college in America and was given a room to share in a dormitory. When two roommates, previously assigned to the same room, returned Sunday evening, they refused to stay and went to a hotel.

The next day when the Indian girl took a seat near the front of the class, two other students stood up and walked to the rear of the classroom. Such were her initial experiences in America.

A year before, I had sat in the stadium watching a football squad practice. A man from downtown, sitting behind me, said to his neighbor, "I wouldn't mind seeing one or two 'niggers' on the team, but I don't care to see so damn many of them."

These college incidents occurred nearly a decade ago. Things have since changed on campuses where, I believe, there is less racial prejudice than in any other community in the land. But prejudice does persist. Eighteen months ago, a bright, handsome, Ph.D. research professor of chemistry came to our home before returning to India. He was courteous, gentle, and a gracious guest. During the evening, when asked to give his impressions of America, he said he loved the friendliness and hospitality of our people and the wide open spaces which symbolized freedom and largeness of spirit. I asked him if there was anything he disliked. With hesitancy he said, "The only thing I don't like is that color seems to make a difference. I do not feel fully accepted because I am black."

A Confession

Let me make a confession. I grew up with considerable prejudice toward people of other races and countries. I recall neither malice nor hatred, but only insensitivity to their feelings. My childhood friends

---

This unpublished essay, written in the early 1970s, focuses on racial prejudice, which Lowell Bennion saw as his own and others' chief failing, along with neglect of the poor.

and I called Negroes "niggers" in rhymes and songs. We blackened our faces and mimicked them in minstrel shows. One of our favorite eating places was the Coon Chicken Inn, where we went completely insensitive to how the name and sign made black people feel. We also called Italians "Dagos"; Japanese "Japs"; and Germans "Huns."

Such attitudes entertained by a Caucasian Mormon youth half a century ago are understandable. Negroes had been slaves in America for over two centuries and since then had been observed primarily in their enforced menial tasks as shoe-shiners, waiters, maids, and porters. Western European powers with superior technological knowledge had conquered and exploited Asiatic and African peoples for generations. Oceans and deserts separated us from day-to-day relations with them and their cultures.

I suspect too that subtle psychological forces were at work. Everyone must think well of himself. This is not easy for youth or even immature adults who have not yet cultivated the kingdom of God within them. It is so much easier to feel superior by imputing inferiority to others. If one cannot grow tall, he can knock others down below his level to see over and beyond them. Nations as well as individuals are capable of this pseudo, illusory path to greatness. Under Naziism in Germany, some fanatical leaders used hatred of Jews to reinforce the notion of Aryan superiority. (Erich Voegelin describes this evil in his book *Rasse und Staat*.)

A New World

A church mission call took me to the Germans whom I had feared and hated during World War I. Once there I learned to love these hospitable, industrious, idealistic, honest, and interesting people who did so much to help me enjoy the simple pleasures of life, including sauerkraut, yoghurt, a dry roll with cheese, a walk in the woods, and such magnificent works as Beethoven symphonies, Wagnerian operas, Kant's thinking, Luther's Bible, and Goethe's poetry. I was able to love them in part because they first loved me as the bearer of good news.

Later, missionary work, study, and travel took us to Austria, Switzerland, Holland, Denmark, France, Italy, and the British Isles. In each country nature was beautiful, people friendly and interesting, culture unique and magnificent. I began to feel like a world citizen.

At the University of Strasbourg I became fast friends with a Hindu from Calcutta, who taught me unwittingly of the moral and spiritual implications of the Word of Wisdom. I shall never forget also a beautiful Negress from Morocco, who with her husband came to our modest apartment in Strasbourg. I can still see her smile through tears as she beheld our blue-eyed, red-haired, pink-cheeked daughter lying in a crib. (She had no children of her own.)

Since student days contacts with individuals of minority groups continue to instruct and inspire me. A Negro lady of fifty came to a Mormon Doctrine class at the Institute of Religion years ago. Learning that she was a daughter of a Protestant minister and devout in her own faith, I asked her why she had come to us. Her answer I shall never forget:

"In the summer I am a recreation worker on a playground in Ogden. White as well as black children come to me with questions and problems. Many are Latter-day Saints. I have come here to learn your teachings so my answers will be right and not hurt their faith in any way."

WOW!

Gospel Fundamentals

One reason I did not recognize my racial prejudice in the days of my youth, I believe, was because my view of the Gospel must have been fragmented if not pulverized. I must not have seen it in one piece, in a framework of fundamental concepts, as I am beginning to now. Nor was I particularly interested in the implications of the Gospel for the social issues of the day. High walls separated religion from daily life except in some areas.

Today the fundamental principles of the Gospel have come to have relevance in my mind for every dimension of our existence, for social as well as personal morality. Consider, for example, only three, along with their implications for our regard for fellowmen. (1) God is the Father of the spirits of all men. Every human being is a child of God, in his image, and with the potentiality to grow in his likeness. And our Father loves his children impartially, no matter what their character or circumstance, because love is not merited necessarily but flows from a loving person. (2) If God is our Father, then all men are brothers, created by the same Being and born of the same earth and humanity. (3) Jesus Christ is the elder brother and the Redeemer of all men. He lived and died not just for Israel, and not just for white men, but equally so for black people and those of any and every hue of color. Christ's redeeming grace knows no restriction, no differentiation among men—except the unwillingness of some to receive it. Nephi bears witness to God's concern and impartiality in these meaningful words:

> For behold, my beloved brethren, I say unto you that the Lord God worketh not in darkness.
>
> He doeth not anything save it be for the benefit of the world; for he loveth the world even that he layeth down his own life that he may draw all men unto him. Wherefore, he commandeth none that they shall not partake of his salvation.
>
> Behold, doth he cry unto any, saying: Depart from me?
>
> Behold, I say unto you, Nay; but he saith: Come unto me all ye ends of the earth, buy milk and honey, without money and without price.
>
> Behold, hath he commanded any that they should depart out of the synagogues, or out of the houses of worship? Behold, I say unto you, Nay.
>
> Hath he commanded any that they should not partake of his salvation? Behold I say unto you, Nay; but he hath given it free for all men; and he hath commanded his people that they should persuade all men to repentance.
>
> Behold, hath the Lord commanded any that they should not partake of his goodness? Behold I say unto you, Nay; but all men are privileged the one like unto the other, and none are forbidden. . . .
>
> For none of these iniquities come of the Lord; for he doeth that which is good among the children of men; and he doeth nothing save it be plain unto the children of men; and he inviteth them all to come unto him and partake of his goodness; and he denieth none that come unto him, black and white, bond and free, male and female; and he remembereth the heathen; and all are alike unto God, both Jew and Gentile. (2 Nephi 26:23-33.)

And Paul, living in that ancient melting pot of the world, the Mediterranean, knew no distinctions within the bonds of faith: "For ye are all children of God by faith in Christ Jesus. For as many of you as have been baptized unto Christ have put on Christ. There is neither Jew nor Greek, there is neither bond nor free, there is neither male nor female: for ye are all one in Christ Jesus. And if ye be Christ's then are ye Abraham's seed, and heirs according to the promise." (Galatians 3:26-29.)

Differences Among Men

There are distinctions among men. Some are more intelligent, literate, smaller or larger than others; some are blue-eyed, others black-eyed. But I see no differences of quality among peoples and races which cannot be explained by diverse environments and cultural heritages. Chinese and Japanese are among our most brilliant students.

I meet Negroes in the community and at conference tables who are superior in intellectual performance and committed to justice and integrity.

Even if peoples of other races were inferior to Caucasians—an assertion made which I do not believe is fact—my obligation would still be to treat them with full respect and do what is possible to help them realize their full potential. Christ admonished us to care for those in any kind of need, because "when ye have done it unto the least of these my brethren, ye have done it unto me." (Matthew 25.)

If we look beyond the visible differences among men—differences of language, education, color, size, and culture—we find so much that is common. No matter what the color of his skin, every man has the same need for food, clothing, and shelter. When President Eisenhower visited Korea, the story is told that he found lieutenants sleeping under one more blanket than privates. He asked, "Does it take any less to keep a private warm than it does a lieutenant?" Substitute Negro and Caucasian for Jew and Christian in Shakespeare's words [given to Shylock] and we have Eisenhower's idea expanded:

"I am a Jew. Hath not a Jew eyes? Hath not a Jew hands, organs, dimensions, senses, affections, passions. Fed with the same food, hurt with the same weapons, subject to the same diseases, healed by the same means, warmed and cooled by the same winter and summer a Christian is?" (*Merchant of Venice*, Act III, scene 1.)

No matter what color a man's skin may be, he has the same spiritual hungers as all men: He needs self-respect, the opportunity to be creative, to enjoy freedom, to belong to other human beings. He needs faith in the Gospel to see him through the vicissitudes of mortality and to qualify him for celestial life.

Minority groups among us need jobs, a chance to succeed in educational and vocational training, the freedom to live in decent housing of their choice. They need and deserve the same access to all of the bounties of life which we or anyone else enjoys. As Christians and Latter-day Saints it is our responsibility and privilege to help them gain these things.

We are not suggesting that affluent white people give away their wealth to the impoverished. This would not enhance the latter's self-respect. "Man does not live by bread alone." Our task is to find effective ways of helping our minority brothers to help themselves. They cannot lift themselves by their own bootstraps. We do not live in a land of equal opportunity for all because in today's world opportunity depends on resources, on health, money, education, and self-respect—which are not equally available in America or in the world.

One World

Today is not a half-century ago. No deserts nor oceans separate men and nations. Technology has obliterated time and space as barriers between us. Nor is there any Shangri-la or Zion to which men can flee from Babylon.

The reality of living in one world brings us face to face with Gospel principles. In former isolation, we could call them ideals in our international relations. We could try to love our neighbors in our homes, wards, and communities and remain coldly indifferent, if we wished, to men across the desert and overseas. That day is past. Either we apply the Gospel to our relations with all men or we perish both spiritually and perhaps mortally. Respect, love, and mercy for our neighbors are laws of life and cannot be ignored with impunity.

Latter-day Saints should be in the forefront of the battle for equal civil rights for all groups in society. Latter-day Saints should give freely of their time and means to help the disadvantaged in our society and in the world to gain sufficient food, clothing, shelter, medical care, and self-respect. There is no other way ultimately to peace and good will among men.

Indeed all other efforts in the name of the Gospel—missionary work, ordinances, payment of tithes and offerings, genealogical and temple work, prayers and singing—all are vain unless we remember "to do justly and love mercy." For this we have the witness of Micah, Amulek, Jesus, and our own hearts. (See Alma 34:28; Micah 6:6-8; Matthew 22:37-40.)

A Negro friend of mine once told me that he believed that God being the source of life and all creation implies an essential kinship of all the people in the world, "and if that kinship is true, is genuine, then *I can never be the kind of person that I ought until you are the kind of person you ought to be.*"

I am so glad to hear of Latter-day Saints in Arlington, Virginia, in New York and Pennsylvania, San Diego, and in Salt Lake City who are reaching out to establish meaningful relationships with black people and other minority groups. I am looking to the day when our concern for all minority groups will match our present praiseworthy interest in the American Indian.

Remember, the worth of souls is great.

Prejudice is not easy to overcome. Even after one has restructured his thinking to cast it out, feelings and attitudes of bygone years may remain. Perhaps our only hope to be able to conquer negative feelings is by finding ways to express positive feelings of good will toward our brethren of all races and cultures.

I ask God and my brothers of another color to forgive me the folly of my youth, my pride, and my insensitivity in the past to their feelings, their innermost needs. And I promise to never again prejudge a man because of the color of his skin and I would hope for no other reason either. We are all children of the same God and we are all brothers. God hasten the day when we may know and feel this to a degree that we free ourselves from prejudice.

VIII
LEARNING HOW TO DO

With Merle, at their daughter Ellen's wedding, 1975

30

What It Means to Be a Latter-day Saint

I am grateful to hear this prayer and music and to be with you. When Brother Herald R. Clark called me early last week and gave me a gracious invitation to come to speak to you, he said, "Talk to them as you would at a fireside chat." This I intend to do. I am going to leave profundity and scholarship to your classrooms and tell you about a fireside chat.

I go to a lot of them. Weary of talking one evening, I decided to do something different. We had a small group of young people in attendance seated in a circle, and, starting from the left side of the circle, I said to the first person, "I would like each one of you in turn to tell us one thing you do not do because you are a Latter-day Saint."

The first person said, "I don't smoke."

The second one said, "I don't drink."

The third one said, "I don't drink coffee."

The fourth one said, "I don't drink tea."

And then there was a long pause before the fifth one thought of something. He finally said, "I don't go to shows on Sunday."

And the sixth one said, "I don't swear."

And then there was a still longer pause and I turned to the other end of the circle and said, "Please tell us each in turn what you *do* do because you are a Latter-day Saint."

The first one said, "I go to church."

The second one said, "I go to priesthood meeting."

The third one said, "I go to Sunday School."

The fourth one said, "I go to choir practice."

There was a long pause before the fifth one could say, "I pay tithing." And they thought of one or two other things, and then there

---

On February 4, 1959, Dr. Bennion gave this address, one of four devotional addresses he was invited to give at Brigham Young University during the 1950s.

was another pause. I used block and tackle and couldn't draw anything else out of this group. I thought perhaps I had caught them off guard. So a few weeks later I went to another fireside and tried the same method and got roughly the same answers. Once in doing this with a younger group of Explorers, I obtained a new answer. One of them said on the positive side, "Because I am a Latter-day Saint, I collect fast offerings."

Brothers and sisters, I have nothing against the things that were said. I am deeply grateful for the Word of Wisdom. I pay tithing, and I do it gladly. And I believe in going to church and worshipping God there and enjoying the fellowship of my brothers and sisters. I delight in church service. The thing that grieves me about these answers is not what was mentioned but what was unmentioned. I do not know how you folks feel here, but in Salt Lake under the shadow of the temple and where I teach, I find that many students and many young people have reduced our religious life to a pattern of performances and of obedience to a few rather unique things in our gospel.

I fear that we Latter-day Saints, modern Israel, may fall into the same sin into which former dispensations of the house of Israel fell. Back in the days of Isaiah and Amos, the Israelites were "religious." They had their new moons and their Sabbath days; they sang hymns and offered prayers and burnt offerings. They probably felt deeply religious, I am sure. But their kind of limited pattern of religious living was not pleasing to God nor to his prophets.

The prophet Amos went from the hills of Judea down into Israel and, speaking for God, said: "I hate, I despise your feast days, and I will not smell in your solemn assemblies. Though ye offer me burnt offerings and your meat offerings, I will not accept them: neither will I regard the peace offerings of your fat beasts. Take thou away from me the noise of thy songs; for I will not hear the melody of thy viols. But let judgment [or justice] run down as waters, and righteousness as a mighty stream." (Amos 5:21-24.)

The prophet Hosea, in most beautiful words, said: "O Ephraim, what shall I do unto thee? O Judah, what shall I do unto thee? for your goodness is as a morning cloud, and as the early dew it goeth away. Therefore have I hewed them by the prophets; I have slain them by the words of my mouth: and thy judgments are as the light that goeth forth. For I desired mercy, and not sacrifice; and the knowledge of God more than burnt offerings." (Hosea 6:4-6.)

And then this very familiar but unsurpassed passage in the Old Testament, wherein Micah calls the mountains to witness when he says: "Wherewith shall I come before the Lord, and bow myself before the high God? shall I come before him with burnt offerings, with calves of a year old? Will the Lord be pleased with thousands of rams, or with ten thousands of rivers of oil? Shall I give my firstborn for my transgression, the fruit of my body for the sin of my soul?" Here is the answer: "He hath shewed thee, O man, what is good; and what doth the Lord require of thee, but to do justly, and to love mercy, and to walk humbly with thy God." (Micah 6:6-8.)

Mere performance and attention to some particular and important things in the religious life are not enough, according to these prophets; we must also remember justice and mercy and humility.

Jesus ran into the same type of restricted religious interpretation in his day. Not all of the Pharisees, but some of them, were devoted to the letter of the law and to certain performances. And Jesus said unto them: "Woe unto you, scribes and Pharisees, hypocrites! for ye pay tithe of mint and anise and cummin, and have omitted the weightier matters of the law, judgment, mercy, and faith: these ought ye to have done, and not to leave the other undone." (Matthew 23:23.)

Wherewith should a Latter-day Saint come before the Lord and bow himself before the high God? How should a Latter-day Saint think of his religious life? If I mistake not, the foundation of our faith, the first principle of our religion, is "faith in the Lord, Jesus Christ." And if our religious life is genuine and deep and meaningful as Latter-day Saints, it will be because we believe in and practice the things which Jesus taught and, as much as we can, the things which he did.

As disciples of the Lord Jesus Christ, how shall we bow ourselves before our God? What does it mean to be a disciple of him? It would take several volumes to try to say, but let me merely suggest a thought or two in a few moments.

It seems to me that the moral teachings of Christ might be summarized under two great ideas. The first is integrity and the second is love. There are many virtues which he taught which are aspects of integrity, of wholeness. The first of these, which he taught over and over again, is humility—to hunger and thirst after knowledge; to have the curiosity of a child; to be uninhibited in one's search for truth by pride and vanity; to be open-minded; to learn from one's enemy, from one's colleagues, from one's students, from one's children, as well as from one's teacher; to feel one's dependence upon God; to feel one's spiritual need—all these things are expressions of humility.

Another virtue he taught so powerfully is that of sincerity, which Confucius called the mother of all virtues. Without sincerity, one cannot love, one cannot have mercy, one cannot forgive, one cannot be honest. Jesus told us that when we pray, we should not pray to be heard of men, but with singleness of purpose, that we should go into our closets and shut the door and pray to our Father in heaven in secret. And when we give, we ought not to let our "left hand know what the right hand doeth."

He taught us to live our religion because we believe in it, because we are born again. We build churches to worship God, not to be counted. We should do our ward teaching because we love to teach the gospel and are concerned for the welfare of our fellowmen—not for any record, not out of fear, but out of the righteous desires of our heart.

Meekness is another wonderful virtue which Christ taught as part of integrity. It means to have no false pride to protect, not to be arrogant, and to have one's life under self-control so that one is free to love God and man.

The other great virtue which Christ taught, of course, is love. I don't think we know much about it, but love means certainly to have an unselfish interest in the happiness and welfare of others. It means to have a deep interest in the well-being of every human being whether he merits it or not, whether he is friend or enemy, stranger or kin.

When we talk this way and say that a Latter-day Saint is a disciple of Christ and that he is to cultivate above all things integrity and love, the reply often comes back that these things are not distinctively Latter-day Saint. Any Christian, says the critic, can be honest and concerned with his fellowmen. In fact, one needn't be a Christian. One could be Buddhist or a Taoist or any other thoughtful person, a philosopher, a humanist, and practice integrity and love of man, and what we want to be is a Latter-day Saint.

I was in a stake officers' meeting one evening when we were replacing stake board members. A certain person was nominated for a position, and the presiding officer turned to me because I knew this person and said, "Is he a good Latter-day Saint?" A lot of ideas flashed through my mind and I said to him, "He is a good neighbor. He is honest. He is hospitable. He is merciful." And I named other Christian virtues.

The presiding officer said quickly, "That isn't what I want to know. Anybody can be a good Christian. I want to know if he is a good Latter-day Saint."

I knew what he meant and I quite agreed with him in part. He wanted to know if the candidate for office paid his tithing and if he were orthodox in his faith. And these things a person ought to do to be a good Latter-day Saint. The thing that hurt me was his remark that anybody can be honest and loving, as though the emphasis were only on the peculiar things in our faith and not also the fundamental aspect of our religion.

I would like to bear you my witness that unless the priesthood which we bear, and the Holy Ghost which has been conferred upon us, and our theological beliefs in God, in mortality, and in the Son of God—unless these things create in us meekness and humility of heart, integrity of mind and heart, and a deep love for our fellowmen, they are vain to us individually. This I believe with all my soul. The priesthood and the Holy Ghost were not given to honor us. They were given to us to make us men and to create in us the power to serve our fellowmen, to make us hungry for righteousness and for truth.

Two years ago a lady in Germany sitting before her television station saw and heard a little discussion on Mormonism and Utah. And in this discussion a Mormon elder said, among other things, "We believe that men are children of God. We believe in eternal progression. We believe that men are that they might have joy." These things, so familiar to us, rang a new bell in her mind and heart, and she rushed to investigate our faith. She came to Utah, wanted to know firsthand what kind of a people we were who had these wonderful beliefs.

It was my pleasure to get acquainted with her and to listen to her. She said to me one day, "I am not disappointed in your theology. I'm going to be baptized soon. The thing that has disappointed me here is that I don't think you people believe your own doctrine." She said, "Your movie houses are full, your libraries are empty. I go to your Sunday School classes and there isn't this eager desire to know, to understand. I don't see much reverence and the humility as you partake of the sacrament. Young people love pleasure more than learning." I don't know that she was right, but she woke me up for a day with her well-meant criticism.

Another thing that Jesus taught us, besides integrity and love, was that we are indeed children of God. "Our Father who art in heaven," he prayed. He told us to trust God. May I remind us that we Latter-day Saints believe that we were created in the image of God. Sometimes we think only in terms of his form, of physical image. Let us not forget that we were also created in his spiritual image. And if we are children of our Father in heaven, we have partaken of his intelligence, his freedom, his immortality, his integrity, his love, his creativity. And if we are to fulfill our own natures as children of God, we must hunger and thirst after knowledge and after righteousness and be deeply concerned with our fellowmen. We must learn to love the attributes and purpose of God.

I would like to go to another fireside someday and get the group in a circle and start at one end and say, "Each of you, because you are a Latter-day Saint, tell us one thing that you do not do." And I would love to hear answers like this: "I don't smoke; I don't drink; I don't swear." But I would also like to hear the circle continue by saying, "Because I am a Latter-day Saint I don't cheat. I don't plagiarize. I don't think of a girl as a means to my own selfish gratification. I don't hurt, if I can, any human being."

More especially would I like to turn to the same group and start at the other end and hear someone say, "Because I'm a Latter-day Saint I go to church, I pay tithing, and I keep the Sabbath day holy." And then I would love to hear somebody say, "Because I am a Latter-day Saint I am kind to my neighbor. I am patient with my husband. I pay my bills. I speak the truth. I hunger and thirst after knowledge. I am going to learn something about the laws of the universe and the nature of human nature so that I might help God bring to pass the immortality and godlike life of man."

"Because I'm a Latter-day Saint I believe in living in simplicity, not in idle luxury, and in using my time and means to remove suffering in this world. Because I'm a Latter-day Saint I will be chaste. Because I'm a Latter-day Saint I love criticism. I will not be defeated by my past failures, for I believe in repentance and forgiveness."

God help us, my brethren and sisters, not to reduce religion to a formula nor to a pattern, but to be true Latter-day Saints, disciples of Christ, I pray in his name. Amen.

31

The Church and the Larger Society

Religion is a complex phenomenon embracing a multitude of things—doctrines, beliefs, history and tradition, scriptures, rituals and ordinances, meetings and activities, leadership and authority, organization and priesthood. But the heart of religion which gives meaning to all of these facets is twofold: man's relationship to Deity and his relationship to fellowman. In the last analysis, all else in religion must be measured by the quality of these two relationships. Jesus bore witness of this so emphatically when he said that everything written in the Law and the Prophets—the accepted scripture of his day—hung or depended on the love of God and the love of man. And Micah expressed the same thought so eloquently when he said:

"He hath shewed thee, O man, what is good; and what doth the Lord require of thee, but to do justly, and to love mercy, and to walk humbly with thy God?" (Micah 6:8.)

These two relationships might be called the vertical and the horizontal. The former might also be called spirituality—man's humility, reverence, awe, and worship before the holiness of God and also his faith and trust in and love and gratitude toward the Father and His Son. The horizontal relationship stands for social morality, a man's practice of honesty, sincerity, justice and mercy, understanding, and love in his dealings with his fellowmen. There is, of course, great overlapping between the spiritual and the moral aspects of religion, as Jesus clearly perceived when he said that the second commandment was like unto the first. It is fascinating to trace the relationship of the spiritual and moral aspects of religion in history. We shall confine ourselves to the Judeo-Christian / Latter-day Saint tradition, which is no small territory.

But let us begin our review with ancient Israel. In the law of Moses and the writings of the Old Testament prophets, man's relation both

---

This essay was published in the Summer 1969 issue of an independent Mormon journal, The Carpenter, *founded in 1968 at the University of Wisconsin.*

llowman are given due emphasis. The Decalogue
at the first three commandments point to God and
The fourth is a transition principle involving both.
ry of religion illustrates well the emphasis in the
ion was grounded in God: "Ye shall be holy: for
Lord your God am holy." (Leviticus 19:2.) But the greater emphasis is placed on man's obligation to fellowman.

Ancient Israel, God's peculiar (or very own) people made a fatal mistake. They thought they could sing praises, say prayers, burn offerings, and keep the new moon and the Sabbath and the passover to honor God and yet ignore "the affliction of Joseph." They did more than ignore their fellowman—they took bribes in the court, falsified their weights and measures, mixed refuse with the wheat, foreclosed on widows and orphans, sold men into slavery for the price of a pair of shoes, and could hardly wait for the Sabbath to pass so they could begin their round of exploitation again.

Amos, Hosea, Isaiah, Micah, and Jeremiah saw through the sham and hypocrisy of their people and, in poetic, colorful, and courageous words, spoke the mind of God against Israel.

In the entire history of religion and in all of scripture no one has excelled these Hebrew prophets in their emphasis on the moral or social dimension of religion. In fact, none have equaled them in their effort to save a nation by leading their people to practice justice and mercy in all walks of life on a social scale.

The Savior was a true follower of the Hebrew prophets as well as a spokesman in his own right. (This is not surprising since we believe that [as Jehovah] he was a revelator in Old Testament times.) Read the Sermon on the Mount. It too is grounded in faith in God, but so much of it has to do with man's responsibility to fellowman; likewise his parables. Christ had a twofold loyalty inseparably linked: to God and to man. Often he turned to the Father for strength that he might return to heal the bodies and souls of men.

There is one difference between the Hebrew prophets and Jesus in moral emphasis. The former were trying to save the nation; Jesus seems to have focused on the individual's morality. The reason for this difference in emphasis may have been that in the days of the prophets there was a nation yet to be saved, whereas in Jesus' day Israel was under the iron yoke of Rome. To have rebelled as a nation would have been vain and suicidal, so Jesus taught a religiously founded morality for all men—men of any nation and "for all seasons."

After this all too brief review of Jewish-Christian teaching, let us turn to the relationship of religion and morality in Mormon history. The restoration of the gospel and Church of Jesus Christ began with a spiritual and theological emphasis: which is the true Christian religion and church was the burning question in the mind of the boy Joseph Smith. His remarkable revelations—the first vision and the visitations of Moroni and ancient apostles and prophets—intensified the spiritual dimension of religion. A man who had spoken with Deity and angels might well have turned to mysticism and theological and ecclesiastical interests exclusively. But this was not to be. Within a year of the Church's organization, Saints went to Independence, Missouri, and there established a City of Zion and consecrated all their earthly possessions to the Lord and henceforth became stewards of his property to live for the building of Zion in anticipation of the coming of Christ.

In the Joseph Smith period of history, our people tried to practice Christian social morality in the presence of their neighbors in Kirtland, in Missouri, and in Nauvoo. Their efforts were heroic in many instances but not without failure because of their own weaknesses and because of interference by enemies.

The second period of Mormon history was one of relative isolation. We went west because we had to, and there with each other and under God we established Zion—in our own self-consciousness and quite distinctive patterns of thought and behavior. Converts from the many nations sang:

> O Babylon, O Babylon
> We bid thee farewell,
> We're going to the mountains
> Of Ephraim to dwell.

Bypassing more productive lands, we forged our character and strengthened our faith in the hard task of cultivation of desert lands.

Gentiles agreed with us that we were a peculiar people but in a different vein. (Peculiar means eccentric as well as God's very own.) From 1846 until into the twentieth century, our sense of separateness from the nation and the world was strengthened by many factors—the original exodus from Nauvoo, the gathering, Johnston's army, antipolygamy laws and their enforcement. We became a people within a nation, a subculture of the larger American society.

This separate state was never absolute. Jew and Gentile came early to the Salt Lake Valley. The railroad opened the door wide in

1869. Mormon youths in the latter part of the century began the trek eastward to school. The tempo of interchange between Mormonism and the world gradually increased politically, economically, and culturally.

Beginning especially in the 1920s, immigration sharply curtailed the gathering, and Mormon youth and others went east and west to find employment and to learn the thought and culture of the world. I was on a mission in Germany (1928-1931) when word came from John A. Widtsoe to keep the Saints in Europe, to build up local leadership, that the time had come when Zion was to be established in all the world, wherever the pure in heart dwelt. Our religion was to become what it was originally intended to be—not an American religion, but a world religion.

Separateness is a thing of the past for Latter-day Saints. Our children can escape neither the evil nor the good of the world. Radio, TV, movies, and the press bring all things to their attention. There is no Zion to which one can flee. We tried unsuccessfully in the Joseph Smith period to establish our own Zion alongside the Gentiles. Then we tried with considerable success to build our own kingdom in relative isolation, but that kingdom is no longer possible in any territorial sense, which leaves us with the task of how to live as part and parcel of the world.

Since we cannot escape the world, my basic position is that we should pitch in and help to shape it by making our contribution to it. We have much to gain and, hopefully, much to contribute. The following are a few suggestions on what we might do.

1. Every Latter-day Saint should serve his community as well as his church. Often active Latter-day Saints give all of their free time to the Church. This is admirable and likely necessary for the bishopric, stake presidency, and perhaps others, but the rest of us should always do *one* job, and do it well, in the Church, and then also assume another responsibility in the community. We live in the larger society. Our children go to school there. We need to rub shoulders and share thought and effort with our non-Mormon neighbors to resolve social problems and to achieve social purposes.

2. If we are to help solve the problems of mankind, we must prepare ourselves both spiritually through prayer and gospel study and also intellectually by reading and studying out of the best books. The problems which face us are exceedingly complex, requiring not only the ideals of the gospel, but also a realistic knowledge of economic, political, legal, and behavioral principles. The world needs

desperately historians, psychologists, sociologists, political scientists, lawyers, doctors, educators, and many other professionals who combine pragmatic knowledge with Christian idealism.

You need not fear, in my judgment, the incompatibility of gospel ideals with the learning of men. I find a very genuine compatibility of what most behavioral scientists are saying about human nature and my understanding of Jesus' view of man. The gospel gives men faith and ideal goals and brotherhood; and the sciences are filling in the details and helping us to achieve the ideals through effective means.

Recent attacks by some of the brethren on sex education, sensitivity training, and group counseling should not be taken—in my view—as a total rejection of education or of education even in these areas named. The wrong kind of sex education or sensitivity training in the hands of untrained or persons of immoral values can be disastrous to personality. I have seen instances of this. On the other hand, there is a place for the right kind of sex education and group counseling in appropriate hands. This I have seen too.

3. The biggest problem I know—to me even larger than communism—is the basic need of every human being, regardless of race, color, creed, or nationality, to feel his own worth, to enjoy the dignity of self-respect. The Caucasian people of Western Europe and America have written a shameful chapter in modern history in their exploitation of the colored peoples of Asia and Africa and the Indians of the Americas. This year I have been teaching blacks out of the ghettoes of Chicago and have captured a little of the resentment and hostility which they feel toward "whitey" because of what we did to their forebears in slavery and since. Over two-thirds of the human family are colored, and they despise the presumption of whites, as they suppose, that color is a mark of virtue or a sign of inferiority before God and man.

In the days of our isolation we could be ignorant or prejudiced toward men of other races, as I was; but now, with the world as intimate as it is, we can no longer afford the luxury of ethnocentricism. We shall have to learn to respect and to love all men as brothers, as the gospel teaches us, or we shall perish.

Now it is easy to love all men in general and in the abstract; the difficulty comes when we specialize. We must become interested in the minority groups in our own communities, building relationships of trust with blacks, Mexican-Americans, Indians, and any other minority or disadvantaged groups. Their problems are real. I was told that 39 percent of Mexican-Americans do not complete high school in the USA. In Salt Lake, about 50 percent of Negroes do not, and you know what this means in today's world.

4. Another area of real concern to me is the so-called "new morality" or "situational ethics." This means, I believe, that one should not meet the problems of life with fixed principles and firm rules, but decide one's moral course of action in any situation on the circumstances of the moment and how they affect life. Instead, for example, of being committed irrevocably to chastity or fidelity, there may be circumstances which would justify pre- and extra-marital relations.

I have some appreciation for part of this philosophy. I believe that moral precepts and rules do sometimes become obsolete because they were born under different circumstances or of sincere but shortsighted minds. Some of the Old Testament morality on things clean and unclean, regarding the eating of pork or pertaining to menstruation and childbirth, are not valid in our time. Certainly the proliferation of the legalism of the Pharisees regarding the Sabbath and other things—which gave Jesus so much difficulty—is a development of religion and morality which one must guard against.

On the other hand, the author of gospel ideals did not teach a lot of rules which were soon to be outdated. He taught rather a few core principles—faith, humility, sincerity, love, and purity of heart. These he illustrated in parable, in conversation, and in his personal life. These he never taught as a rigid system of ethics, a catechism, but always in relation to life.

The challenge to Latter-day Saints in the area of personal morality, I believe, is to follow the example of the Savior, to think and live fundamental concepts of life. [Each] situation should be considered and direct us in the application of the gospel to life. Situations, however, do not indicate their own solutions. One does not resolve a problem by talking about the problem. Problems are resolved in the light of principles, and principles get their meaning from life itself—a qualitative, ideal life.

It is my experience and observation that the ideals of Christ, including chastity, hold up very well. Sex is only part of love, and love is only part of life. And the good life was exemplified in the life of Jesus.

It is my prayer that we will have the wisdom and courage to follow him and that we shall try to realize his ideals in the larger society in which we are both compelled and privileged to live. This, in my judgment, is a great challenge to the Church in the twentieth century.

32

What It Means to Be a Christian

Latter-day Saints are accused by some critics of being un-Christian. This doesn't concern me. What is of real concern is whether we Latter-day Saints believe and act like disciples of Jesus. Hence I welcome this opportunity to meditate with you on what it means to be a Christian.

Grace

A Christian acknowledges and is profoundly grateful for the grace of Deity. By grace, I mean unmerited gifts freely given to mankind. Not enough is said in our church about grace, but the restored gospel of Jesus Christ, in my judgment, is full of grace. We do not earn all of our blessings by faith and works. Not all of our blessings come by obedience to law, I believe.

Three great acts of creation are wrought by Deity on our behalf—the spiritual creation in the pre-earth life, the mortal creation, and the resurrection. Christ is playing a leading role in the latter two. Life in all three of its stages is a gift. I hope you believe that—that life is a gift. You and I were incapable of creating ourselves either on earth or in the resurrection.

The gift of the Holy Ghost, the light of Christ, and the spirit of God come to us freely. We have to open our minds and hearts to receive them, but they are gifts of love nonetheless. The priesthood, the very power of God, is also a precious gift. It is Deity's to give.

One of the greatest gifts of grace is forgiveness of sins. True, we must repent to be in a frame of mind to receive and to be healed by forgiveness. But as the word itself illustrates, giving is always involved in forgiveness, whether between persons or between Deity and human beings.

The whole gospel teaching has come to us as a gift of Deity through

---

This address was given at the Sunstone Theological Symposium in Washington, D.C., in May 1987 and published in Sunstone, *July 1987.*

Jesus and the prophets. I didn't create or originate faith, repentance, meekness, humility, integrity, or love, and neither did you.

Grace plays a large role in both Catholic and Protestant faiths. In Catholicism, it comes to the Christian through the sacraments of the Church, which have been called vehicles of divine grace. I love that definition of an ordinance—a vehicle of divine grace. In some Protestant faiths, salvation is entirely a matter of grace. When salvation is conceived in terms of redemption from death and sin, it is natural and quite logical to give Christ full credit for it, following the lead of the Apostle Paul: "For by grace are ye saved through faith; and that not of yourselves: it is the gift of God; not of works, lest any man should boast." (Ephesians 2:8-9.)

Salvation for Latter-day Saints includes redemption from sin and death, but it also has a very positive meaning: It is a process of self realization of one's full potential as a human being and a child of God. It is to increase in knowledge and wisdom, in integrity and love, in the divine attributes of Deity. Life is a gift of grace, but what we do with that gift is our responsibility and opportunity. Grace precedes, accompanies, and follows the faith and works of the individual, but human growth is unthinkable without human effort, I believe.

Atonement

A Christian recognizes and accepts Christ's central role in the atonement. I like the literal meaning of the word "atonement," namely "at/one/ment." Man's goal is to become one with the Father and the Son, to bring his life in agreement with that of Deity. It begins with knowledge: "And this is life eternal, that they might know thee the only true God, and Jesus Christ, whom thou hast sent." (John 17:3.)

To become one with the Father and the Son, we must overcome three things: mortality, sin, and ignorance, because the Father and Son are immortal, sinless, and intelligent. Christ is the great mediator lifting us toward the Father. He died to bring to pass the resurrection.

There is a wonderful saying in Alma, chapter 34, in the talk by Amulek. He said the whole meaning of Christ's sacrifice was to bring about the means unto men that they might have faith unto repentance. . . .

Jesus taught and exemplified the real values of life as no other person has done. He revealed the character and will of God. He came that we might have life and have it more abundantly. Now I suggest that we as Christians should be grateful for the grace of Christ and for his atonement, but I think we ought to concentrate on overcoming ignorance and living as he would have us live.

Concern for People

Jesus had two supreme loyalties in life: to his Father in heaven and to human beings. He turned to his Father for direction and to renew his strength so that he could continue his teaching and healing and eventually die for his fellow human beings. He was particularly interested in the alienated of society: the poor, the blind, the deaf and dumb, the lame, and the sinner. He comforted the poor, fed the hungry, healed the leper, liberated the possessed, even raised the dead to comfort the bereaved.

Much to the consternation of scribes and Pharisees, he dined with publicans and sinners. In so doing, he placed the well being of persons even above the sacred law of Moses. To the woman caught in adultery, who according to the law should be stoned, Jesus said, "Neither do I condemn thee: go, and sin no more." (John 8:11.) Jesus came not to destroy the law but to make it serve life. In the Prodigal Son parable, he has the father (I think representing the Heavenly Father) run out to meet the wayward son, fall on his neck, and kiss him and celebrate his homecoming, because "It was meet that we should make merry, and be glad: for this thy brother was dead, and is alive again; and was lost, and is found." (Luke 15:32.)

For Jesus, the sacred Sabbath was not an end in itself. Man was not made for the Sabbath, but the Sabbath was made for man. It is a day to do good, to heal, to save life. I think it is safe to say that man was not made for the gospel, but the gospel was made for man. Faith, repentance, humility, and love derive their meaning and value because they build life—the lives of individuals and society.

A person, to be a Christian, must place the highest value on persons, I believe, and his or her relationship to them. Nothing matters ultimately in any setting—in marriage, the family, school, the church, the community, the world—except what happens to persons. Even the Church is an instrument to bless people. It is not an end in itself. Man was not made for the Church, but the Church was made for people. We should not serve the Church, but rather serve people through the Church. We don't teach lessons; we teach people. . . .

A Christian's loyalty is to persons: to Deity and to human beings. His loyalty goes beyond his own family and church community. Like Jesus, he is concerned with Jew and Gentile, with people in the larger community and in the third world. He is willing to share his time and means with people anywhere who need his interest and help. He is interested in the retarded, the mentally ill, the elderly, the poor, the lonely, the "sinner." He does not judge others. He will serve some of these people as his strength permits.

Alma understood the humane emphasis in the Christian gospel when he stated one's readiness to follow Christ in this way: "And now, as ye are desirous to come into the fold of God, and to be called his people, and are willing to bear one another's burdens, that they may be light; yea, and are willing to mourn with those that mourn; yea, and comfort those that stand in need of comfort, . . . what have you against being baptized . . . ?" (Mosiah 18:8-10.)

A Sense of Values

Human life has an economic base. Food, clothing, and shelter are essential to survival. Humans are creatures of desire and wants and crave comfort, health care, and the amenities of life. We must come to terms with the economic aspects of our existence. This is a problem of all people in all cultures. It was obviously a thing of great interest to Jesus, who had things to say about it:

> Lay not up for yourselves treasures upon earth, where moth and rust doth corrupt, and where thieves break through and steal: but lay up for yourselves treasures in heaven, where neither moth nor rust doth corrupt, and where thieves do not break through nor steal: for where your treasure is, there will your heart be also. . . . No man can serve two masters. . . . Ye cannot serve God and mammon. (Matthew 6:19-24.)

Take no thought for your life, what you shall eat and what you shall drink? Don't store up in your basements welfare supplies? Take no thought of what Jesus is saying here? But you know that the interpretation and more accurate, up-to-date English interpretation of that passage is: Be not anxious about your life, what you shall eat and what you shall drink and wherewithal you shall be clothed, but seek ye first the kingdom of God and his righteousness. That makes a lot of sense. Don't spend your nervous and soul energy on material things. "Take heed," Jesus said, "and beware of covetousness: for a man's life consisteth not in the abundance of the things which he possesses." (Luke 12:15.) Jesus also commented on how hard it was for a rich man to enter heaven and the folly of building bigger and bigger barns to accommodate one's possessions. (See Luke 12:16-21.)

A Christian's highest ambition and first love will not be the amassing of a fortune or the making of money. He will know that the kingdom of God lies within a person's feelings and thoughts and in relations to Deity and to human beings. He will place human and spiritual values above material ones. He will not, for example, live in luxury while a third of mankind go to bed hungry. He will not be wasteful nor extravagant when he could be helping people with work or otherwise. He will not buy luxury cars or a home for show or to feed his vanity. Plain living and high thinking are becoming to a Christian.

A Christian will not make money by injuring others. He will not deceive people about investments, promote tobacco, liquor, and drug sales, encourage gambling, or misrepresent a car, house, or a sale. A Christian will heed Jesus' words: "For what shall it profit a man, if he shall gain the whole world, and lose his own soul?" (Mark 8:36.)

Humility

There are four virtues that Jesus stressed repeatedly, and I think they are the very essence of Christian living: humility, faith in God, integrity, and love. A Christian will cultivate them all the days of his or her life.

The first Beatitude, "Blessed are the poor in spirit," means humility. How appropriate that this should be the first because it signifies teachability, a sense of a person's spiritual need, a dependence on God, a hunger and thirst after righteousness and truth. Humility leads to a recognition of sin and error, a desire to repent—which is the second Beatitude: "Blessed are they that mourn" doesn't mean blessed are they that mourn for the dead. It means blessed are they who mourn for their sins, their mistakes, and are penitent—and that follows naturally from humility.

We don't learn gospel principles as we do the times table: two times two is four. Our understanding of each principle can grow and should grow with experience. Honesty, for example, for a child may mean not to lie or steal. For an adult it also means integrity, being true to one's convictions and values.

When I was about five years of age my mother sent me to the grocery store to buy two yeast cakes for a nickel. She gave me a quarter. I decided on the way to keep the change. You know, you could get a root beer or an ice cream cone for a nickel in those days. I decided to keep the change unless she asked me for it. If she asked me for it I wouldn't lie, I'd give it to her. Well, she asked me for it.

But my idea of honesty was pretty limited at five, and at seventy-five I am having my problems with integrity.

Humility remains the foundation of a vital, growing, religious, ethical life. These gospel terms are just words, and their meaning has to grow with us and with experience.

Faith

The second great Christian principle is faith. Jesus had implicit faith in his Heavenly Father and taught us to exercise the same kind of faith. "Wherefore, if God so clothe the grass of the field, which to day is, and to morrow is cast into the oven, shall he not much more clothe you, O ye of little faith?" (Matthew 6:30.)

Anticipating the cross, Jesus said, "Father, if thou be willing, remove this cup from me: nevertheless not my will, but thine, be done." (Luke 22:42.) Faith in God doesn't mean that we always have implicit trust that he will grant us our every desire. It means rather that we trust his judgment, that we believe God is on the side of truth and justice and mercy.

A disciple of Jesus can also say,"Father, thy will, not mine, be done." With the ancient prophet Habakkuk, he can say, "Although the fig tree shall not blossom, neither shall fruit be in the vine; the labour of the olive shall fail, and the fields shall yield no meat; the flock shall be cut off from the fold, and there shall be no herd in the stalls: yet I will rejoice in the Lord, I will joy in the God of my salvation. The Lord God is my strength." (Habakkuk 3:17-19.)

Read all of Habakkuk, chapter three, and read the seventy-third psalm, because in both instances the authors love God and put trust in him because of who he is, not in terms of receiving blessings. A Christian does not walk through life alone.

Integrity

The third basic virtue of the Christian life, I think, is integrity. There are two virtues, two ethical principles, that embrace all the virtues of life. They are integrity and love. Integrity includes the more personal virtues of humility, repentance, sincerity, honesty, and moral courage. Love encompasses the more social virtues of tolerance, kindness, mercy, forgiveness, helpfulness. Love presupposes integrity, and integrity needs the direction love can give it. If you want to simplify your ethical life, work hard on those two virtues—integrity and love—and you will have eternal life.

Integrity means oneness, wholeness, unity in the inner life. A person of integrity is free of guile, pretense, deceit, and hypocrisy. His life is an open book. He has convictions and values clearly defined, and he is true to them in every walk of life. Integrity creates meekness or self-control. It gives peace of mind, a sense of strength. A person of integrity knows no fear, no shame, no guilt. A Christian is true to himself, to fellow humans, and to God. His conscience is clear. He can sleep at night.

Love

The fourth and last principle I will mention is love. Love is the central principle of the gospel of Jesus Christ. This is clear from many statements of the Savior. You will recall Christ's reply to the lawyer who asked, "Master, which is the great commandment in the law?" Jesus said unto him, "Thou shalt love the Lord thy God with all thy heart, and with all thy soul, and with all thy mind. This is the first and great commandment. And the second is like unto it, Thou shalt love thy neighbour as thyself. On these two commandments hang all the law and the prophets." (Matthew 22:36-40.)

Jesus didn't originate these two commandments. They are found separately in the Mosaic law, in Deuteronomy and Leviticus. But he brought them together and made them the central focus of the religious life. Shortly before his death he said to the twelve, "By this shall men know that ye are my disciples, if ye have love one to another." (John 13:35.)

Following his resurrection, he found Peter and others who had returned to their fishing. Jesus asked Peter, "Lovest thou me more than these" (the fish that they had caught)? "Yea, Lord," said Peter, "thou knowest that I love thee." Jesus said, "Feed my lambs." Three times Jesus asked Peter, "Lovest thou me?"and three times he said, "Feed my sheep."

We could cite other sayings of Jesus which illustrate the central role of love in his life and teaching, but let us turn to the role of love in the life of a Christian.

It is interesting to me that a human being's need after food, clothing, and shelter is to be accepted, needed, wanted, and loved by other human beings. To give and receive love is the deepest of all psychological human needs. Isn't it interesting that it is also the central and basic principle of the gospel? Verily, the gospel of Jesus Christ is congenial to human nature. It fulfills human nature.

What do I mean by love? There are three basic kinds of love between people—romantic, friendship, and love of neighbor, or

Christian love. Romantic love tends to be possessive, demanding, self-concerned, and sometimes fickle. Friendship at its best is reciprocal. But Christian love is outgoing, selfless, centered in the other person. A Christian's love is unconditional, not earned, graciously given. It is universal. If you don't love all people, you may not love any of them, in a Christian sense. A Christian loves all people and any individual: an authoritarian husband, a nagging wife, a disobedient son, a thief in the night. The real test of Christian love is if you can forgive an enemy who has despitefully used you and hurt you, with or without cause. A Christian can and will love people he doesn't like, that he disagrees with and finds troublesome. To love someone in a Christian spirit, one need only to wish him well and to seek his well-being.

Perfection

I find that a lot of Latter-day Saints are trying to be perfect, and I hear a lot of preaching about perfection. Sometimes a stake conference is built around the theme, "Be ye therefore perfect, even as your Father which is in heaven is perfect."

I have a high priests quorum I attend every Sunday, and they talk sometimes as though they were near perfection. Even if you'd like to be perfect, I suggest that seeking perfection is not a wise way to go about it. It is not a good way to live a Christian life.

I have five reasons why I think it is foolish, unwise, un-Christian almost, to seek perfection as a goal in this life.

The first reason is, I don't think we know what perfection is. I associate perfection with God and with Christ, but I don't understand them fully—their character, their thinking, their understanding of life and the universe, and so I really don't know what overall perfection is or what perfection in anything is.

Secondly, I think you are bound to fail if you try to be perfect as a human being, and you will have a sense of guilt, a sense of shame. You will be burdened with failure.

Thirdly, you might think you are succeeding. Jesus, in the eighteenth chapter of Luke, tells a parable about two men who went out to pray, a publican and a Pharisee. The Pharisee said, "I thank thee, God, that I am not as other men are. . . . or even as this publican here." And the publican would not as much as look unto heaven, and beat upon his chest and said, "God be merciful to me a sinner." Jesus said the latter was justified, and that he that exalteth himself shall be abased and he that humbleth himself shall be exalted. (Luke 18:10-13.)

The fourth reason I have for not seeking perfection is that wonderful Mormon doctrine that I love—eternal progression. Progression means the act of stepping forward, eternally. I think that is the vision of Mormonism, that we may grow eternally under the tutelage of our Father in heaven and Christ, and enlarge our lives forever more—certainly in this life, and I hope in the life to come.

Finally, people who strive to be perfect, in my observation, put themselves at the center of things. They are conscious of themselves too much. I had a fine freshman student who spent half of his time keeping track of himself. He had three big looseleaf notebooks, and he jotted down every thought he had and every feeling and every word. He reduced his life to his own parameters. I am very fond of Jesus' wisdom when he said, "He that findeth his life shall lose it: and he that loseth his life for my sake shall find it." (Matthew 10:39.)

I think the only time you experience life as a whole, in all its potentiality, is when you give yourself to a cause that is greater than yourself, one that is outside of yourself.

Conclusion

May I summarize by saying that a Christian believes in the atonement wrought by Jesus Christ on his or her behalf and gratefully acknowledges the abundant grace of the Savior. I think a Christian has to have real feeling for the Savior, feelings of gratitude, of loyalty, of reverence—of friendship, if I may say so. Like Jesus, his highest loyalty on earth is to persons. The Church and the gospel are, for a Christian, here to build the lives of human beings—one's own included but not singled out for preference.

A Christian is not caught up in a quest for material possessions. He believes in plain and simple living and high thinking. Above all, a disciple of Jesus cultivates humility, lives by faith, holds fast to his integrity, and makes love the central core of his life. For him, love is a verb and must find expression in service to others. God help us to learn to be true disciples of the Lord Jesus Christ.

33

God the Ethical and Merciful

God the Ethical

When we contrast the Old Testament with Greek myths, the closest written records in time and space to come down to us, we see an immediate contrast in the nature of the deities each presents. The gods of Olympus are spiteful, jealous, capricious, vindictive, domineering, and exploitive. Certainly, many episodes recorded in the Old Testament might justly earn one or more of these objectives as well; but as I read the Old Testament, I see the massacre of the Canaanites and the sacrifice of Jephthah's daughter as isolated incidents against a background of moral standards.

God is ethical in his relations to human beings and unrelenting in his requirements that human beings be ethical with each other. The message of the writing prophets—Amos, Hosea, Micah, Isaiah, Jeremiah, and Ezekiel—is unmistakable. Flattery, offerings, bribes, and praises are not part of the worship of Israel's god. On the contrary, not even praise and sacrifice are meritorious unless accompanied by moral relations with one's fellow human beings.

Moses, speaking for God, said: "Ye shall be holy; for I the Lord God am holy."(Leviticus 29:2.) In the rest of that powerful and thought-provoking chapter, he defined holiness in terms of honesty, justice, and mercy in human relations.

Amos (760-740 B.C.) was the first of the writing prophets to declare the moral character of God. Speaking for God, Amos exclaimed:

> I hate, I despise your feast days, and I will not smell in your solemn assemblies.
>
> Though ye offer me burnt offerings, and your meat offerings, I will not accept them: neither will I regard the peace offerings of your fat beasts.

Reprinted here are two chapters from The Unknown Testament *(Deseret Book, 1988), written in Lowell Bennion's eightieth year.*

> Take thou away from me the noise of thy songs; for I will not hear the melody of thy viols.
>
> But let judgment run down as waters, and righteousness as a mighty stream. (Amos 5:21-24.)

And why is this worship rejected? Because in daily dealings with each other, these chosen people were unjust, deceitful, unfair, and oppressive to those least able to defend themselves:

> Woe to them that are at ease in Zion, and trust in the mountain of Samaria, which are named chief of the nations, to whom the house of Israel came! . . .
>
> That lie upon beds of ivory, and stretch themselves upon their couches, and eat the lambs out of the flock, and the calves out of the midst of the stall; that chant to the sound of the viol, and invent to themselves instruments of musick, like David; that drink wine in bowls, and anoint themselves with the chief ointments: but they are not grieved for the affliction of Joseph. (Amos 6:1, 4-6.)

The psalms recognize and praise the righteousness of the Lord, reciting a veritable litany of ethical qualities:

> Justice and judgment are the habitation of thy throne: mercy and truth shall go before thy face. (Psalm 89:14.)
>
> The Lord is upright: he is my rock, and there is no unrighteousness in him. (Psalm 92:15.)
>
> For he cometh, for he cometh to judge the earth: he shall judge the world with righteousness, and the people with his truth. (Psalm 96:13.)
>
> The Lord reigneth; let the earth rejoice; let the multitude of isles be glad thereof. Clouds and darkness are round about him: righteousness and judgment are the habitation of his throne. (Psalm 97:1-2.)
>
> His work is honourable and glorious: and his righteousness endureth for ever. He hath made his wonderful works to be remembered: the Lord is gracious and full of compassion. . . . The works of his hands are verity and judgment; all his commandments are sure. They stand fast for ever and ever, and are done in truth and uprightness. (Psalm 111:3-4, 7-8.)
>
> Blessed are they that keep his testimonies, and that seek him with the whole heart. They also do no iniquity: they walk in his ways. Thou hast commanded us to keep thy precepts diligently. O that my ways were directed to keep thy statutes! Then shall I not be ashamed, when I have respect unto all thy commandments. I will praise thee with uprightness of heart when I shall have learned thy

> righteous judgments. I will keep thy statutes: O forsake me not utterly. (Psalm 119:1-8.)

Think of the cumulative effect on a people of bearing in their imaginations the image of an ethical and righteous God who requires justice, obedience, truthfulness, honor, and compassion from his people. As generations passed, the "fear" of God capriciously punishing on a whim or for omitting a trifling part of the cult would disappear into a superstitious background, to be replaced by a relationship of truth in a God who needs to be feared only in the sense that rigorous standards and consistency of judgment always require appraisal of one's motives and behavior. Instead of being mysterious and alien, this is a God who is the model of righteous behavior for his people.

Isaiah, in eloquent language, describes God's rejection of Israel's religious ritual when keeping it has been used to justify neglecting the ethical life. How could a God of integrity and compassion accept praise from people who cheat their neighbors and take advantage of widows and orphans?

> To what purpose is the multitude of your sacrifices unto me? saith the Lord: I am full of the burnt offerings of rams, and the fat of fed beasts; and I delight not in the blood of bullocks, or of lambs, or of he goats.
>
> When ye come to appear before me, who hath required this at your hand, to treat my courts?
>
> Bring me no more vain oblations; incense is an abomination unto me; the new moons and sabbaths, the calling of assemblies, I cannot away with; it is iniquity, even the solemn meeting. Your new moons and your appointed feasts my soul hateth: they are a trouble unto me; I am weary to bear them.
>
> And when ye spread forth your hands, I will hide mine eyes from you: Yea, when ye make many prayers, I will not hear: your hands are full of blood.
>
> Wash you, make you clean; put away the evil of your doings from before mine eyes; cease to do evil; learn to do well; seek judgment, relieve the oppressed, judge the fatherless, plead for the widow.
>
> Come now, and let us reason together, saith the Lord; though your sins be as scarlet, they shall be as white as snow; though they be red like crimson, they shall be as wool. (Isaiah 1:11-18.)

Micah speaks eloquently of the kind of religious offering acceptable to an ethical God:

> Wherewith shall I come before the Lord, and bow myself before the high God? shall I come before him with burnt offerings, with calves of a year old? Will the Lord be pleased with thousands of rams, or with ten thousands of rivers of oil? shall I give my firstborn for my transgression, the fruit of my body for the sin of my soul?
>
> He hath shewed thee, O man, what is good; and what doth the Lord require of thee, but to do justly, and to love mercy, and to walk humbly with thy God? (Micah 6:6-8.)

It is important to remember that ethics are not the same as religion. There are many aspects of the religious life and several legitimate ways to be religious, either individually or in a congregation. One aspect is intellectual: a knowledge of theology, scripture, and religious history is valuable. Ritual, church activity, and attending services bind an individual to his or her cobelievers. Christian service and personal worship of God through prayer are also essential to the religious life.

The unique and powerful emphasis in the Old Testament is the repeated declaration of God through his prophet-spokesmen that none of these ways of expressing religious values are acceptable to him unless they are accompanied by justice and mercy in our everyday relations with fellow human beings. In short, the Old Testament affirms that there can be no true spirituality without genuine social morality.

These ethical concepts are drawn directly from the nature of God himself. They constitute the core of the prophetic message of Elijah, Amos, Micah, Isaiah, and Jeremiah. They underlie the whole Mosaic law as spelled out in Deuteronomy. This concept is called ethical monotheism, Judaism's finest contribution to the world, in my opinion. God is ethical. And those who would serve him must also be ethical in their human relations.

Theology is of no value if it substitutes for social morality. Devils also believe and tremble. To be righteous, belief must include concern for our fellow human beings. Religious ordinances and rituals are vain if they do not encourage spirituality and morality. Church life is not an end in itself but a place to be inspired to go forth and deal honestly and compassionately with each other.

This is a lesson we must learn over and over. Reading the Hebrew prophets with their passionate clarity is, in my opinion, an excellent way to renew our commitment to justice and mercy.

God the Merciful

It is interesting to me that the ancient Hebrews rejoiced in the mercy of God and invoked it with the same faith and confidence that they applied to his judgment. Obviously, these two virtues were not seen as incompatible or contradictory in their thought.

The Lord's mercy is beautifully portrayed in Hosea, whose marriage was a graphic example in miniature of the Lord's relationship to Israel. His wife, Gomer, bore him several children, then was unfaithful to him with several lovers. At some point, she came to her senses and returned to Hosea, who normally would have disowned her. However, in love and mercy he received her back and resumed the marriage.

Similarly, Israel deserted the Lord's law for the permissiveness of the cult of other gods. Hosea expresses the Lord's anger and disappointment with backsliding Israel:

> O Ephraim, what shall I do unto thee? O Judah, what shall I do unto thee? for your goodness is as a morning cloud, and as the early dew it goeth away. . . . For I desired mercy, and not sacrifice; and the knowledge of God more than burnt offerings. But they like men have transgressed the covenant: there have they dealt treacherously against me. (Hosea 6:4, 6-7.)
>
> My people are destroyed for lack of knowledge: because thou hast rejected knowledge, I will also reject thee, that thou shalt be no priest to me: seeing thou hast forgotten the law of thy God, I will also forget thy children. (Hosea 4:6.)
>
> For Israel slideth back as a backsliding heifer: now the Lord will feed them as a lamb in a large place. (Hosea 4:16.)

Hosea also spells out the method by which Israel can repent, meriting the Lord's mercy by doing mercifully. It is impressive to me that this call to repentance is not threatening or angry, but tender and pleading. The Lord reminds Israel of his love and promises them his mercy, appealing to them with gentleness and generosity:

> Sow to yourselves in righteousness, reap in mercy; break up your fallow ground: for it is time to seek the Lord, till he come and rain righteousness upon you. (Hosea 10:12.)
>
> Therefore turn thou to thy God: keep mercy and judgment, and wait on thy God continually. (Hosea 12:6.)
>
> O Israel, return unto the Lord thy God; for thou hast fallen by thine iniquity.
>
> Take with you words, and turn to the Lord: say unto him, Take away all iniquity, and receive us graciously: so will we render the calves of our lips.
>
> Asshur shall not save us; we will not ride upon horses: neither

> will we say any more to the work of our hands, Ye are our gods: for in thee the fatherless findeth mercy.
>
> I will heal their backsliding, I will love them freely: for mine anger is turned away from him.
>
> I will be as the dew unto Israel: he shall grow as the lily, and cast forth his roots as Lebanon. His branches shall spread, and his beauty shall be as the olive tree, and his smell as Lebanon.
>
> They that dwell under his shadow shall return; they shall revive as the corn, and grow as the vine: the scent thereof shall be as the wine of Lebanon. (Hosea 14:1-7.)

No one could question the Lord's right to be angry and punitive, to set conditions of acceptance and probation. Instead, he appeals to Israel's memory of the loving, trusting faith that had existed between them and stands ready to heal the breach.

Just as God is merciful, so he requires us to be merciful, particularly to those who have no particular claim on us: the poor, the widow, the stranger, the fatherless, and the afflicted. . . . Humility before God and person-to-person mercy result in spirituality and social morality. It would be difficult to make a case for removing them from any spiritual life.

The law of Moses mandates mercy:

> And when ye reap the harvest of your land, thou shalt not wholly reap the corners of thy field, neither shalt thou gather the gleanings of thy harvest. And thou shalt not glean thy vineyard, neither shalt thou gather every grape of thy vineyard; thou shalt leave them for the poor and stranger: I am the Lord your God. (Leviticus 19:9-10.)
>
> Thou shalt not oppress an hired servant that is poor and needy, whether he be of thy brethren, or of thy strangers that are in thy land within thy gates: At his day thou shalt give him his hire, neither shall the sun go down upon it; for he is poor, and setteth his heart upon it: lest he cry against thee unto the Lord, and it be sin unto thee. . . .
>
> Thou shalt not pervert the judgment of the stranger, nor of the fatherless; nor take a widow's raiment to pledge. (Deuteronomy 24:14-15, 17.)

As we read these passages, the law of Moses seems to be describing the kinds of activities we would today term "charitable work." I find it particularly appropriate that the God of love defines mercy in terms of loving behavior. Beyond our baptism, confirmation, ordinations, prayers, and offerings to the Lord, he requires our mercy, compassion, love, and generosity to one another. We learn mercy by practicing the works of mercy.

This means that we visit the widows and others who are lonely, succor the disabled of mind and body, provide work for the unemployed, take an interest in children who need attention, and help people become more self-sufficient both at home and abroad. It means that we are troubled by the suffering of fellow human beings and do something to relieve it. It also means that our sharing is somewhat selfless in that we do not praise ourselves for these works or criticize others for needing our mercy. Nothing sours the sweetness of a loving act so quickly as the merest taint of self-congratulation on our generosity or sensitivity or tact!

It is not enough to pay a generous fast offering and leave compassionate service to the bishopric and Relief Society presidency. We must set aside time, energy, and means to help low-income and lonely people, the elderly, the disabled, and the alienated—all marginal members of our community, whether they be members of the Church or not.

I know a father of nine who seeks out one or two widows each month and works in their yards, or makes minor repairs on their homes. He has been doing this for several years. He is a true disciple of the prophets and of Jesus. . . .

Appendix A

A Chronological List of Contents

Appendix B

A Chronological List of the Writings of Lowell L. Bennion

Copies of all these writings, published and unpublished, may be consulted at the Archives of the Lowell Bennion Community Services Center at the University of Utah.

"Diary." Handwritten letters and entries in leatherbound volume in Lowell L. Bennion's possession, comprising a daily record of his mission, from October 18, 1928, to May 23, 1931.

Max Weber's Methodology. Paris: Les Presses Modernes, 1933, 179 pp.

What About Religion? Salt Lake City: General Boards of the Mutual Improvement Associations of The Church of Jesus Christ of Latter-day Saints [cited hereafter as MIA General Boards], 1934, 136 pp.

Supplement to the M Men and Gleaner Girls manual, chapters 4-6. *The Improvement Era* 37 (November 1934): 689.

"Religion and Life in the World." *The Millennial Star* 100 (February 24, 1938): 114-16, 125.

"The Meaning of God." *The Millennial Star* 100 (March 17, 1938): 165-66.

"How Can a Man Be Saved?" *The Millennial Star* 100 (April 21, 1938): 242-44.

"Whence Religion?" *The Millennial Star* 100 (June 23, 1938): 386-88.

"How God Speaks to Man." *The Millennial Star* 100 (October 13, 1938): 642-43.

Review of *Life of Christ* by Hall Caine. *Week-day Religious Education* 3 (June 1939): 7.

"Teaching Religion by Word of Mouth." *Week-day Religious Education* 3 (December 1939): 7-10.

Youth and Its Religion. Salt Lake City: MIA General Boards, 1939, 194 pp.

Contributions of Joseph Smith. A series of radio talks, with William E. Berrett and T. Edgar Lyon. Salt Lake City: Deseret Book, 1940, pp. 69-83.

The Religion of the Latter-day Saints: A College Course. Salt Lake City: Department of Education of The Church of Jesus Christ of Latter-day Saints [hereafter cited as LDS Department of Education], 1939, 146 pp.

The Religion of the Latter-day Saints. Salt Lake City: LDS Department of Education, rev. ed., 1940, 309 pp.; second ed., 1965, 319 pp.

The Church of Jesus Christ. Salt Lake City: Deseret Sunday School Union Board, 1941, 99 pp.

Today and Tomorrow. Salt Lake City: The Church of Jesus Christ of Latter-day Saints, 1942, 150 pp.

"The Fruits of Religious Living in This Life." *The Improvement Era* 44 (April 1941): 208-9. Reprinted in 73 (November 1970): 90-93.

"Christ's Example." *Relief Society Magazine* 32 (July 1945): 436. First in a series of visiting teachers' messages, followed by "Charity Suffereth Long and Is Kind," 32 (August 1945): 502; "Charity Envieth Not," 32 (September 1945): 570-71; "Charity Vaunteth Not Itself, Is Not Puffed Up," 32 (October 1945): 628-29; "Charity Doth Not Behave Itself Unseemly," 32 (November 1945): 699; "Charity Rejoiceth in the Truth," 32 (December 1945): 771-72; "Charity Hopeth All Things, Charity Endureth All Things," 33 (January 1946): 60-61; "Charity Never Faileth," 33 (February 1946): 132-33.

Trail Builder Lessons. Salt Lake City: The Primary Association of The Church of Jesus Christ of Latter-day Saints, 1948. *For Blazers*, pp. 35-125; *For Trekkers*, pp. 39-173; *For Guides*, pp. 57-61.

"Joseph Smith—His Creative Role in Religion." Joseph Smith Memorial Lecture, *Herald-Journal,* Logan, Utah, December 18, 1948, p. 9.

The Church of Jesus Christ in Ancient Times. Salt Lake City: Deseret Sunday School Union Board, 1951, 95 pp.

Goals for Living. Salt Lake City: The Church of Jesus Christ of Latter-day Saints, 1952, 401 pp., including other materials; 1962 ed., pp. 227-456.

"Practical Mormonism." No. 11 in series, "BYU Speeches of the Year." Provo, Utah: Brigham Young University, 1953. Address delivered November 5, 1952.

Teachings of the New Testament. Salt Lake City: Deseret Sunday School Union Board, 1953, 182 pp. Reprinted in hardcover by Deseret Book, 1956, 376 pp.

An Introduction to the Gospel. Salt Lake City: Deseret Sunday School Union Board, 1955, 1964, 322 pp.

An Introduction to the Gospel: Teacher's Supplement. Salt Lake City: Deseret Sunday School Union Board, 1956, 80 pp.

"How Shall We Judge One Religion As 'Better than Another'?" Unpublished talk at University of Utah (Humanities-Social Sciences Seminar), Salt Lake City, February 7, 1956.

"But the Greatest of These. . . . " Salt Lake City: University of Utah, 1956. Baccalaureate address, delivered June 3, 1956.

"Life Eternal." MIA theme lesson for *M Man-Gleaner Manual, 1957-58.* Salt Lake City: The Church of Jesus Christ of Latter-day Saints, 1957, pp. 142-49.

"Toward a Happier Marriage." *The Instructor* 93 (June 1958): 166-69. [General conference priesthood session address, April 5, 1958; also published in *One Hundred Twenty-eighth Annual Conference,* Salt Lake City: The Church of Jesus Christ of Latter-day Saints, 1958, pp. 83-87.]

"How Can We Increase Reverence?" *The Instructor* 93 (July 1958): 212-13.

Introduction to the Book of Mormon and Its Teachings. Provo, Utah: LDS Department of Education, 1959.

Religion and the Pursuit of Truth. Salt Lake City: Deseret Book, 1959; reprint, 1968, 180 pp.

"Developing Abilities and Skills in Leadership (As a Preparation for Missionary and Other Church Service)." Salt Lake City: The Church of Jesus Christ of Latter-day Saints, 1959.

"What It Means to Be a Latter-day Saint." No. 15 in series, "BYU Speeches of the Year." Provo, Utah: BYU Extension Publications, 1964. Address delivered February 4, 1959.

"Pursue Truth in Sincerity and Love." No. 5 in series, "BYU Speeches of the Year." Provo, Utah: BYU Extension Publications, 1960. Address delivered October 14, 1959.

"Teacher Helps" for *Spiritual Values of the Old Testament,* by Roy A. Welker. Salt Lake City: MIA General Boards, 1960, 359 pp. [Three to five pages of outlined teacher aids by Lowell L. Bennion after each chapter, making up thirty lessons.]

"In the Sweat of Thy Face." *The Improvement Era* 63 (August 1960): 2-5 in "Era of Youth" section.

Six Fundamentals of Good Teaching and Leadership. Salt Lake City: MIA General Boards, 1961, 73 pp.

Training for Church Service and Leadership. Provo, Utah: LDS Department of Education, 1962. Reprint of *Six Fundamentals* as instructor manual for teacher training.

"Cultivating Love in Marriage." In *Handbook for Young Marrieds, 1962-63.* Salt Lake City: Mutual Improvement Association of The Church of Jesus Christ of Latter-day Saints, 1962, pp. 89-101.

"The Working Wife." In MIA *Handbook for Young Marrieds,* 1962-63, pp. 102-11. Reprinted in MIA *Young Marrieds Manual 1964-65,* pp. 153-63.

"The Sabbath in the Home." In MIA *Handbook for Young Marrieds,* 1962-63, pp. 152-60.

"Thou Shalt Love . . . Thyself." *The Improvement Era* 65 (April 1962): 248-49, 277-80.

"Where Is Goodness?" *The Instructor* 97 (July 1962): 226-29, 250.

"Honesty—From Idea to Action." *The Instructor* 98 (March 1963): 92-93.

"The Joy of [Teaching]." *The Instructor* 97 (April 1963): 124-25. Talk given at Deseret Sunday School Union Conference, October 7, 1962.

"Jesus the Christ." *The Instructor* 97 (November 1963): 406-10. [A series of twelve teaching supplements for James E. Talmage's *Jesus the Christ,* used in the gospel doctrine class of the Sunday School. This first article begins with "Our Study of 'Jesus the Christ,' " "The Quality of One's Faith," "Greatness in the Kingdom of Heaven," and "A Controversial Figure," and continues in the next issue with "The Light of the World," "And the Truth Shall Make You Free," "Blindness," and "Who Is My Neighbor?" (December 1963, 436-39); then "Versatility in Gospel Living (January 1964, 38-42); "The Parables of Jesus" (February 1964, 80-83); "Slow to Learn" (March 1964, 120-24); "Render unto Caesar . . . And unto God" (April 1964, 164-67); "The Last Supper" (May 1964, 196-201); "Jesus Before Pilate" (June 1964, 242-47); "Teachings of the Resurrected Christ" (July 1964, 285-87); "Christ on the Western Hemisphere" (August 1964, 322-25); "In Search of Truth" (September 1964, 368-71); and "Jesus the Christ to Return" (October 1964, 408-11).]

"What Is Man? (A Mormon View)." Unpublished address given at an interfaith meeting, Salt Lake City, December 2, 1963.

"The Liberal and Conservative View in Mormonism." Transcript of debate with Chauncey D. Riddle at Brigham Young University in about 1963. Tape of the debate and transcript.

Teacher's Manual for Jesus the Christ by James Talmage. With Chauncey D. Riddle. Salt Lake City: The Church of Jesus Christ of Latter-day Saints, 1964, 176 pp.

"The Art of Casual Conversation." In *M Man-Gleaner Manual,* 1964-65. Salt Lake City: MIA General Boards, 1964, pp. 121-26.

"Death and Life Hereafter." Interfaith dialogue, Salt Lake City, October 19, 1964.

Fundamentals of Leadership. Salt Lake City: MIA General Boards, 1965.

"Accepting Students." *The Instructor* 100 (February 1965): 68-69.

"Jesus Taught People." *The Instructor* 100 (May 1965): 194-95, 197. [First in a series on "Teaching Insights" titled "Jesus, the Master Teacher." The series followed with "Jesus Loved People" (June 1965, 240-41); "Jesus Taught Principles, Not Rules" (July 1965, 284-85); "Jesus Taught Positively" (August 1965, 326-27); "Jesus' Use of Words" (September 1965, 376-77); "Jesus' Use of Illustrations" (October 1965, 406-7); "Jesus—Master Artist in Proverb and Parable" (November 1965, 448-49); "Jesus Taught with Singleness of Purpose" (December 1965, 494-95); "Jesus Made Men Think" (January 1966, 26-27); "Jesus Kindled the Imagination" (February 1966, 66-67); "Jesus Taught for God, Not for Himself" (March 1966, 106-7); "Jesus Lived What He Taught" (April 1966, 146-47).

"Religion and Social Responsibility." *The Instructor* 100 (October 1965): 388-91.

"And Always Remember Him." *The Instructor* 101 (October 1966): 382-83.

"For by Grace Are Ye Saved." *Dialogue: A Journal of Mormon Thought* 1 (Winter 1966): 100-104.

"There Is a Law." *The Improvement Era* 70 (January 1967): 6-10.

"The Outcome." *The Instructor* 102 (January 1967): 23. [First in a series of twelve "Teaching Insights," followed by "Adapting the Gospel to Human Nature" (February 1967, 83); "The Glory of Man" (March 1967, 117); "Singleness of Purpose" (April 1967, 156); "Discipline" (May 1967, 187); "Teaching: Giving or Quickening?" (June 1967, 223); "How Does the Teacher Learn to Ask a Thought-provoking Question?" (July 1967, 294); "I Don't Know" (August 1967, 307); "Inspiration" (September 1967, 370); "Relationships" (October 1967, 401); "Religion and Morality" (November 1967, 440, 443); and "Simplicity" (December 1967, 495).]

"Forgive Thyself." *The Improvement Era* 70 (October 1967): 12-15.

"The Mormon Family in a Changing World." *Dialogue: A Journal of Mormon Thought* 2 (Autumn 1967): 41-42. [Guest editor's introduction to special issue on the Mormon family.]

"This-worldly and Other-worldly Sex: A Response." *Dialogue: A Jour-*

nal of Mormon Thought 2 (Autumn 1967): 106-8. A reply to "Three Philosophies of Sex, Plus One," by Carlfred Broderick.

"Teaching Ideas and Persons." Address given to the College of Family Living faculty, Brigham Young University, September 19, 1967. Published in *Family Perspective* 4 (Fall 1969): 5-12.

Scriptures of The Church of Jesus Christ of Latter-day Saints. Salt Lake City: Deseret Sunday School Union Board, 1968, 250 pp.

Review of David Brewer's *The Mormons.* In *The Religious Situation: 1968.* Boston: Beacon Press, 1968, pp. 547-54.

"Use the Scriptures." *The Instructor* 103 (February 1968): 91.

Seek Ye Wisdom." *The Improvement Era* 71 (June 1968): 90-94. [General conference priesthood session address, April 6, 1968; also published in *One Hundred Thirty-eighth Annual Conference,* Salt Lake City: The Church of Jesus Christ of Latter-day Saints, 1968, pp. 94-99.]

"Drugs: Their Use and Abuse." *The Improvement Era* 71 (October 1968): 18-22.

"The Place of the Liberal in Religion." Address at Salt Lake Institute of Religion, February 28, 1969, published by the LDS Student Association.

"Seek Learning . . . by Study and by Faith." *The Improvement Era* 72 (April 1969): 5-7.

"Gracious Partners." *The Instructor* 104 (June 1969): 191.

"The Church and the Larger Society." *The Carpenter* 1 (Summer 1969): 64-72.

"My Memories of President David O. McKay." *Dialogue: A Journal of Mormon Thought* 4 (Winter 1969): 47-48.

"What Should Be the University Policy with Respect to Student Violence?" Speech given as part of the University of Utah Great Issues Forum, February 25, 1970; tape at University of Utah library.

"The Gift of Repentance." *Dialogue: A Journal of Mormon Thought* 5 (Autumn 1970): 61-65.

"The Fruits of Religious Living in This Life." *The Improvement Era* 73 (November 1970): 90-93. Reprinted from *The Improvement Era* 44 (April 1941): 208-9.

"A Black Mormon Perspective." Review of *It's You and Me, Lord!* by Alan Gerald Cherry. *Dialogue: A Journal of Mormon Thought* 5 (Winter 1970): 93-94.

"Question and Answer." *The New Era* 1 (January 1971): 11. Answer to "How can I develop enthusiasm to magnify my present church calling when I'm honestly not all that excited about it?"

"Religion and the Social-political Order." Address at Tucson Institute of Religion, March 17, 1971. First in annual Henry Eyring Speaker Series.

"Prejudice." Unpublished essay, early 1970s.

"Faith and Reason: Carrying Water on Both Shoulders." *Dialogue: A Journal of Mormon Thought* 6 (Spring 1971): 110-12.

"Faith and Reason: The Logic of the Gospel." *Dialogue: A Journal of Mormon Thought* 6 (Autumn 1971): 160-62.

"Situation Ethics." Unpublished essay, dated November 7, 1971.

Husband and Wife. Salt Lake City: Deseret Book, 1972, 69 pp.

Looking Toward Marriage. Salt Lake City: Deseret Book, 1972, 51 pp.

On Being a College Student. Salt Lake City: Deseret Book, 1972, 75 pp.

"Learning by Study and Faith." *M Men-Gleaner Manual.* Salt Lake City: The Church of Jesus Christ of Latter-day Saints, 1972, pp. 56-61.

"An Introduction to Max Weber." Chapter for book on eminent sociologists.

"Question and Answer." *The New Era* 2 (February 1972): 34-35. Answer to "What does 'Love thy neighbor' mean?"

"Overcoming Our Mistakes." *The New Era* 2 (November 1972): 12-16. Devotional Address at Salt Lake Institute of Religion, April 14, 1972.

"Faith and Reason: Religion and Morality." *Dialogue: A Journal of Mormon Thought* 7 (Summer 1972): 90-93.

"I Dare You to Believe—in Jesus Christ." Devotional address at the Salt Lake Institute of Religion, April 20, 1973, and published by the LDS Student Association.

"The Uses of the Mind in Religion." *Brigham Young University Studies* 14 (Autumn 1973): 47-58. Address given at the Phi Kappa Phi banquet at Brigham Young University, April 12, 1973.

"Three Loyalties in Religion." *Dialogue: A Journal of Mormon Thought* 9 (Spring 1974): 62-65.

"Question and Answer." *New Era* 4 (July 1974): 11. Answer to the question, "I think I have a strong inferiority complex. If I wait long enough, will it go away?"

"Latter-day Saints as a Subculture: Our Survival and Impact upon the American Culture." A panel presented at the annual AMCAP convention and printed in *Association of Mormon Counselors and Psychotherapists Journal,* Fall 1976, 22-24.

"The Position of Blacks in the Church of Jesus Christ of Latter-day Saints." Unpublished essay written before 1978.

The Things That Matter Most. Salt Lake City: Bookcraft, 1978, 63 pp.

"The Weightier Matters." *Sunstone* 3 (January-Febuary 1978): 28-29.

"Reflections on T. Edgar Lyon: A Tribute at His Funeral." *Dialogue: A Journal of Mormon Thought* 11 (Winter 1978): 12-13.

"A Response." Reply to "Priesthood and Philosophy," by E. E. Ericksen, an address reprinted from 1948. *Sunstone* 4 (July-August 1979): 13.

"A Response." Reply to "Knowing, Doing & Being: Vital Dimensions in the Mormon Religious Experience," by Arthur R. Bassett, a paper given at the Sunstone Theological Symposium, August 1979. *Sunstone* 4 (December 1979): 68.

"Jesus and the Prophets." *Dialogue: A Journal of Mormon Thought* 12 (Winter 1979): 96-101.

Jesus the Master Teacher. Salt Lake City: Deseret Book, 1980, 63 pp.

"The Hebrew Prophets." *Sunstone* 5 (July-August 1980): 41-42.

Quoted on role of women in Mormonism, in Kenneth L. Woodward, "What Mormons Believe," *Newsweek*, September 1, 1980, 71.

"A Response." Reply to "The Mormon Christianizing of the Old Testament," by Melodie Moench Charles, a paper given at the Sunstone Theological Symposium, August 1980. *Sunstone* 5 (November-December 1980): 40.

Understanding the Scriptures. Salt Lake City: Deseret Book, 1981, 88 pp.

"So—You're Going To Get Married." Pamphlet published by the White House Conference on Children and Youth, December 1981, 10 pp.

"From the 'Golden Days' of My Youth." Chapter in *Turning Points*. Salt Lake City: Bookcraft, 1981, pp. 37-40.

The Essence of Love. Salt Lake City: Bookcraft, 1982, 40 pp.

"My Odyssey with Sociology." Invited speech at a meeting of the Utah Sociological Association, Weber State University, November 5, 1982.

I Believe. Salt Lake City: Deseret Book, 1983. 87 pp.

"Thoughts for the Best, the Worst of Times." *Dialogue: A Journal of Mormon Thought* 15 (Autumn 1983): 101-4.

The Book of Mormon, A Guide to Christian Living. Salt Lake City: Deseret Book, 1985, 130 pp.

"Reflections on the Restoration." *Dialogue: A Journal of Mormon Thought* 18 (Autumn 1985): 160-67.

"Faith and Reason: Three Essays." Published in the twentieth anniversary collection of best essays from *Dialogue: Personal Voices: A Celebration of Dialogue*. Salt Lake City: Signature Books, 1987, pp. 95-110.

"What It Means to Be a Christian." *Sunstone* 11 (July 1987): 5-7. Address given at Sunstone Theological Symposium, Washington, D. C., June 1987.

"Caring: Share Yourself This Holiday Season." *This People* 8 (Holiday 1987): 18.

The Unknown Testament. Salt Lake City: Deseret Book, 1988, 170 pp.

"The Weightier Matters." Reprinted in *The Student Review,* an unofficial BYU newspaper, February 23, 1988), p. S2, from *Sunstone,* January-February 1978.

Do Justly and Love Mercy. Centerville, Utah: Canon, 1988, 97 pp.

"The Moral Component of Religion." Paper given at the Sunstone Symposium, August 20, 1988, and published in *Sunstone,* July 1988.

Index